CW01651328

STAGING FEMININITIES

MANCHESTER
UNIVERSITY PRESS

In memory of Peggy Harris (née O'Connor) April 1919–April 1996.
With love, as always.

Staging femininities

Performance and performativity

GERALDINE HARRIS

MANCHESTER UNIVERSITY PRESS
Manchester and New York

distributed exclusively in the USA by St. Martin's Press

Copyright © Geraldine Harris 1999

The right of Geraldine Harris to be identified as the author of this work has been asserted by her in accordance with the Copyright, Designs and Patents Act 1988.

Published by Manchester University Press
Oxford Road, Manchester M13 9NR, UK
and Room 400, 175 Fifth Avenue, New York, NY 10010, USA
http://www.man.ac.uk/mup

Distributed exclusively in the USA by
St. Martin's Press, Inc., 175 Fifth Avenue, New York, NY 10010, USA

Distributed exclusively in Canada by
UBC Press, University of British Columbia, 6344 Memorial Road,
Vancouver, BC, Canada V6T 1Z2

British Library Cataloguing-in-Publication Data
A catalogue record for this book is available from the British Library

Library of Congress Cataloging-in-Publication Data applied for

ISBN 0 7190 5262 9 *hardback*
0 7190 5263 7 *paperback*

First published 1999

06 05 04 03 02 01 00 99   10 9 8 7 6 5 4 3 2 1

Typeset in Palatino with Frutiger
by Action Publishing Technology Limited, Gloucester
Printed in Great Britain
by Biddles Ltd, Guildford and King's Lynn

Contents

List of illustrations

Acknowledgements

I am profoundly grateful to the enormous number of people who have in various ways contributed to this book, but I would like to acknowledge my particular debt to the following: my 'original' and still important teacher Mrs Murray Smith; all the performance practitioners with whom I have had such enjoyable, educational and, I hope, productive contact over the last ten years but particularly Rose English, Bobby Baker and Annie Sprinkle, as well as Annie Griffin and Geraldine Pilgrim, both of whom only appear briefly in this work but had a tremendous impact on its genesis; the students at Lancaster who over the last ten years have taught me on the Feminist Theatre or Gender and Identity courses or while pursuing their research, for the rigorous fashion in which they have constantly forced me to rethink my assumptions; all my colleagues past and present in Theatre Studies and the Nuffield Theatre at Lancaster for their generosity during my existential, professional and computer crises, with especial thanks to Darrell Macquire and Steph Sims. Most specifically, I owe Dr Andrew Quick and Pete Brooks an incalculable debt of gratitude for their support and challenges – while they both continue to owe me money. I would also like to thank my colleagues in Women's Studies at Lancaster, especially Maureen MacNeill; Adrian Heathfield at Warwick University; all those at Manchester University Press connected with this book and especially Matthew Frost, for supporting this project and for their patience in putting up with my truly terrible proof-reading; Colin Knapp, without whom I would not manage to get out of bed in the mornings, let alone achieve anything else.

An earlier, shorter version of chapter five appeared in *Shattered Anatomies* (1997), edited by Adrian Heathfield with Fiona Templeton and Andrew Quick in a limited edition, published by Arnolfini Live, Bristol.

Introduction
Political meanings: practices and theories, feminisms and postmodernisms

Whatever the specific topic or area of study officially under consideration at almost every conference, symposium or workshop that I have attended over the last ten years, at some point discussion has focused on the problematic relationship between theory and practice. While this holds equally for women's studies events as for theatre studies and performance events, at the latter this dialogue tends to be far more acrimonious and divisive. This may be because at the former the majority of the participants are both theorising about women and (however provisionally) 'practising' as women, while the number of academics who actively engage in theatre production is still relatively limited.

The ideal perception of the relationship between theory and practice in any sphere is one of equal exchange if not interchangeability. Yet, in my experience, many performance practitioners feel alienated by academic language, or 'jargon' as it is frequently designated, and subsequently feel that their work is being appropriated to deliberately opaque and therefore suspect discourses, created by people whose relationship to this work can appear parasitic. Even worse, theorists and critics sometimes lay out programmes detailing what this practice should or could do, which either ignore or appear ignorant of what is already being done or may seem hopelessly intellectualised and impractical when faced with the pragmatics of production. The same sort of issues can arise with women's studies and particularly feminism, where 'theory' often seems loftily divorced from everyday struggles of women outside and even sometimes inside academia.

I would not even begin to suggest any solutions to these problems, except to indicate that the constant remarking of the relationship between theory and practice as an insurmountable divide is not in the interest of any of the parties concerned. Yet neither am I entirely convinced by the apparent too easy dissolution or 'transcendence' of this divide that seems to be implied as having occurred in much recent theoretical writing nominated as 'performative'. I would prefer to acknowledge that while the perceived 'gap' between theory and practice is at times a locus of difficulty, it is also a potentially productive space. It is this productive space between theory and performance practice that I wish to explore in this book, and in this way I hope to strive towards a dialogue and a structure in which the theories serve to explore and illuminate the practice but, more importantly, the practice serves to test out and illuminate the theories. Moreover, I do not intend to formulate any 'new' theories or suggest 'new' directions for practice, since there seems to me to be plenty of work yet to be done on what already exists. Advances in performance practices may be *influenced* by theories but are ultimately produced through the process of creating work. Even practices self-consciously created in relation to a particular ideological programme seldom emerge as 'pure' embodiments of the proposed perspective, and this is famously the case with even canonical theorist/practitioners such as Antonin Artaud and Bertolt Brecht.

However, since this is an academic publication a great deal of space is inevitably given over to elucidating theory, sometimes at the expense of discussing the practice. In mitigation of this I would like to assert that my starting point has been the *work* of a number of female performance practitioners and the manner in which it has been received by other commentators. Rather than seeking out practices that offered themselves as examples of theoretical perspectives, I have looked for approaches and methodologies that seemed suitable to the discussion of this practice and its reception. On the other hand, I have not chosen these works at random, and even the most innocent reasons for my choices have to some extent defined in advance the boundaries of the theoretical terrain to be explored. So although my selection has been heavily conditioned by my own pleasure in these works in so far as I found all of these productions provocative and entertaining, this in itself produces a dilemma for my theorising. While all of these productions were witty and amusing if not downright funny, this tends to get lost within my analyses and interpretations. This is, of course, because humour in live performance often stems less from what is said and done than from the way something is said or performed: in short, it depends on the charismatic presence of the live performer. Humour may also be context specific, dependent on the conjunction of time and place, a specific audience and the particular circumstances of a production – basically, you had to be there. This is even more acute in the genre of work I am considering than in more traditional forms. Rather than 'drama' or 'theatre', the three practitioners studied here are usually placed under the heading of 'performance', or rather 'live or performance art', terms I shall be investigating in the next chapter. This suggests, among other things, works by practitioners, often deemed to be experimental or avant-garde, who do not necessarily have a traditional theatre background or training, do not privilege written text or employ conventional theatre forms and whose works are not always performed in theatre buildings. Indeed, such work normally puts into question the traditional assumptions of theatre and drama, particularly the conventional relationship between the performer and the performance, the live event and the spectator. As a result, all the works studied here, even when based on a predetermined script, frequently involved elements that produced a certain randomness or depended on some type of audience participation and therefore, in turn, entailed a spontaneous response from the performer.

So, for example, any reading I might make of the Rose English show *My Mathematics* (5 August 1992), will always be coloured by the fact that on the night I saw it at the Queen Elizabeth Hall in London, the live stallion which shared the stage with English in the second half of the show developed the most enormous erection. I gather this was not a regular part of the show mainly because previously English had worked with mares. When this occurred the stallion was upstage and English was down stage delivering some 'serious' lines concerning the nature of desire, so that for some time English remained unaware of this phenomenon. Her obliviousness plus the contrast between the two 'performances' produced a hysterical reaction in what was actually an 'insider' audience made up of a large proportion of performance practitioners and scholars. This moment became transgressive in all sorts of ways, not least because of her obvious bewilderment at the gales of laughter, which encouraged audience members to shout 'behind you', invoking the rituals of British pantomime. English's subsequent acknowledgement of her own surprise and momentary loss of equilibrium contrasted strongly with her performance up to this point of the persona of the authoritative and dominating 'Rosita Clavel'. This moment continued to affect the reception of the rest of the piece, producing smirks and ripples of laughter at moments which in other performances might have been received in a different fashion. Yet this performance cannot be considered to have 'failed', since in the first place, like much of English's work, this show deliberately drew upon popular genres, and so the audience's introduction of pantomime convention was apt within the framework of the piece. Secondly, part of the thematics of this show was the examination of the complex and shifting power dynamic that exists between performer and spectator, and this had already been explored in terms of passive/active, sadistic/masochistic. This episode clearly underlined the potential for sadism in the audience's part of the exchange. Thirdly, although 'Rosita Clavel' was to an extent defined as a 'character', there was never any attempt in the piece to convince us of her psychological reality, and we were always aware of watching Rose English pretending to be Clavel in quotation marks. Therefore the temporary loss of this pose did not represent a fracturing of an illusion but a further opening up of the issue of performing. Finally, her work often includes live animals, young children, magic and illusions that are not always reliable, in an attempt to explore the unstable relationship between the 'real' and the performed. In this instance the signifier of the horse's 'real' desire worked in counterpoint to ways in which the 'performance' of desire was represented throughout the piece. As a result, this 'accident' provided a unique experience of this show, producing new meanings but also working to consolidate and make explicit ideas that actually may have been less clearly marked in other performances.

This field in general presents a problem for theory and criticism, in so far as most people working in this area recognise the impossibility of accurately and fully documenting the experience of the live event. A written interpretation of a performance is, in effect, a translation from one sort of 'language' or set of codes to another, and jokes notoriously 'get lost' in translation. Moreover, any account will be influenced by which particular performance of a show is taken as the object of study, where and when this took place and even the positioning of the spectator within the auditorium. Equally, any interpretation will always be mediated both through the subjectivity of the spectator and the form the record takes. It is not possible therefore to produce an objective or definitive reflection of the event, since ultimately all such accounts are selective, partial and impure. This may be equally true of all theatre, if not all criticism, but up until fairly recently many drama and theatre studies departments tended to focus on the study of play-texts, which do at least provide some material basis for re-readings to challenge earlier interpretations. In this instance, my reading of *My Mathematics* above remains falsely authoritative since, in the absence of a written text or even a video recording of the piece, it can only be challenged by someone who saw the same performance, and any disagreement would be a matter of the accuracy of their memory and their subjective interpretation against mine. While I do not intend to address these and the other difficulties involved in the documentation and interpretation of live performance at length as a separate theoretical concern within this book, in practice such issues are always central to my readings of the shows. These problematics are acknowledged and explored by means of always providing more than one reading for each piece in an effort to remark and communicate the complexity of the works themselves while simultaneously opening up to question not only my own authority but also the authority of the theorists on whose work I draw in order to construct these interpretations.

My desire to study these works that have given me pleasure is also the product of my own feminism. This project started in earnest when, after seeing this performance of *My Mathematics*, a friend informed me that while English's work was always entertaining, 'it was never about anything'. This shocked me because I thought the deceptively simple structure of *My Mathematics* was potentially exceptionally dense in terms of reference and possible meanings. As my reading of *The Double Wedding* (1991) will imply, I have, partially, come round to agreeing with my friend's position, with the proviso that if English's work is not 'about anything', it is not about anything in an extremely complex, highly sophisticated, philosophical manner. At the time, I felt this comment represented a tendency to devalue certain types of performance as not worthy of serious and detailed consideration and that a production initiated and led by a white, male, heterosexual practitioner would not have been dismissed in this manner. While I still ascribe to this view to some extent, on reflection I also believe that this comment reflects a prevalent attitude in Britain towards 'performance' in general as opposed to theatre, even among those who apparently support this form. While it is perfectly acceptable to write a book focusing on the work of a single playwright such as Alan Ayckbourn, Harold Pinter or Caryl Churchill, in which a whole chapter may be devoted to exploring a single play, the norm in writing on performance appears to be to discuss a number of practitioners together and to comment briefly on selected aspects of a wide range of productions. The argument for such an approach may be based on the 'ephemeral' nature of the form, although a similar issue of ephemerality has never impeded commentators who offer detailed and apparently authoritative analyses of historical, non-text-based performances, and this argument does not seem to apply to US criticism. It is noticeable that of the three practitioners who are the main focus of this work, only Sprinkle has been given specific and lengthy critical consideration. While this may relate to the nature of her work, it can also be attributed to certain cultural differences between Britain and the USA explored in chapter one. However, the noticeable critical neglect of a practitioner like Rose English in Britain may also have been exacerbated by the academic practice of collecting women's work together under the rubric of 'feminist theatre'. This often creates expectations concerning female authored performance that can be extremely limiting. In a sense it has created preconceived ideas about what women's work should be 'about' that can blind the spectator or the critic to what the work may *actually* be attempting to explore. For example, the Christian themes and imagery which recur in Bobby Baker's work have been largely ignored by academic commentators, perhaps because they do not sit easily within dominant feminist paradigms.

A feminist impulse, then, produced the desire to write a work that took some (funny) shows by women seriously without entirely appropriating them to the category of feminism. This is a rather tricky paradox to negotiate and, to paraphrase some lines from *The Double Wedding*, although some people might call my position hypocritical, I would prefer to call it contradictory. On the one hand I am interested in these productions because they are all initiated and performed by women. Moreover, my pleasure in these works inevitably has to do with a sexed/gendered identification with the practitioners, and since I focus on the representation of 'femininity' within these works, I inevitably privilege certain aspects of the productions at the expense of others. On the other hand, the readings I execute take as a starting point the notion that terms like 'femininity', 'woman' and 'feminist' are contested and unstable categories, not givens. It is the various ways in which 'woman', or the 'feminine', is represented, performed and received in these works and the different sorts of feminist *readings* these representations may be given which constitute my primary concerns. I am not therefore claiming that the shows themselves are feminist, and my readings are also always informed by the manner in which the shows relate to the field of performance in general and the specific contexts in which they occurred.

One significant context could be deemed to be the 'postmodern' era: not only do all the shows under consideration make some sort of direct or indirect reference to postmodernism but, drawing on Charles Jenks and Fredric Jameson among others, they are all also definable as stylistically postmodernist (see Jameson 1991 and Jenks 1986). That is, these productions are hybrids, both multimedia and fluctuating between various genres of visual and performing arts. They are eclectic in terms of borrowing from other, past texts and performances, employ irony, parody and pastiche, paradox and contradiction, and while they deliberately play upon intertextuality, they are also self-reflexive and self-referential. They eschew linear narratives, operating through juxtaposition and collage, and resist the production of fixed or single meanings or reading positions. In short, all sorts of boundaries are challenged and confused, between art forms, between high and popular culture, between the stage and the auditorium, between the reality of the performance and the 'real', between the identity of the performer and the role. This postmodern turn produces the necessity of referring to some postmodern theory in order to understand why, how and if they are indeed 'postmodern' and what implications this may hold for the construction of sex and gender and even notions of performance within them. Indeed, so far in theory, my suggestion that a) my readings of the shows rather than the shows themselves are feminist and these readings are subjective and context specific, and b) terms like 'the feminine', 'feminist' and 'woman' are contested and unstable categories, indicates the taking up of a position that could be designated as postmodern feminism or feminist postmodernism. Yet, as I hope to demonstrate, in practice, in so far as this can be described as a 'position', it is itself characterised by instability, not least because, as Linda Singer points out,

> It is both ironic and paradoxical that the terminology of 'feminism' and 'postmodernism' works dramatically against the grain of much of the writing, theory and practice to which they are supposed to refer, since such terminological collection works to occlude, deny or obscure the very differences, particularities and specificities upon which feminist and postmodern projects so often insist. (Singer 1992: 464)

In theory *any* and all attempts to discuss either postmodernism or feminism as if either of these terms represented single, coherent and unified positions is inimical to most of the theories and practices in question and most particularly to the theories and practices that might be indicated by the joining of the two terms. In the first place, each term in and of itself signifies in a number of different ways, in so far as 'postmodern' can, as already indicated, refer to a historical period, an aesthetic and a wide range of diverse, often opposing theories, including the writings of Jean-François Lyotard, Fredric Jameson, Jean Baudrillard, Richard Rorty and Umberto Eco, to name but a few. Paradoxically, many of these theorists would actually argue against the first two definitions, since effectively they constitute unifying 'grand' narratives or 'metanarratives'. Certain theorists frequently referred to as 'poststructuralist', such as Jacques Derrida, Roland Barthes, Michel Foucault and even Jacques Lacan, are also often included in the sweep of postmodernism, and these two terms are sometimes used interchangeably. However, for some (postmodernists), such as Andreas Huyssen, poststructuralism remains a discourse of and about modernism and may even be symptomatic of 'high' rather than 'post' modernism, remaining concerned ultimately with aesthetics and the linguistic, and as a result is both formalist and elitist. Conversely for Huyssen, postmodernism is both a historical condition and an analysis of that condition and therefore far more engaged with the social and the political (Huyssen 1990). Yet, as becomes clear in my discussion of *The Double Wedding* in chapter three, not only do both postmodernism and poststructuralism draw on the same historical sources and references, but many of the tools used to analyse the postmodern condition derive directly from the development of linguistic theory by poststructuralists. So, for example, both the term and the basic principles of 'deconstruction', one of postmodernism's more 'political' methodologies, are usually attributed to Derrida. Moreover, the blurring of distinctions between postmodernism and poststructuralism may also be due to the fact that major hallmarks of postmodernism are said to be eclecticism, the crossing of boundaries and the breaking down of barriers between genres and disciplines. Equally, this conflation of postmodernism and poststructuralism may arise from the fact that *if* indeed the period is postmodern, *any* theory, practice or cultural artefact produced within this period can be automatically subsumed under this heading, which in itself rather belies the notion that there is such a thing as a single, postmodern aesthetic. It is possible therefore to suggest that poststructuralism is simultaneously among the discourses that describe and define the 'postmodern condition' and itself a product of that condition and thereby to an extent responsible for producing the condition of which it is part. Actually, one of the more significant differences is that poststructuralism remains a term mainly employed by academics, while the term 'postmodernism' has had a more popular currency. In any case, many of the theories I utilise in this study are in fact more properly poststructuralist than postmodern, and this includes the work of feminists such as Judith Butler, Luce Irigaray, Julia Kristeva and Susan Bordo.

In comparison, 'feminist' and 'feminism' refer first and foremost to a politics which developed out of consciousness raising and political activism and has only latterly, with the establishment of women's and gender studies within academia, been equated with a body of theory. Although it signifies an ideological movement and therefore a metanarrative, this movement has never had a single, clearly defined, common ideology or been constituted around a political party or a central organisation or leaders or an agreed policy or manifesto, or even been based upon an agreed principle of collective action. As a result, feminism has always for the most part consisted of diverse individuals, addressing sexual political issues in different ways on the level of the local and the specific, coming together in loose coalitions to address particular issues. This diversity in feminist practice has always been reflected within emergent feminist theory, and, as with postmodernism, this generic term embraces a number of antagonistic positions. Further, although some theorists define a limited number of feminist categories, such as radical or cultural, socialist or materialist, bourgeois or liberal or even postmodern, it is hard to find any two examples of any sort of practice from different sources where there are not anomalies, disagreements and contradictions. In practice, these different categories of feminism seldom remain discrete and separate, so that, for example, in the realm of theatre, a play like Sarah Daniels's *Masterpieces* (1984), while nearly always defined as a clear example of 'radical' feminism, has inherent socialist feminist tendencies. These occur both in the Brechtian elements of its structure and the manner in which, through these elements, it explores the economic base of the oppression of sex workers. Similarly, a play like Kay Adshead's *Thatcher's Women* (1988), starts off as a piece of socialist realism before moderating into something that might represent a move towards a 'radical' or 'cultural' feminist perspective.

Conversely and on a more general level, it has always been acknowledged that there are significant differences between French, US, British and indeed 'post-colonial' feminisms due to the different social, political conditions in which they developed, and each of these has moderated through time according to alterations in these conditions. British feminist theory and indeed British feminist theatre practice in the 1970s and early 1980s were often dominated by socialist feminism. With the erosion of British socialism under the pressure of successive Conservative governments and the collapse of Communism in the Eastern block, British feminists turned to other paradigms. These have drawn upon both French and US feminisms, so that there has been a great deal of cultural exchange and cross-fertilisation, although significant differences remain. On an even more specific level there has, for example, been much complaint concerning the critical tendency to group together the so-called French feminists, as I do above. This term has often been used as shorthand to refer to only three theorists: Luce Irigaray, Julia Kristeva and Hélène Cixous. This not only suggests a theoretical unity between these three women which does not exist in practice but also ignores a number of other extremely influential feminists who happen to be French and who have little in common with these three, such as Monique Wittig and Catherine Clement. The same principle of diversity holds for US and British feminism, and the same issues of social, cultural and historical specificity surely apply to postmodernism; in theory, any sort of postmodernism (and poststructuralism) should always acknowledge and work through such differences. Yet this is often ignored in practice and both feminism and postmodernism are discussed as if they were easily identifiable, singular, transcultural phenomena.

In theory, neither postmodernism nor feminism can be

discussed in the singular as if these terms referred to a consistent and coherent body of thought or genre of practice, and no single example of either can stand for the whole or even for a particular strand in a completely satisfactory manner. So, despite the fact that I have defined all the shows as belonging to the postmodern period and all sharing certain characteristics that may be deemed as common to a postmodern aesthetic, none of them is actually postmodern in quite the same way, and there are as many differences between them formally as there are similarities. Equally, if they can all be given feminist readings, these readings refer to a range of types and variations of feminism, even within a single show. Sometimes, as with Sprinkle, these variations may be national, sometimes they relate to other discourses, so that, for example, the references to British (Protestant?) Christianity that recur in Bobby Baker's productions inevitably complicate and colour any discussion of these works in relation to either feminism or postmodernism.

Yet to return to Singer's remark, paradoxically this play between multiplicity and specificity may be said to be a defining characteristic of postmodernism and one that it holds in common with feminism. Further, the working within such ironies, paradoxes and contradictions may, ironically, paradoxically and in a contradictory manner, also be said to be a common features of much feminist and postmodern practice and theory. Therefore, in so far as it is possible to speak of them in the singular (which is not at all), they have much in common while remaining distinct and fundamentally contradictory. Both, for example, offer critiques of humanist rationalism, scientific objectivity, historical truth and the transparency of language in order to expose the hidden and unequal power relations within the belief systems at the foundations of Western culture and society. However, whereas post modernism is sceptical about the power relations behind all and any belief system or, in Lyotard's terms, all and any metanarratives that are presented as being able to speak in general, feminism has tended itself to perform as a metanarrative, presenting itself as speaking for and about women as a general category. Yet the concepts, which some postmodernists seem implicitly to support, of the postmodern as a definable, Western transcultural aesthetic and a general, transcultural experience of a period of time both represent narratives that are as 'meta' as anything offered by feminism.

Both feminism and postmodernism for the most part produce their critiques 'deconstructively', working to demonstrate the hierarchical nature of the binary oppositions that inform the dominant linguistic, social and philosophical structures of Western culture and thought. But whereas, in theory, *all* binaries are 'deconstructed' within postmodernism – including the notion of Western culture and thought, as opposed to, for instance, Eastern culture and thought – *some* feminisms continue to maintain and depend upon making a distinction between masculine and feminine, reversing the normative hierarchy, to revalue the concept of the feminine and render it in positive terms. Further, *all* feminisms, in practice, must to some degree depend on remarking and upholding the binary relationship between male and female, since they are concerned with the oppression of women as group, class or identity category. The remarking of this binary implies that there are aspects of human subjectivity based on the experience of sexual difference which tend to be general if not universal, even if this experience of sexual difference is itself mediated through the socially specific. So while for most but not all feminisms gender is seen as socially constructed, sex often appears to remain a truth, a 'fact' or a natural given, while for many postmodernists there can be no perception of the truth, the real or of nature that is not always already culturally constructed. Postmodernism usually posits a notion of subjectivity that is constantly being produced and reproduced through competing discourses. The tendency to privilege any one subjectivity or aspect of subjectivity as a universal stable position and therefore as a basis for articulating human perception and experience is perceived as being caught up in a hierarchical system which always depends on the exclusion and abjection of some 'other'.

In this comparison it could easily seem that a notion of a postmodern feminism, or vice versa, constitutes an aporia, and in theory it should be impossible or at least severely contradictory to discuss 'postmodern' shows in terms of feminism. In the same article cited above, Linda Singer goes on to explore the relationship between feminism and postmodernism metaphorically in terms of kinship, familial relations and even a 'marriage', recalling the manner in which, in Britain, socialist feminism used to be referred to as an 'unhappy marriage'. Marriage as an institution has been identified by feminists as legally, financially and symbolically representing the securing of heterosexual, patriarchal norms through the exchange of women. The marriage contract signifies an unequal partnership in which the erasure of the identity of the female subject is reinforced in the exchange of one patronymic for another. This also reflects the manner in which some feminists have viewed the potential outcome of an alliance between feminism and postmodernism. For some, feminism cannot operate without a notion of a stable 'female subject', and the de-centring of the subject in postmodernism is seen as an attempt to prevent women's access to the privileges of a position hitherto denied to them. As Margaret Whitford puts it, this 'continues to leave women in a state of fragmentation and dissemination that reproduces and perpetuates the patriarchal violence which separates women' (quoted in Elam 1994: 71). In these terms, postmodernism takes on the aspect of a backlash against feminism if not a straightforward patriarchal conspiracy which, as Craig Owens puts it, 'may yet be another masculine invention engineered to exclude women' (quoted in Suleiman 1990: 183). This concern is reinforced by the fact that any canonical roll-call of major postmodernist thinkers has always tended to be exclusively male, and few of these theorists show much, if any, interest in or sympathy for sexual politics. Meaghan Morris has pointed out that this view itself is to some extent a self-fulfilling prophecy, since it 'emerges from texts by male critics referring primarily to each other commenting on the rarity of women's speech', and she responds by citing over thirty-eight female thinkers, some of whom have produced poststructuralist analyses of modernity and 'many of whom have had, in fact, quite a bit to say about postmodernism' (Morris 1994: 377–8). However, citation of feminist, if not simply female, thinkers in the context of postmodernism tends to occur in writings entitled Feminism *and* Postmodernism or vice versa. In her book *Feminism and Deconstruction*, Diane Elam points out that 'this "and" not only breaks but joins' and that in using it she intends to indicate a relationship that is interdependent but not hierarchical (Elam 1994: 13). Yet Elam also acknowledges the possibility that one term is actually implicitly presented or read as subordinate to the other. This is always a danger with feminism and postmodernism, since feminism remains the (supposedly) more 'marginal' term, the 'minority' interest, the subordinate women's issue to the (male) postmodernist broader concerns. This can also lead to the perception that postmodernism and poststructuralism have shown feminism the error of its modernist ways.

Theorists such as Fraser and Nicholson suggest the possibility of a more equal partnership in which feminism and postmodernism are each in possession of 'valuable resources' which can help remedy the deficiencies of the other in a complementary fashion, on the principle that

> Postmodernists offer sophisticated and persuasive criticisms of foundationalism and essentialism, but their conceptions of the social tend to be anaemic. Feminists offer robust conceptions of social criticism, but they tend at times to lapse into foundationalism and essentialism. (Fraser and Nicholson 1990: 20)

While postmodernism may be relatively more engaged in the social and political, the focus in *both* postmodernism and poststructuralism on notions of discourse, linguistic theory and signifying systems is seen as producing a movement away from any active engagement with the material world. To put it another way, there is a perceived dissolution of the 'social' into the 'cultural', where the production or 'reading' of 'texts' is framed as the equivalent to, or rather a substitute for, acting in and on the world. Indeed, the postmodern as a condition is often described as a symptom of late capitalism, in which the increasing symbolisation of the economic and the commodification of culture have produced a loss of 'real' value, since everything is reduced to the level of the exchange of signs. This, together with an analysis in which all 'truth claims' are revealed as constructions that normalise unequal power relations, is seen as resulting in a loss of the ability to distinguish between right and wrong, good and bad, fake and copy, leading eventually to the sort of apathetic passivity described in the works of Baudrillard (see Baudrillard 1988). Similarly, the concept of the subject as an effect rather than an author of discourse is perceived as a loss of agency, and the fragmentation of identity into multiple and differing identities as producing moral incoherence and political relativism. Politics as we have known it in the West in the modern era has always been based on a notion of 'the polis' as a unified body, who collectively make choices based on a universal perception of 'reason' and 'truth'. The fragmentation of the people as a body, as formulated by postmodernism and experienced within the postmodern era, is seen as negation of the social and the evacuation of the political, with community and collectivity superseded by a new and extreme form of capitalist, bourgeois individualism.

Alternatively, it could be said that postmodernism and post-structuralism are part of a reconfiguration of the political, in which, as Lyotard suggests, notions of the *polis* or of community will be redefined as 'a multiplicity or diversity – each member of which is essentially autonomous, yet somehow relates to the others justly'. This is quoted by Philip Auslander in his seminal essay 'Toward a Concept of the Political in Postmodern Theatre', in which he joins a debate elucidated by, among others, Lyotard, Hal Foster and Fredric Jameson concerning the possibility of a postmodern political critique (Auslander 1987: 21). Auslander, like the others cited, recognises that it is in the nature of postmodernism that any such critique always operates within that which is critiqued, because postmodernism accepts that there is no way of positioning oneself 'outside' the discourses that construct culture – and this brings with it attendant dangers. As such, it is perhaps not surprising that Susan Rubin Suleiman points out a contradiction between some postmodernist theory and practice on this point of the possibility of a postmodern political critique. As Suleiman indicates, most postmodernist critics agree that meanings, political or otherwise, are discovered in the process of reading by diverse and multiple, socially constructed subjects, rather than existing within texts as bearers of transparent meanings. According to Suleiman, however, this position is implicitly contradicted by the claim, articulated by Foster, Jameson and Lyotard, that it is possible to discuss certain cultural artefacts in terms of a good 'resistant' postmodernism and a bad 'reactionary' postmodernism. This would appear to suggest that texts do carry fixed and self-evident meanings and by implication indicates a common, if not universal, subject position for the decoding of these meanings. In this instance, postmodernism shows a tendency to 'lapse' into foundationalism and essentialism, similar to that of feminism. It seems strange, then, that, like Fraser and Nicholson but on more cynical grounds, Suleiman suggests that the problem of the politics of postmodernism art may be overcome by a coalition with feminism:

> In short, feminism brings to postmodernism the political guarantee postmodernism needs to feel respectable as an avant-garde practice. Postmodernism, in turn, brings to feminism a certain high 'theoretical discourse' on the frontiers of culture, traditionally an exclusively male domain. (Suleiman 1990: 189)

It is significant that Suleiman makes this comment in relation to the 'avant-garde', a type of work, like poststructuralism, often accused of bourgeois formalism and elitism, and a category to which all the works under consideration in this book belong. This in itself reveals that one danger with Suleiman's cheerfully opportunistic proposition is that, in this exchange, feminism may lose, or indeed already have lost, its political respectability. The fact that, under the influence of postmodernism and poststructuralism, many of the early feminist thinkers and practitioners have been rejected in favour of theories drawn from the work of male theorists, is often cited as evidence of the appropriation and inoculation of feminism within the male domain of the academic institution. Indeed, academic feminist 'high' theorists and avant-garde practitioners are often accused of an 'anaemic conception of the social', and here I am only too aware of the dangers of being firmly 'within' that which I may critique. Even represented in positive terms as an encroachment on a 'male domain', this union remains uneasy for feminism's political respectability since it is still, presumably, political in a manner inadmissible within postmodernism in that it remains an identity politics dependent on a notion of a universal female subject.

Both those who construct postmodernism as a backlash against feminism and those in the mutual benefits camp always presuppose that feminism is somehow 'outside' postmodernism with the problem of subjectivity as the point of division. Yet feminism as we think of it today has arisen within the so-called postmodern period, and until fairly recently feminism was also thought not to be properly political, partly because it was a discourse that demanded a radical rethink of the relationship between the personal and the political, the private and the public, the cultural and the economic. Most types of feminism also agree that historically, within patriarchal discourse, 'woman' has functioned as a sign with no reference to the 'real', even if they also insist on the existence of a 'true' feminine elsewhere. Feminism has also always been concerned with linguistics, and the much mocked, radical feminist insistence on terms like 'Wimmin' and 'Herstory' were actually 'deconstructive' before this term had general currency. Meaghan Morris also points out that while expressing surprise at the lack of feminist critics in the 'postmodern' debate, male theorists like Huyssen and Owens constantly assert that 'crucial aspects of postmodernism now would be "unthinkable" without the impact of feminist thought' (Morris

1994: 379). In short, feminism may have always been very much 'inside' postmodernism, even as Morris indicates operating as an 'enabling' discourse for both postmodernism and poststructuralism, and in fact the areas of greatest apparent conflict are also the points at which its contribution has been the most significant.

When Fraser and Nicholson argue for a coalition of postmodernism and feminism they focus on this issue to produce a definition of 'the subject' which proposes that we

> replace unitary notions of woman and feminine gender identity with plural and complexly constructed conceptions of social identity, treating gender as one relevant strand among others, attending also to class, race, ethnicity, age and sexual orientation. (Fraser and Nicholson 1990: 34–5)

Yet, as I have already suggested, feminisms rather than feminism have always offered plural, competing notions of what 'woman' and 'the feminine' might mean. Surely the formulation above developed as much under the influence of 'lesbian', 'black' and 'working class' feminists, who felt that the category of 'woman' as defined by 'white', 'heterosexual', 'middle class' feminists was exclusive and inadequate in describing the complexity of oppression of individuals who are 'other' in different ways at different times. On the simplest level, feminism has always been a continuing enquiry into the *problematic* of what it means 'be a woman' in both theory and practice. In the realm of theory, the speed at which feminist thought has developed, working through and discarding epistemologies, means that any answers or solutions to this problem have been temporary, no sooner formulated than challenged from within feminist discourse.

To some extent feminism has always been a politics in search of a subject rather than based on one, and this is evident in practice. In her 'Gender Diary', discussing the 'divide' in feminism between the essentialists and social constructionists, Anne Snitow suggests that, whatever their theoretical position, in daily life women tend to travel back and forth between these positions (Snitow 1990: 34). This is because, as Judith Butler has pointed out, it is important to remember that the taking up of a subject or an identity position is not a matter of choice (Butler 1993: 232). Feminists exist in societies in which as 'women' they are constantly being defined in powerful and persuasive ways, which can be impossible to resist. This has produced within feminism a very pragmatic and a very postmodern acceptance of paradox and contradiction, since as women they may have to negotiate the paradoxes and contradictions both between their own theories and their daily experience and also between the competing discourses that construct this experience.

If in practice feminists 'lapse' into foundationalism and essentialism it is not only the case, as Butler citing Gayatri Spivak suggests, 'that feminists need to operate on an operational essentialism, a false ontology of women as universal in order to advance a feminist political programme' (Butler 1990: 325). It is also because, as Diane Elam indicates, once something has been deconstructed it does not necessarily stay deconstructed forever, and indeed she could add everywhere and for everyone (Elam 1994: 20). In short, even the most postmodern of feminists operate in a social, cultural world in which foundationalism and essentialism may be being critiqued but have not been transcended or disappeared. As Susan Bordo puts it, 'we still live in a culture in which our language, intellectual history and social forms are gendered: there is no escape from this fact and from its consequences on our lives' (Bordo 1995: 242).

It may be by reason of the unavoidable, social and material consequences of 'being a woman' in our culture that feminism has been more robust than postmodernism in terms of offering a social critique. At the same time, postmodern discourse has not solved, finished with, done away with or said the last word on the problem of the 'subject', and identity politics remains a central political concern and even increasingly a central political problem as we approach the millennium. One of the most frequently cited descriptions of postmodernism defines it not as a radical break from modernism but as a reworking from within, a resignification of modernism. If the postmodern condition or period or subject exists and we can talk of such a thing as postmodernist theory, then in practice all these things are in a condition of flux between modernism and postmodernism, now one, now the other, without ever being entirely one thing or the other. The difference between (male) postmodernist and (female) feminist and postmodernist thinkers, however, may lie in the fact that because of the material effects of 'being a woman', feminist, postmodernist theorists seem more aware of this process as a *practice* and attempt to explore it pragmatically and productively. So, for example, Rebecca Schneider refers to a recent 'philosophical positioning of "both at once" – feminists who bear an Irigarayan "double gesture", paradoxically essentialist and constructivist at once' (Schneider 1997: 36). I would include under this category Judith Butler, Diane Elam and Susan Bordo, all of whom in various ways explore 'woman' as both a discursive construct and an embodied, historically located object and therefore as an identity category which cannot be simply transcended in one fell swoop but which is not an 'absolute' either. The exploration of this idea of double gestures which are paradoxically both at once is one of the main points of focus of this book and the main means of negotiating the tricky terrain between theory and practice.

However, formulations such as the one proposed by Fraser and Nicholson are often seen as having been produced by the corrective influence of postmodernism on feminism and have been used as part of a campaign against any vestiges of essentialism, and it is here, with an insistence on theoretical purity, that the gap opens up between theory and practice. In response to such ideas, Susan Bordo warns that there can be no view from 'nowhere', since all viewing is perspectival and, as a result,

> No matter how local or circumscribed the object or how attentive the scholar is to the axes that constitute social identity, some of those axes will be ignored and others selected [...]. This selectivity, moreover, is never innocent. (Bordo 1995: 222)

This is as much a problem for postmodernism as for feminism, since any time the local and specific is examined exclusion takes place and the object under consideration easily starts to appear as a generalised example. Hence my reason for placing inverted commas around 'black', 'lesbian' and 'working class' feminisms, since these perspectives, which have been so crucial in deconstructing 'white', 'middle class', 'heterosexual' feminism through insisting on the specificity of certain identities, in themselves represent generalisations that ignore the multiple differences within the groups supposedly represented by these terms. Of necessity feminists, like those who wish to espouse a 'resistant' postmodernism, are always operating within and potentially reinforcing that which they critique. In the course of this book therefore, and in line with both Judith Butler and Susan Bordo, I am going to argue not only that 'theoretical' purity is an impossible ideal but that any attempt to achieve such purity is essentially undemocratic. On the one hand, pursuing such 'purity' ignores the complexity, diversity and, of necessity, pragmatically impure nature of practices. On the other, in direct contradiction to most recent configurations of postmodernism and feminism, this pursuit represents the desire for the discovery of a metanarrative that will solve the problem of the political once and for all, rendering all differences comprehensible, if not identical, in advance through reference to a single and overwhelmingly authoritative perspective.

My own position throughout this work will inevitably be 'centric', not least since the main works considered are by white women working within the avant-garde and I cannot claim any sort of 'innocence' on this point. My main justification for this choice of material, as I suggest in chapter one, is that this is a field that has at least offered *some* (and, in Britain at least, mainly white) women opportunities and openings not readily available in other more established, canonical or commercial forms of art or performance. In fact, the more commercially successful and 'popular' the form, the shorter the list seems to be of female practitioners from any class, racial or sexual group who function as acknowledged 'authors', rather than 'interpreters' of the works of others. In the fields of film or television drama for instance, women writers, editors, directors, producers and 'controllers' are still in a tiny minority, if not entirely absent. The avant-garde is of course by its nature on the margins and so may be subject to slightly less direct social control and censorship than mass entertainment forms with their greater economic productivity and powers of dissemination. As such, the avant-garde is more likely to serve as a space for mounting work considered to be of a 'minority interest' and which interrogates some dominant norms. However, the nominations 'avant-garde' or 'experimental', like those of 'feminist' or 'postmodern', do not guarantee that this will actually be the case, any more than 'popular' or 'mass' necessarily signify works that address or represent the interests and concerns of the majority of the population.

I am not, therefore, suggesting in any way that the performances considered in this book exemplify or speak for 'women' in our culture or even 'female performance', and in fact my limiting of the scope of this work to close readings of three particular shows is, in part, intended to guard against such generalisations. I am simply interested in testing out and exploring certain theories in relation to these specific practices. I also make no great claims for the political impact or efficacy of the shows studied, partly because of their limited and even exclusive audiences but also because no single performance or act of representation, in itself, has much political effect except as part of a wider discourse of change. On the other hand, my own acknowledgement of my 'lack of innocence' and of the limitations of my study is not intended, in Susan Rubin Suleiman's terms, as an 'excuse for anything goes' or as an evasion of responsibility (Suleiman 1990: 196). Rather, it is intended as a starting point for exploring the problematic of, as Auslander puts it, 'walk[ing] a tightrope between complicity and critique' that is implicit in notions both of feminist 'double gestures' and of a post-modern politics predicated on 'resistance' or 'subversion' in the realm of the cultural (Auslander 1987: 21).

This book is therefore structured around a process of interrogation, which is often self-reflexive in so far as it offers interpretations of performances while questioning the grounds on which these interpretations are constructed. This is achieved by exploring the ways in which the shows may be said to resist attempts at authoritative, interpretative 'mastery' and cannot ultimately be appropriated to a single, 'pure', uncontradictory theoretical position. This means that the critical perspective shifts from modernist to postmodernist, to poststructuralist, to feminist, from practice to theory and back again, in an attempt to follow the movements I perceive as occurring within the shows. As a result, the book itself proceeds by means of both analysing and making a series of double gestures, exploring oppositions and contradictions through a process of repetition and difference, presenting and building upon a series of perspectives, while also putting them into question. In this fashion I hope to create spaces for differences and for debate within and between the shows themselves, within and between these perspectives, and within and between practice and theory. Eventually and perhaps inevitably, considering the form in which I am writing, my approach does amount to something like a coherent thesis not entirely arising from but best explained through reference to Derrida, Judith Butler, Diane Elam and the notion of the politics of undecidability. However, this is a thesis which attempts to preserve and respect differences, and which resists synthesis and the establishing in advance of a single model for either creating or analysing any sort of performance practice, political or otherwise.

In chapter one, I start by examining the fashion in which, like postmodernism and feminism, resistance to definition appears to be a defining characteristic of contemporary 'performance'. This exercise is undertaken in order to explore why and how these three forms, concepts and/or sets of practices have come to be perceived as closely related by both British and US theorists. I then engage in the first of numerous double gestures, analysing the similarities and differences in the traditions of female performance art in Britain and the USA and the similarities and differences between Baker, Sprinkle and English, in order to place them together in a 'sub-genre of female performance art'. While, in theory, I agree with Philip Auslander's contention, made again through citing Lyotard, that to read art as 'political' messages is to 'leave the politics of representation uncriticised', I suggest that, in practice, female performance art always potentially carries some sort of 'political' message because, in being 'authored' by 'women', it inevitably implies a critique of the politics of representation (Auslander 1987: 21). In doing so, I deliberately deploy a contingent essentialism as a means of interrogating the assumption which, post Brecht, has tended to dominate political performance criticism, that certain forms of representation necessarily convey specific and clearly identifiable ideologies.

A brief overview of the work of each practitioner over a twenty-year period is then used to introduce some feminist and postmodernist perspectives concerning the subversive or resistant potential of certain formal means of representation, drawing together ideas on the uses of humour and the concept of the 'unreadable' text. This is pursued with particular reference to '*ecriture feminine*' and also to Susan Rubin Suleiman's interpretation of Roland Barthes's discussion of the 'writerly text'. In the course of her analysis, Suleiman argues that Barthes represents the 'writerly' as a 'masculine' form, despite its traditionally 'feminine' qualities, underlining the way in which the same forms have often been claimed by different sexual political factions. Suleiman also asserts that Barthes positions the female reader of such texts 'as a woman, impersonating a man, impersonating a woman' (Suleiman 1990: 39).

In chapter two, drawing on the coincidence that all three of the practitioners in question have been described by critics in terms that construct them as 'men in drag', I introduce and explore a range of theories of identity which draw upon 'performative metaphors'. As such, I try to evaluate whether or not the description of Baker, English and Sprinkle in these terms can be defined as resistant or normative. The ideas considered include, among others, Judith Butler's notion of gender as performative as developed in *Gender Trouble* (1990), both Joan Riviere's and Jacques Lacan's ideas of 'masquerade', as well as Irigarayan mimicry. In discussing these notions I consider the argument posited by Carole-Anne Tyler that, aside from Lacan, these theorists tend to represent gender as a 'fiction' while reinscribing sex as foundational, and as a result, in practice, these concepts assume the transparent communication of 'author's intentions' (Tyler 1991). As a means of both acknowledging and countering this point, I focus on Judith Butler's thesis in *Bodies that Matter* (1993), where both sex and gender are described as performative in a manner that undermines the notion of all and any author's intentions. Touching on the problems that can arise in applying Butler's ideas in a general way, due in part to her privileging of the performer over staging, I consider the problem of distinguishing between performance and performativity. Returning to the issue of form, I then explore the differences and similarities between Butler's ideas and Brechtian theory, partly in order to critique the exclusive and limiting fashion in which, over the last twenty to thirty years, Brecht's ideas have been reified as the dominant paradigm for political theatre.

Chapter three offers a close reading of Rose English's *The Double Wedding* (1991), analysing the ways in which the piece could be said to foreground the performativity of performance, in an interpretation that moves between Plato's cave, Nietzsche's void, Walter Benjamin's cinema, Brecht's epic theatre and Artaud's 'Theatre of Cruelty'. The reader should be warned that in many ways I found this the most 'difficult' and theoretically challenging chapter in the book. I have tried my best to render the material accessible, but ultimately the result reflects the attempt to grapple with an extremely dense and profoundly theatrical work which, as such, strongly resists translation into 'another' sort of language. Moreover, the theoretical terrain in which this piece appears to be placed, in and of itself, suggests that in the final analysis this is a show which cannot be interpreted, only described. I argue that *The Double Wedding* foregrounds the performativity of performance which means that potentially this show has an almost infinite number of meanings and no meaning at the same time, or rather it refers only to the process of representation whereby meanings proliferate but no 'thing' is ever made present. While I continue to draw on Butler, the main source for this reading is Derrida's essay, 'The Double Session' (1981). As such, I suggest that the confusion of identity that appears to have been produced by this show arose because the piece can be interpreted formally as functioning as a Derridean 'hymen', and therefore it literally 'stages' phallic authority in a manner that renders the difference between binary oppositions 'undecidable'. However, since 'undecidability' resists synthesis, I also argue that if the show does operate in this manner, any such reading remains a matter of individual interpretation, so that this effect cannot definitely be said to be a matter of author's intentions, nor can it definitely be claimed as subversive or normative. In short, this piece firmly places the responsibility for 'final' meanings on the spectator in a manner that starts to explore a 'different sort of ethics' and opens up crucial areas of debate for contemporary political performance.

After describing Bobby Baker's *How to Shop* (1993), chapter four investigates Susan Bordo's critique of Derridean-influenced postmodern, feminist theory in her book *Unbearable Weight* (1995). Bordo picks out Butler's work in *Gender Trouble* in particular, asserting that Butler's ideas depend on a conception of the body as an unsituated, linguistic fiction rather than as a located historical object. She also accuses Butler of representing her own perspective as a 'correct unimpeachably pure position' (Bordo 1995: 290). While suggesting any such criticism of Butler is for the most part countered in *Bodies that Matter*, I take up Bordo's point concerning theoretical purity and her worry that some of this genre of 'postmodern' thought, in practice, might actually represent an *un*subversive repetition of the repudiation of 'the body', and by association of the maternal feminine, which has characterised Western, patriarchal philosophy at least since Plato. This introduces a reading of Baker's *How to Shop*, focusing initially on the way the show plays between the material and the immaterial, repudiation and celebration of the maternal body, sadism and masochism, masculine and feminine. This reading is carried out in relation to Riviere's notion of masquerade and Julia Kristeva's notion of the abject, with specific reference to the emphasis on religious iconography within the piece (see Kristeva 1982). I then demonstrate how concentrating on the social and physical location of this show in a lecture theatre and on its staging as a public lecture, rather than purely on discourses that privilege Baker's sex or gender, provides a different yet contiguous reading for the piece. This interpretation depends on the spectator taking all the roles Baker performs equally seriously and also on their willingness to take responsibility as an active agent for making meanings *after* the event. In this reading, Baker appears, in Michel de Certeau's terms, to be 'involved in a different kind of production', one that 'shows itself not in its own products but in the art of using those imposed upon it' (de Certeau 1994: xii). The products imposed upon Baker in this instance include all the discourses considered in the first half of the chapter but also Lauren Langman's academic essay on shopping which sets out to define the 'subject' of consumption and which is quoted in the show (Langman 1992). This essay employs both performative metaphors and religious imagery and I suggest that Baker deconstructs this deconstruction, which claims to describe 'her' subjectivity as a consumer, subverting it on its own terms. She can then be said to perform a subjectivity that repeats all these various discourses but cannot be contained by them. This is a subjectivity shown to be 'incoherent', radically contradictory, not so much Brechtian as 'undecidable', and so this is a repetition that creates a 'hiatus in iterability', which allows space for Baker's 'agency' without reinscribing a notion of author's intentions.

The theme of the relationship between production and consumption is continued in chapter five, with specific reference to the use of autobiography in the writing of academic criticism. In this chapter I offer a reading of Annie Sprinkle's *Post Post Porn Modernist* (1994) through a number of academic accounts of this show, which I compare and contrast with my own response. The result is an exploration of the way in which this piece might be said to produce a 'double movement' in the spectator which undercuts their intentions and confronts them with the groundlessness of their own authority. In this case this 'double movement' describes a fluctuation between identification and dis-identification with Sprinkle, a process directly affected by the specific conditions of seeing the performance and one which produced an awareness of Sprinkle as not a woman – *like me* but also *not a woman* – like me.

The conclusion returns to some of the issues addressed in this introduction, especially the relationship between theory and practice and the problematic of working within that which you wish to critique. As part of this discussion, I revisit the issue of distinguishing between performance and performativity, to stress the importance of finding connections while respecting differences. I then offer a summary of 'my' authorial position throughout this book through a combination of ideas drawn from Judith Butler and Diane Elam, both of whom draw on Derrida. This description of 'ethical activism' and 'the politics of undecidability' is supported through reference to Rose English's show *Tantamount Esperance* (1994). In a final double movement, however, I suggest that as well as helping to achieve an understanding of these concepts, a close reading of this show might also illuminate some of the assumptions, paradoxes and contradictions on which they depend. As such, I suggest that English's work, like Baker's and Sprinkle's, is worth taking as seriously as Derrida's or Butler's or any of the other authorities cited in the book, including myself, even though, or perhaps because, the former, unlike the latter, produce works that are funny.

1

The means of reproduction: the female performance art tradition, form, humour and ideology

The three practitioners I am considering in this book are usually described as 'performance artists', and unfortunately this term threatens to produce a problem of definition akin to that posed by 'postmodernism' and 'feminism'. In fact, there is a striking parallel between Linda Singer's comment cited in the introduction concerning the ironic paradox in the way these terms are employed and Jeanie Forte's opening statement in her article 'Women's Performance Art: Feminism and Postmodernism' which reads:

> Limiting one's critical focus to a particular group of performance artists or their performances has always seemed inappropriate, since that project would appear to perpetrate the very act of defining and categorising that anything called performance art actively resists. (Forte 1990: 251)

Resistance to definition appears to be a defining characteristic of all three terms, and, as with feminism and postmodernism, this is apparent in common usage where performance art is sometimes treated as a sub-genre of, or used interchangeably with, the broader category of performance and sometimes described as a completely separate phenomenon.

The first two usages have become more prevalent in recent years; this might be explained by Bert O. States's suggestion in his essay 'Performance as Metaphor' that the term performance has emerged as a 'keyword' in the sense employed by Raymond Williams. Keywords are words whose meanings 'are inextricably bound up with the problems [they are] being used to discuss' (Williams, quoted in States 1996: 2). As a result, they belong to 'the fields of both ideology and methodology: they are at once an attitude and a tool'. Further, a keyword, 'seconded by ideology, never stops ramifying itself until it has claimed as much territory as possible' (States 1996: 2). Putting the issue of performance *art* aside for the moment, clearly both feminism and postmodernism could be described as keywords in the same fashion as performance, and the way in which the territorial claims of each term has expanded over roughly the same period of time means that they often occupy the same ground.

It is not surprising, therefore, that the term 'postmodernism' frequently appears in discussions concerned with performance, and Nick Kaye is not alone in his opinion that 'performance may be thought of as primarily a postmodern mode' (1994: 23). Nor is it surprising to find Jeanie Forte asserting that 'Arguably all performance art, particularly in the earlier years, evidenced a deconstructive intent', and going on to say that 'women's performance emerges as a specific strategy that allies postmodernism and feminism' (1990: 251–2). Similarly, States contends that the spread of this term within theatre studies arises out of the impact of 'multiculturalism, interdisciplinary and *gender studies*' (1996: 2, my emphasis). Certainly the work of American, female performance artists of the 1970s and 1980s and its reception by feminist critics and theorists have had a notable influence on the subject area in the USA. All of this would imply that the spread of 'performance' as a keyword has been 'seconded' by 'postmodernism' and 'feminism', and as a result not only are the meanings of all three terms 'inextricably bound up with the problems they are used to discuss', but all three terms are to a certain extent inextricably bound up in the discussion of a similar, if not the same, set of problems. Indeed, Jill Dolan has specifically identified the increasing use of 'performative metaphors' as arising from postmodern/poststructuralist and feminist debates on subjectivity, arguing that

> The proliferation of performative metaphors is prompted in part by poststructuralist vocabulary that refuses a notion of inherent, essentialist ontology, but that suggests instead a constructionist notion of identity as anti-metaphysical, emphatically material and historical, constantly refashioning itself in various contexts and configurations of reception. (Dolan 1993: 419)

Yet Dolan is also wary of the spread of such metaphors where they are developed by other disciplines 'creatively borrowing concepts from theatre studies' without conceding the specificity of this field in and of itself, and she expresses her desire to see theatre studies 'acknowledged and visited, rather than raided and discarded' (419–20).

It is significant that in a book which attempts to define and trace the history of performance, Marvin Carlson starts by offering a whole raft of definitions and descriptions of this term derived from cultural studies, anthropology, sociology, philosophy, linguistics, feminism, and gay and lesbian studies, and States's essay adds one or two to this list from the field of science. This eclecticism and confusion of boundaries might be taken as evidence of the fundamentally postmodern nature of performance. However, like Dolan, both writers are predominantly interested in how these conceptualisations circulating in other fields specifically relate back to theatre studies, and ultimately both are concerned with distinguishing between performance used as a metaphor to discuss a broad range of social and cultural activities and what Carlson calls, for lack of a better term, 'theatrical performance' (1996: 196). In fact, States warns against the seductions of 'illusory transitivity' when dealing with performative metaphors. He points out that it is only too easy to 'move through culture identifying all sorts of performances and performative modes' and 'find family resemblances between things that gradually become more different than they are alike'. In short, the interdisciplinary terrain occupied by performance as a keyword is now so broad that, as States puts it, 'it is easy to find similarities that apply in one case but do not apply in another' (States 1996: 2–3). Bearing this in mind, I intend to consider some key performative metaphors developed in relation to the performance of subjectivity in everyday life separately in the next chapter and to focus here on the categorisation of Sprinkle, Baker and English as performance artists within a theatrical context.

Even here the keyword status of the term 'performance' means that new territories open up at an alarming rate. For example, when Carlson sets out to trace the history of performance and performance art, he acknowledges the map delineated by writers such as RoseLee Goldberg, setting out turn of the century, European, modernist, avant-garde antecedents, with particular reference to 'artistic' cabarets, Artaud, Dada and surrealism, the Bauhaus, the experiments of Cage, Cunningham et al. at Black Mountain College in the 1940s and 1950s and the 'happenings' in the USA in the 1960s and 1970s (see Goldberg 1988). However, he also proposes that both categories owe much to popular theatre and street entertainment spanning ancient Rome and Greece, the European fairs established in the medieval period, nineteenth-century circus, music hall and vaudeville and their twentieth-century incarnations including variety theatre and stand-up comedy, and finally some types of political theatre and street demonstrations. In short, he includes virtually all of live entertainment, except for mainstream or 'legitimate' theatre, opera and classical ballet. As a result, when he focuses on the 1970s and 1980s as a period when 'Performance and performance art emerged … as major cultural activities in the United States as well as in Western Europe and Japan', he concludes that the complexity, variety, popularity and ubiquity of such activities 'have made them very difficult to define' (Carlson 1996: 100).

While States acknowledges the problems posed in defining performance, he does offer a definition of performance *art,* on the principle that

> there is one huge respect in which *performance* as used in the term *performance art* signifies something different from its meaning under normative circumstances (say of theatre or concert performance). Performance art was, and to great degree still is, aimed at deconstructing the normal assumptions of traditional theatre. … Understanding performance art outside of the context of 'normal' theatre and art would be as fruitless as trying to understand the Declaration of Independence outside the context of British Imperialism. Thus the true performance of performance art occurs between whatever form it takes and the background presuppositions whose gravitational pull it sought to escape. (States 1996: 11)

While Carlson agrees that, in the 1970s at least, 'theatre was probably the most common "other" against which [performance art] could be defined', he is careful to point out that many of the practitioners he cites who were producing works both before and after this period do not have theatre backgrounds or interests, and the arts whose 'presuppositions' they are seeking to escape are often painting, sculpture, music or dance (Carlson 1996: 104). At the Standing Conference for University Drama Departments of March 1998 in Glasgow, Franc Chamberlain also pointed out that the annexing of territory accomplished by 'performance' as a keyword within academic criticism could be termed 'colonialist'. He argued that the use of this term often disguises a privileging of theatre and by extension the modes of analysis developed in relation to this form, at the expense of the specificity of other genres of performance such as music and dance. As such, in a similar fashion to 'feminism' and 'postmodernism', while supposedly signifying multiplicity and difference, this term often actually functions as a metanarrative that appropriates differences to a single perspective.

Consequently it is important to note that none of the three practitioners I am considering has a background in theatre. Rose English and Bobby Baker trained at art schools and originally worked in other media, and before becoming a performance artist Annie Sprinkle was a sex worker and performer in the American porn industry. Equally, Rozsika Parker and Griselda Pollock's book *Framing Feminism* (1987), which at the time of writing is the only book to examine the history of women's performance art in Britain, does so in the context of fine or visual art rather than theatre. On the other hand, Rose English has indicated that when she and her peers started engaging in live performance work, 'we thought it was something new, but actually we discovered it had been going on for thousands of years and was called theatre' (see Armistead 1992). So, although RoseLee Goldberg states that this type of work 'defies precise or easy definition beyond the simple declaration that it is live art by artists' (Goldberg, quoted in Carlson 1996: 79), this very 'liveness', and the fact that the means used to escape the gravity of one particular art form has often been to combine it with others, has tended to create a pull towards theatre, always the most obviously hybrid of the arts. This has meant that practitioners who are designated as performance artists, whether they regard themselves as such or not, have been perceived and often forced to define themselves, if only negatively, in relation to theatre.[1]

In case this seems like firm ground, however, it is Marvin Carlson's view that

> Despite the enormous variety of performance activities during the 1970s and 1980s, it is still possible to trace two over-all and related trends. First, the initial widespread opposition of performance to theatre has steadily eroded; and second, the initial emphasis on body and movement … has gradually given way to image centred performance and a return of language. (Carlson 1996: 116)

Yet I am sure Carlson would agree that it would be easy to find numerous exceptions to these trends since, although he does usefully identify a number of themes, movements and continuities in this field, he ultimately agrees with Forte that, even while doing so, 'I recognised that in a fundamental way it ran contrary to the nature of the subject' (1996: 188). However, Carlson does proceed to offer some sort of broad definition of 'theatrical' performance, which I am going to draw on in order to situate the work of English, Baker and Sprinkle within the wide and potentially confusing terrain covered by performance as a keyword, since, despite the diversity of their backgrounds, in my opinion their practice can be usefully, if loosely, described in this fashion. Significantly, Carlson's definition also corresponds to the sort of definitions offered by theorists from other disciplines who develop performative metaphors when they wish to distinguish their use of such metaphors from traditional notions of 'theatrical' performance. 'Theatrical' performance, then, refers to live performance in front of an audience who are conscious of the fact that they are participating in a mimetic event. Such performances are not necessarily mainstream, traditional or 'canonical' theatre, musical or opera, but like these forms they are by some means 'framed' or marked off from 'everyday life', and part of this 'framing' occurs in terms of place and time. In such performances there is, then, in Alan Read's terms, a 'tripartite' relationship between self, performer and the rest of the audience (Read 1993: 90). As a whole, the event constitutes a deliberate, self-conscious and self-reflexive representation of particular social phenomena and so, as Carlson puts it, can be said to offer some sort of 'metacommentary' on these phenomena (Carlson 1996: 190). The liveness and the tripartite relationship also mean that the performance's function and meaning as 'metacommentary' are produced as much in the process of perception and reception within specific contexts, at specific times and as an interaction between specific individuals, as through the act itself.

This does not mean that the work of the three practitioners in question cannot also be described as performance art. However, when it comes to this more specific category, I am going to take seriously American performance artist Ellie Govan's statement: 'I don't think it's necessary to define it; every time it happens it defines itself' (see Beatty 1990). This means that I am going to follow the principle that *if* English, Baker and Sprinkle are indeed performance artists, any examination of their practice should constitute an exploration of what this means in these particular incidences. Equally, any analysis of the forms their art takes should, in theory, reveal the 'background presuppositions whose gravitational pull they are seeking to avoid'. Moreover, if performance is 'primarily a post-modern mode' and the work of female performance artists does indeed 'ally feminism and postmodernism', similarly, evidence of the influences of these discourses should be evident in their productions. Finally, if, like feminism and postmodernism, performance art resists categorisation, although there may be certain correspondences between the work of these three women, there should also be significant variance.

So far I have identified a number of provisional and questionable commonalities between these practitioners and their work. They are all women, they are all white and none of them comes from a theatrical background; their work is often very funny, is situated within the avant-garde and can be described in relation to Charles Jenks's definition of a postmodern aesthetic. I can add that they have all been engaged in some form of live performance, if not always strictly performance art, for over twenty years, and all their performances directly acknowledge the presence of the audience and, with one or two exceptions, involve some degree of active audience participation. English has on occasion played roles in mainstream productions, but within their own work none of them creates 'traditional theatre' in terms of interpreting pre-existing play-texts by other authors and all of them utilise improvisation during the course of their performances. Yet this does not mean that their shows are not 'scripted' and rehearsed in some fashion. Indeed, English often writes texts for her shows, one of which has been published (see Levy 1992), and she has expressed an interest in seeing it reproduced by others. However, in performance these three practitioners usually play very much upon their own particular, individualised stage personas and, in the case of Sprinkle and Baker, draw directly on their own lives. As a result, it is difficult to imagine these works being reproduced or reworked with someone else in their 'roles'. This may be a key factor in their categorisation as performance artists, since it constitutes one of the aspects of their work that allows them to be described as 'auteurs' in the sense used in film studies. This nomination indicates that while they all engage collaboratively with other performers and artists and, in the case of Baker and Sprinkle, with directors, they are usually credited with authorship of the work. As in film studies, 'auteur' status is supported by evidence of a continuity and development of recurring themes, interests and modes of expression throughout a body of work, in which their presence as a contributor is apparently the single constant factor. It may be that ultimately the distinction between the general category of performance and performance art is to a large extent bound up with such ascribing of authorship and is based in part on the principle that the artist herself features directly or performs within the art work.

It would be disingenuous if I didn't acknowledge that, based on these similarities, I am already treating English, Baker and Sprinkle, provisionally, as part of a 'sub-category' of female performance artists; Jeanie Forte offers a further justification for this move on the grounds that 'the overtly political nature of much women's performance art since the 1960s has invited just such a critical distinction' (1990: 251). Yet Forte is speaking solely of American practitioners, and Baker and English are British, so my placing them in this 'sub-category' demands further examination.

At the start of *Performance,* Carlson explains his emphasis on artists in the United States as due to the location of his own experience of this activity but also because,

> despite its international diffusion, performance art is both historically and theoretically a primarily American phenomenon, and a proper understanding of it must, I believe, be centered on how it developed both practically and conceptually in the United States. (1996: 2)

My *own* experience as an academic studying female performance artists seems to affirm this statement. I live and work in a small town in the North of England and have only ever paid one brief visit to the United States. Yet the first time I watched *Sphinxes Without Secrets,* a video introducing the work of over twenty-five US female performance artists, I found that I was already familiar with the names of at least half of these practitioners and could list several more not covered in the programme (Beatty 1990). Moreover, I was also often familiar with their *practice*, either through attending live performances in Britain or through video recordings, transcripts of shows, reviews, published interviews, scholarly articles and books. Indeed, I had even marked essays on their work written by students at Lancaster and elsewhere. Yet, embarrassed as I am to admit this, if asked completely off the top of my head to supply the names of an equal number of British, female performance artists, I would have trouble citing even nine or ten. Of this number, I am familiar with the work of only six or seven, and here I am for the most part dependent for my knowledge on seeing shows or reading reviews, which are few and far between. I feel impelled to add (defensively) that I am not including women working as members of experimental companies and who do not tend to have 'auteur' status, where I might do a lot better. Even if this ignorance is simply indicative of my own shortcomings, it would seem to suggest that, at the very least, there has been greater interest in documenting, studying and publishing indigenous women's performance art in the USA than in Britain.

There could be any number of general, social, cultural, political, geographical, historical, artistic and academic reasons for this situation. For example, in staking his claim for performance as an American phenomenon, Carlson refers to the historical development of theatre in the United States as predominantly 'informal', 'non-literary' and one where 'the performer is the dominant figure' (1996: 2). Interestingly, he twice cites Ruth Draper as part of this tradition, an American monologist from the 1930s, who Rose English has described as a major influence on her own practice (see Rogers 1986: 31 and Performance Magazine Survey 1985: 9). Certainly, always struggling under the long shadow cast by Shakespeare, British theatre history and criticism has tended to privilege the play-text at the expense of informal and non-literary forms – although such forms have, as in the USA and elsewhere, always been enjoyed in Britiain by mass audiences.

Equally, if, as Goldberg argues, the European modernist cabaret was an important antecedent of performance art, the fact that Frida Strindberg's attempt to found such an establishment in London in 1912 failed dismally in comparison to successes in Paris, Barcelona, Munich, Cracow, Vienna, St Petersburg, Moscow, Zurich and Berlin may indicate a long history of a British lack of engagement with this form.[2] Indeed, Britain was relatively slow and reluctant to show an interest in modernism at all and most particularly in relation to theatre. Even so, there is a history of performance art in Britain, even if its genesis, usually pinpointed around the founding of the company The People Show in 1965, occurs later than in the USA. Also, although throughout *Performance* Carlson identifies cultural and aesthetic differences between Britain and the USA in this field, the few works that document the development of this form in

Britain do tend to affirm a strong US influence. So both Sandy Craig in *Dreams and Deconstructions* (1980) and Peter Ansorge in *Disrupting the Spectacle* (1975) stress the impact on this field of visits made to Britain in the 1970s by US companies such as La Mama and The Living Theatre. It is also striking that, with one or two exceptions such as Geraldine Pilgrim and Janet Goddard, few women feature in these British accounts at all, let alone as 'auteurs'.

Yet, as in the USA, there was a 'flowering' of indigenous women's performance art in Britain in the 1970s and 1980s which seems to have been constantly overlooked within theatre studies. Artists like sculptor Shirley Cameron moved into performance art in 1971, and a performance art festival at the Serpentine Gallery in 1976 included works by Rose English, Judith Katz, Lyn MacRitchie and Sylvia Stevens. In 1980 an exhibition of women's performance art at the Institute of Contemporary Art (ICA) in London, with the ironic title 'About Time', included pieces by Bobby Baker, Roberta Graham, Susan Hiller, Tina Keane, Rose Finn-Kelcey, Catherine Elwes, Sylvia Ziranek, Sonia Knox, Carlyle Reedy and Rose Garrard, among others. This initiative was followed by a series of similar events in London and elsewhere in the early to late 1980s. For all this information I am chiefly indebted to the Parker and Pollock book cited above, which also quotes a statement made by Susan Hiller at a Nottingham-based festival of women's performance art in 1981 noting 'the tendency to falsify the history of performance art in current writing which favours US and European antecedents over British and explicitly ignores the early contributions by women' (Parker and Pollock 1987: 38).

A further exhibition held at the ICA in 1980 entitled 'Issue: Social Strategies by Women Artists' featured artists from several countries but was dominated by those from the USA and Britain – provoking comparisons. Parker and Pollock cite Lucy Lippard, the American curator of this event, as contrasting the 'marginal and temporary' interest in 'social art' and 'socialist art movements' in the United States, as opposed to the important place held by left wing politics in art practices in Britain, and as identifying a 'more advanced level of theoretical discussion' as occurring in this country (1987: 41). They also note that, in reviewing the conference held following this exhibition, the artist Monica Petzal complained at the dominance of 'articulate socialist feminist voices' (44). The same interest in left wing politics was also apparent in the burgeoning 'alternative' and 'political' theatre scene of the period, which tended to be based on companies or playwrights, and it is this field that has tended to absorb critical attention in Britain, feminist or otherwise.

In comparison, much of the best known female performance work in the USA of the same period was, apparently, dominated by the 'radical' or 'cultural feminist' voices. In an essay in which she critiques this tendency, Jill Dolan refers to Lippard's and Moira Roth's tracing of this tradition in US female performance art and identifies practitioners Leslie Labowitz, Hannah Wilke and, by implication, Carolee Schneemann and Rachel Rosenthal as all working within this vein (Dolan 1987). However, the characteristics she identifies in their work – a basis in autobiography, foregrounding the body particularly through nudity and the privileging of women's natural, biological and 'spiritual' capabilities – can be discovered in numerous works by female performance artists in both countries. It is also curious that many of the artists defined by Dolan as 'cultural feminists', Labowitz and Schneemann and Rosenthal, are the same ones who are presented by Jeanie Forte as 'postmodernist' and so as showing 'woman' 'to be a culturally constructed category' (Forte 1990: 252). This contradiction between Forte and Dolan could demonstrate one of two things, though possibly both at once: the ease with which academic discourse can appropriate and interpret the same practices as examples of opposing ideological positions, or the 'double gesture' of both postmodernism and (poststructuralist) feminist practices as noted by Rebecca Schneider and discussed in the introduction. It is also significant perhaps that in order to explicate this concept, Schneider refers in detail to Schneemann's early work (Schneider 1997).

Whatever the case, Dolan's and Forte's writings, placed alongside works such as Sue Ellen Case's highly influential book *Feminism and Theatre* (1988), mark a reaction in US feminist performance criticism away from cultural feminism and towards a poststructuralist-influenced, materialist or social constructionist position. This did not necessarily reflect a change in feminist performance practice so much as in the way of interpreting it. Indeed, traces of earlier modes of feminism can still be divined in the work of the artists such as Holly Hughes or Split Britches whom Dolan champions in opposition to the cultural feminists.[3] Nevertheless, these new critical approaches, with their greater emphasis on sexuality and race than usually found in Britain, demonstrated and exposed the limitations of British socialist feminism, although they still tended to pay little serious attention to class, economic and national differences. Paradoxically, this shift, which, in theory, implicitly puts into question the whole notion of a 'sub-category' of female performance art, also marked an outburst of critical energy and academic enthusiasm for this genre in the United States. This enthusiasm corresponded roughly to the beginning of the spread of 'performance' as a keyword and occurred at roughly the same point at which theoretical and critical interest in comparable British work, such as it was, seems to have waned. In any case, while there is plenty of evidence of activity from 'experimental' and 'alternative' companies in Britain in the late 1980s and in the 1990s, at this time, like the early socialist political theatre groups, indigenous 'auteur', female performance artists become harder to track down. Some of the 1980s artists like Sonia Knox, Rose Garrard and Rose Finn-Kelcey, to name but three, continued to perform, and younger British-based 'auteur' artists, such as SuAndi, Lisa Watts, Susan Lewis, Maya Chowdry and Louise Wilson, appeared. Yet in terms of both critical attention and number of appearances at the more prestigious performance events, the field has been heavily dominated by Rose English, Bobby Baker and, until her move into full-time film making, Annie Griffin. There have also been complaints that events focusing on sex and gender politics at the influential ICA in London or the Manchester-based Queer Up North festival have in recent years mainly featured US artists at the expense of British or European performers. The Magdalena project based in Wales is the only venue in Britain which, on a regular basis, provides a platform for female performance artists from all over the world, rather than primarily privileging performers from either the USA or Britain. The fact that its work receives little attention, either from academic performance critics or from the mainstream press, may be something to do with geographic, political and artistic 'centrism' in Britain but also the increasing dominance of US performance criticism in this country.

To return to the 1980s, even if socialist feminist voices dominated in Britain, there is still evidence of a debate between different feminisms rather than a complete rout, and certainly even early work by Rose English and Bobby Baker cannot be simply appropriated to the category 'socialist feminist'. Further, on the level of the individual artist, it is easy to find similarities of form and common themes in the work undertaken by women in both countries. Moreover, artists crossed the Atlantic in both directions, so that in 1981 *The Drama Review* offered a review of a series of women's performances in New York that included Sonia Knox, Rose English and Carlyle Reedy, all based in Britain, alongside indigenous artists such as Leslie Labowitz, Linda Montana and Cheri Gaulke (Schuldt 1981). Even allowing for cross-fertilisation, it is still striking how far the artists interviewed in the video *Sphinxes Without Secrets* reiterate virtually the same comments made in *Framing Feminism* when discussing why many women favoured performance art as a mode of creative and political expression, despite the many national, cultural, racial and ethnic differences between them. It is also interesting to note that in both these texts the majority take their reference points from visual art rather than theatre. To summarise these discussions, the artists' explanations for preferring to work in the field of performance art include the following: as a relatively new genre it did not carry the burden of a historical discourse delimiting what form it should take, where it should occur, what materials it should employ, what its subject matter should be and, most importantly, who was authorised to do it in the first place. Since it was not really 'collectable' in the same way as object-based art, it resisted commodification by commercial or State art institutions, and since this meant there was little money to be made from it, it was less competitive. At the same time, it could be cheap to produce and so the artist could have more control over both the means of production and the artefact produced. The positioning of the artist within the art work rather than 'behind' it also offered a direct, immediate and active relationship between producer and audience, and one by-product of this was that it gave visibility to women as 'authors' of the works. This worked against the gravitational pull of artistic practices in which, historically, women's participation in art was for the most part limited to model, inspiration, interpreter or performer of a male author's work, or at best as a subordinate and often invisible collaborator with a male artist. Therefore, whatever your ideological position, performance art constituted a space in which the exploration of certain dominant cultural norms relating to female subjectivity and identity was a potential, if not an inescapable, part of the processes of both the making and reception of the work (see Parker and Pollock 1987 and Beatty 1990).

I have no idea if these are the reasons why Baker, English and Sprinkle chose to work in this field, but the final point can be said to be common to both British and US cultures and transcends conscious authorial 'intentions' in a manner which, for me, largely justifies the provisional placing of these three very different artists within the same sub-genre of female performance art. This justification is in part based on historical grounds, in so far as their work occurs as part of a tradition of women's art, occurring with slightly different inflections in the USA and Europe. This is a tradition which all three have had a hand in shaping and which represents a reaction against a history of artistic practices, within which women have been exploited and ignored and from which they have tended to be excluded as named authors. Placing all three practitioners within this tradition is important because the press often characterises Baker and English in a slightly patronising fashion as individual and isolated examples of a peculiarly British 'eccentricity'. However, I am actually performing something of theoretical 'double gesture' in so far as I am implying that while the British and US traditions vary, in terms of both practices and critical approaches to works and indeed there are distinctions within, as well as between, these national groupings, there are also significant points of interchange, repetition and connection across them. In fact, at first glance, not only do the work of Sprinkle and Baker have a great deal in common but both seem to favour 'cultural feminism', as described by Dolan in 1987. Both draw heavily on autobiographical material, both speak directly to the audience as 'themselves', both foreground their own bodies, both have appeared nude and both make direct reference to biologically-based female experience and to some sort of 'spirituality'. There are also similarities in the way their shows tend to be structured around the telling of stories, which are punctuated by 'demonstrations', involving a range of visual aids and objects and presented in the spirit of imparting their various skills, expertise and knowledges to the audience. Yet while still potentially within a cultural feminist paradigm, Baker's focus on motherhood, heterosexuality and domesticity appears diametrically opposed to Sprinkle's focus on her professional activities as a sex worker in the public domain and polymorphous sexuality. However, if their work is read as 'deconstructive' rather than taken at face value, this very opposition means they arrive at a similar 'social constructionist' position, albeit from completely different directions. Each celebrates the skills and competencies involved in the activities taking place under the subject categories of 'mother' and 'whore', challenging the manner in which these roles are depreciated and marginalised within the dominant social order. Yet both could be said to simultaneously put into question the discursively produced binary oppositions which divide women into such categories in the first place. As complex and slippery as this statement may seem theoretically, in practice it remains an over-simplification of their differing representations of their own subjectivity.

Sprinkle's official career as 'auteur' female performance artist dates from around 1985, but since providing autobiographical details of models alongside photographic images is common in pornography, the genesis of her later performances possibly reach back further, and elements of subsequent shows are evident in the porn film *Deep Inside Annie Sprinkle* (1981). Certainly, *Post Post Porn Modernist*, examined in chapter five, is not only a reworking of an earlier version, *Post Porn Modernist*, but prefigurings of this show can be found in earlier appearances, including Schechner's show at The Performing Garage in New York, *The Prometheus Project* (1985), the film *ANNIE* (1989), an interview with Sprinkle in *Angry Women* (1991), the video *The Sluts and Goddesses Video Workshop, or How to be a Sex Goddess in 101 Easy Steps* (1992) and a documentary concerned with tantric sex, *Sacred Sex* (1992). To some extent all these 'performances' detailed different stages in her transformation from plain shy Ellen Steinberg to successful sex worker and performance artist Annie Sprinkle and finally to Anya, Goddess and Sacred Prostitute, a journey which is summarised in *Post Post Porn Modernist*.

By contrast, Baker's staged subjectivity, as artist, housewife, lecturer and cookery demonstrator, seems to have remained fairly stable from *My Cooking Competes* in 1980 onwards, a show which itself follows on thematically from her installation *An Edible Family in a Mobile Home* (1976) and *Packed Lunch* (1979). However, her identity as a 'mother' also emerges as a dominant theme in *Drawing on a Mother's Experience* (1988) and continues to be an important motif through *Cook Dems* (1990), *Kitchen Show* (1991) and *How to Shop* (1993) right up to *Take a Peek* in 1995 where, in a sense, she took on a 'character' as 'the fat lady'.

On a simple visual level, this consistency is signified by the fact that while, during the course of some performances, Baker may perform some sort of costume change, her white 'cook dems' overall has become a trademark, whereas Sprinkle's fluid identity is signified by frequent changes in clothes and style both within works and from piece to piece. However, Sprinkle's three personas tend to be represented as a linear, developmental accumulation in temporal terms, so that each one seems to represent a stage in her progress forwards as an individual towards 'growth', if not wholeness, a process over which she appears to have some degree of choice, if not control. On the other hand, in each show Baker's apparently stable and coherent identity splits into contradictory identities as she is caught up in the claims of competing discourses. In short, her multiple, social and sexually determined identities as artist, wife, housewife, mother and daughter, with their different demands and values within our culture, frequently clash, pulling 'Bobby Baker' in different directions, with some violence. While Sprinkle is able to transcend her negative experiences as sex worker through their graphic representation in her show, Baker is always arriving at moments of ambiguity, hesitation or silence, where she declares or performs an intention to spare the audience 'the gory details', whether these are of her post-natal illness or of emotions that may not be considered socially acceptable. However, while these feelings and experiences may not be represented in any direct or literal form, the audience may discern them in the spaces left to mark their 'absence' or in the polyvocal images she creates, like the marks that show through the sheet she has used as a canvas for her 'food painting' in *Drawing on a Mother's Experience*. These have been erased by a layer of flour, but when she wraps the sheet around herself they become visible through the 'wrong side'. Therefore, while for most of her show Sprinkle uses visual material, objects and her own body to illustrate and explicate her verbal narrative, the visual and bodily texts in Baker's often show things that cannot, should not or must not be expressed in words. In short, Sprinkle clearly and directly breaks social taboos, Baker marks the limits set by such taboos and as such breaks them indirectly and in a cryptic fashion. Whereas Sprinkle's use of her body in performance focuses mainly on sexual liberation and the search for a variety of experiences and expression of pleasure given or received, there is, as Susan Melrose points out, a masochistic element in Baker's work (Melrose 1993). She offers on the one hand images of a constrained and disciplined body and, on the other, of a body which is always on the verge, and sometimes over the edge, of being 'out of control'. It is significant that, for a short piece performed in the Royal Chelsea Physick Garden as part of the Barclays New Stages Festival in 1994, Baker produced a life-size planting pot shaped from her own body and overflowing with herbs, all of which were revealed in the course of the show as having been at some point in time recommended as a cure for hysteria. As such, this piece implicitly touched upon the way the medical 'gaze' has defined and constructed the female body, providing a link with Sprinkle's use of the speculum in *Post Post Porn Modernist* to exhibit her cervix to the audience. Yet where Sprinkle asserts herself and confronts the objectifying gaze of the audience, in most of her shows Baker is always excusing herself and constantly cleaning up to erase traces of her own activity. Finally Sprinkle's spirituality is alternative or New Age, whereas Baker's is located firmly within the Judeo-Christian tradition.

Even so, however different and complex both Baker's and Sprinkle's practices may be, they are easier to appropriate to the same sub-genre of female performance art than English's, mainly because their subject matter immediately invites feminist analysis in a way hers does not. English is often addressed as 'Rose' on stage, but in fact she frequently also performs a 'character': for instance, Rosita Clavel has surfaced twice, first in *My Mathematics* and later in *Venus and Vulcan: The Adoration – an Equine Nativity* (1993). At other times she slips in and out of 'named' roles, such as the Hostess and the Hermit in *The Double Wedding* (1991), or quotes recognisable theatrical types, such as the 'princess' and the 'principal boy' in Acts one and two respectively of *Walks on Water* (1988). In *Tantamount Esperance* (1994) she played a more or less 'proper' and consistent character of this name, but this represented a new departure, and in the past these have been 'characters' in the sense indicated by Carlson discussing artists like Eleanor Antin (1996: 152): that is, they are not traditional, coherent, believable, narrative characters but obviously theatrical 'persona'. In English's case they are marked as such by overt and melodramatic exaggeration, including the use of stylised gesture and voice as well as large-scale expressions of deliberately 'fake' emotion. Some sort of deliberate and comic 'bad acting' also occurs to an extent in Baker's work, but whereas with Baker this appears to signify that she is not 'really' performing and therefore has no 'technique', this style in English's work is a parodic display of 'technique' which indicates that she is most definitely 'performing'. Nevertheless when English drops out of these personas to comment on the show or her own performance, or engage in discussion with the audience, there is little sense of encountering the 'real' Rose English.

Of course, even when they appear to be most 'themselves' on stage, all three practitioners are always actually 'performing', and so, as States puts it, expanding on a point made by Richard Schechner, they are all 'not themselves and not, not themselves', and perhaps because they *are* performance artists, one way or another this paradox or double movement or marking is foregrounded in the work of all three (States 1996: 17). However, of the three, English is far more obviously and self-consciously deconstructing the norms of traditional theatre, and so this paradox tends to be remarked as an issue in relation to the conventions of stage 'character' rather than in terms of her own identity. Another way of putting this may be that English is the most 'poststructuralist' of these artists in that her chief concern is with 'form', with signifying systems and testing the limits of representation, and so her work is less directly concerned with specific social and political issues than Sprinkle's and Baker's. Any exploration of 'social' subjectivity in her work arises as a by-product of an ongoing philosophical enquiry into the relationship between the real and the mimetic, which embraces both Lyotard's reworking of Kant's 'Sublime' and the ridiculous. If this seems a rather large claim, I would like to point out that in 1984 she performed a piece entitled *Plato's Chair* and her work always follows a Neoplatonic structure in that questions are constantly posed, sometimes directly to the audience, but apparently answers are seldom provided. These questions are always related to the nature of representation or the particular representation in process but can range in scope from asking if any of the audience came by bus in *Walks on Water* to 'are there enough hats in this show?' in *Thee Thou Thine* (1986) to 'what is the difference between *echt* and *ersatz*?' or again 'what is the difference between a void and a vacuum?' both in *The Double Wedding*, the latter being a question that, for the academic at least, may point to Nietzsche, among other philosophers.

Indeed, her shows are 'dialectical' in so far as they place side by side different modes of representation in a way that foregrounds the various means by which they attempt to represent reality and also marks the manner in which they are always bound to fail, since a 'representation' is always a reproduction and can never be the thing itself. So, for example, in Act three of *Walks on Water* a painted waterfall backcloth is transformed into a waterfall of 'real' water, which of course is still a theatrical illusion. In *My Mathematics* (1992) the couch used to represent a horse in Act one is replaced by a 'real' horse in Act two, but this horse is still 'performing' rather than simply 'being a horse', not just because he *is* a 'performing horse' but because he is representing 'My Mathematics', a fictional performing horse. Three of her shows have been concerned with some sort of reconstruction of films on stage and the ultimate failure of theatre to reproduce the 'realism' achieved in film: *Thee Thou Thine* (which drew on *Oklahoma!*), *Moses* (1987) (which drew on *The Wizard of Oz*) and *The Double Wedding* (which, as will become clear in chapter three, was supposedly based, in part, on a film version of itself). Her work frequently includes performances from acrobats, aerialists, dancers, musicians, ice skaters and magicians. These 'real' performance skills are often contrasted with attempts to copy or 'fake' them, so that in *Tantamount Esperance* 'proper' impeccably performed stage illusions are played out alongside 'cod' illusions. English also often uses these artists as body 'doubles' or stunt persons to perform feats that she cannot herself achieve, yet this doubling is always deliberately revealed and remarked as such.

This concern for illusion and 'doubles' embraces an interest in 'disguise' that extends to cross-dressing. For some of *Adventure or Revenge* (1981) she wore a false beard and a doublet and hose, in Act two of *Walks on Water* she appears in the costume of a pantomime principal 'boy', in one scene of *The Double Wedding* the majority of the male cast appear cross-dressed and in *Tantamount Esperance* English was in full male drag for the entire show. This aspect of English's work can be read through recent feminist theories related to drag and cross-dressing as 'subversive strategies', although, as my discussion in chapter three indicates, I believe that this element cannot be considered in isolation from the broader context of her work. Not only does English's use of 'drag' pre-date the dissemination and popularisation of such theories but it appears as part of a specifically theatrical vocabulary which embraces all types of costumes, false hair including wigs and blatantly false beards on both male and female performers, her own use of ever longer false eyelashes from show to show and indeed horse tails both on 'real' horses and sported by female performers pretending to be horses in *Quadrille* (1975). In fact horses also emerge again and again in her work from her first piece *The Boy Baby* (1974) to *My Mathematics* and *Venus and Vulcan: The Adoration – an Equine Nativity*, which again featured a 'real' mare and a 'real' foal and in which she firmly announced 'this is *not* an allegory', perhaps with reference to Magritte's famous painting of a pipe which contains the words 'this is not a pipe'.

I could offer a reading of the possible 'meanings' generated around the horses in English's shows, perhaps even in relation to theories of sex and gender, but this theme marks a point where I hesitate to commit myself. This hesitation in part stems from a desire to underline the fact that the above remarks are not intended as a comprehensive summary of work created and performed over a twenty-year period. Although I may have pointed out some continuities in the works of these practitioners, I am aware of the danger of making their work seem one-dimensional in that Sprinkle's appears 'positive', Baker's rather 'negative' and English's 'abstract'. In fact all three of them produce shows which are densely layered and open up multiple possibilities for interpretation, and if a flattening effect occurs it is mainly because the constraints of this sort of summary make it difficult to explore ambiguities, including the ambiguities produced by the use of humour. Actually, despite my characterisation of all three of these artists as 'auteurs', thereby ascribing them the position of controlling meanings, and despite my definition of all of them as deploying a postmodern aesthetic, the formal characteristics used by these practitioners might equally be described as 'writerly' in the sense established by Roland Barthes, although at first glance Sprinkle's work may appear less so than Baker's or English's. This term describes a form that is fragmented, plural, contiguous, anti-narrative, non-linear, multiple, poetic and therefore considered to be 'open', creating far more space for the reader to participate in the construction of meanings than other, more traditional forms. An interpretation of such a work, therefore, may reveal more about the 'reader' than the work itself, and frankly I find the recurrence of horses in English's work (and indeed certain other themes or images in the work of the other two) both funny and slightly troubling. My impulse is to pass this off as a joke and to put my discomfort down to my fear of all animals whose teeth are bigger than my own. However, in the hands of a psychoanalyst this joke in itself may be rather revealing, and there is no doubt that my sense of being 'troubled' is related to some extent to the fashion within our culture of using horses metonymically to represent 'masculine' sexual power. As will become clear later in this book, I am not alone in being both amused and 'troubled' by elements in all of the works in question, and this unease, linked to the issue of form, may be related in various and contradictory ways to the problematic of categorising these three as practitioners within a political sub-genre of female performance art. The same considerations might also open up some interesting questions concerning the apparent disagreement noted above between Dolan and Forte over the political meaning of certain forms and the status of the shows under consideration as postmodern and/or feminist and/or 'writerly' and funny.

By coincidence, in chapter three I offer a reading of English's *The Double Wedding* mainly through Derrida's 'The Double Session', which is followed in his book *Dissemination* (1981) by a discussion of the novelist Phillipe Sollers's work *Numbers*, just as *My Mathematics*, which explored the difference between (theatrical and mathematical) 'numbers', followed on from *The Double Wedding*. As far as I know this coincidence may be entirely mine as a reader rather than English's as an auteur, but in theory the 'open' form of her work allows for and validates such correspondences, which in this case opens up a fascinating, if somewhat dense, even convoluted, chain of associations and intertextual references. Following up the *Numbers* connection, I noticed that in *Subversive Intent*, a book concerned with feminism, postmodernism, the avant-garde and laughter, Susan Rubin Suleiman explores Barthes's concept of the 'writerly text' in relation to his discussion of the 'unreadability' of a novel by Sollers. In the course of this discussion, Suleiman writes about the perception of avant-garde texts, which, like Sollers's, utilise unfamiliar or difficult forms, as being 'aggressive', 'intelligible' and 'not worth reading'. She goes on to cite Denis Ferraris's comment that to pronounce a text unreadable is to 'deny its existence' and that to do so a reader must feel 'that the text in question is not only scandalous, but also in a profound way, menacing'. Ferraris suggests that this menace arises because this style of text confronts the reader with 'their own unintelligibility' (Suleiman 1990: 36). As Suleiman indicates, although Barthes's notion of the 'writerly' text is not exactly equivalent to Ferraris's concept of the 'unreadable' text, it is very similar, and both writers developed their ideas around the same genre and often the same works of avant-garde literature.

Bearing all this in mind, the fact that my friend cited in the introduction asserted that English's shows were funny but 'not about anything' directly after seeing *My Mathematics* takes on a new significance. As such, she was to some degree designating English's works as not worth the effort of 'reading', or rather denying their existence as anything other than the most superficial entertainment. Perhaps her response and my own to certain aspects of English's work is a reaction to some sort of 'menace' posed by the form of the shows. Equally pertinent to my current discussion is Suleiman's comment that the characteristics of the form that Barthes nominates as 'writerly' are the same as those which 'in classical terms are usually categorised as "feminine" and negatively valued' and those claimed in positive terms as the defining qualities of '*ecriture feminine*' by 'French feminists' of the 1970s, Hélène Cixous and Luce Irigaray (Suleiman 1990: 38–9). If the shows under consideration in this book are in fact formally writerly, they could therefore equally be described as *ecriture feminine*, and this would further justify the inclusion of English, Sprinkle and Baker within a tradition or sub-genre of political, female performance art. To a certain extent this might also illuminate but not resolve the conflicting views expressed by Dolan and Forte, since, within this tradition, female performance artists, whatever their feminist position, have sought to discover, reclaim and deploy a 'female' or 'feminine' form. Some of the artists they both cite may even have been directly influenced by Irigaray's or Cixous's ideas, particularly since in the mid to late 1980s the latter had a significant impact on both feminist theory in general and female performance in Britain and the US specifically, partly as a result of her own engagement with theatre with *Portrait of Dora* (1979). The strength of her influence as a theorist produced a series of heated debates, provoked by works like Toril Moi's book *Sexual/Textual Politics* (1985), as to whether or not Cixous's notion of *ecriture feminine* was essentialist or social constructionist, simply a reclamation and reversal of the classical feminine or a radical resignification. This argument arose mainly because in developing the concept of *ecriture feminine*, Cixous, like Irigaray, drew upon and continued to work within the terms of psychoanalytical theory, albeit 'deconstructively', and as a result appeared to privilege sexual difference above other differences. However, the polyvocal, poetic and 'open' form of Cixous's own theoretical writings meant that this remained a matter of interpretation, and the debate has never been resolved. To further complicate matters, as with Barthes's concept of the writerly, while most of the texts Cixous used to explicate her ideas are generally held to be 'modernist', the same list of characteristics I have identified above as definable as both 'writerly' and 'feminine' also usually appear within descriptions of works designated as postmodern. Therefore, the contradictory claims made by Dolan and Forte could signify a form that is so radically ambiguous and 'open' that it produces a 'postmodern' confusion of categories, or rather a form that is 'both at once' moderating between essentialism and social constructionism.

If English, Baker and Sprinkle do utilise writerly or 'feminine' forms as much, as well or instead of a postmodern aesthetic, this would reinforce the argument for discussing them in relation to feminism. For the reader prepared to engage with them, both Cixous's *ecriture feminine* and Barthes's writerly text are supposed to produce an erotic *jouissance*, related to the pre-Oedipal relationship to the maternal body. In terms of psychoanalytical theory, since this pleasure draws on the pre-linguistic and it is through language that we are defined as subjects and make sense of the world, this *jouissance* effectively represents a deliberate giving oneself up to 'unintelligibility'. This surrender may be pleasurable but is also always potentially 'menacing', since it implies the loss of a discrete sense of self, as defined by our cultural psycho-sexual norms. On this basis it has been argued by Barthes and Cixous that the 'writerly text' and '*ecriture feminine*' are forms which present a challenge to phallologocentric norms.

For Hélène Cixous, one of the specific ways in which a feminine text, as she puts it, 'could not help but' achieve the disruption of phallologocentric norms was through blowing up patriarchal law and 'truth' with laughter (Cixous 1981: 258). Although personally I have never found Cixous's writing particularly funny, this remark is frequently cited in works dealing with women and humour, including Suleiman's *Subversive Intent* (1990: 17) and Frances Gray's *Women and Laughter* (1994: 37). In this latter book, Gray uses Freud's *Jokes and Their Relation to the Unconscious* as a starting point and then goes on to draw on Laura Mulvey's influential theory of 'woman as the object of the gaze' in relation to cinematic representation to demonstrate how, historically, woman has been constructed as the 'object' rather than the author of the joke (1994: 19–36). Gray asserts that, 'Like sexuality, laughter has sometimes been highly valued, sometimes denigrated: but like sexuality – indeed *with* sexuality – laughter has been closely bound up with power' (6). It is worth adding here that Anne Beatts has suggested that the positioning of woman as 'object' rather than 'author' of jokes is based on an unconscious male fear that 'the ultimate joke may be the size of their sexual apparatus' (quoted in Auslander 1997: 110). As Gray puts it, 'to define a joke, to be the class that decides *what is funny*, is to make a massive assumption of power' (1994: 8). This is partly because such judgements represent a decision over meanings, a position of authority that is supposedly denied women in our culture because, according to Jacques Lacan, this power is attributed to 'the phallus' as the transcendental signifier which guarantees the meaning of all other signifiers (see Grosz 1990). While the phallus is said to have no signified, it does have a metonymic relationship to the penis which allows for a delusion of grandeur, that having the penis is effectively having the phallus, a fallacy supported by the simultaneous fantasy that women are 'castrated'. This is the basis for the assumption that the speaking position or the user of signs and decider of meanings is 'masculine', and it this assumption which, according to Cixous, *ecriture feminine* 'laughs at' by revealing the ludicrous and purely imaginary foundation on which it depends. Except, in practice, if a text is genuinely writerly or feminine, presumably for the most part it is the reader or audience, *not* the writer, who decides on meanings and therefore whether or not a text is funny and whether or not it is subversive. Unless the text does carry single and fixed meanings it cannot be intrinsically and always subversive in this way, and so *ecriture feminine* might only work for those predisposed to laugh at the patriarchal law in the first place.

To return to English, Baker and Sprinkle, although audience reaction suggests a switching between comic and serious material, it is often difficult to pinpoint the exact moment this transition occurs and whether or not the laughter is always 'appropriate'. On at least one performance of *The Double Wedding* a speech which, on the surface, does not 'read' as particularly funny was greeted by gales of laughter, leading English to remark, 'It's sometimes the biggest speeches in a night out that get the biggest laughs. Isn't it? So perplexing. And the things that are meant to be funny are the things people weep at. Such an unpredictable affair theatre, isn't it?'[4] Bobby Baker has remarked on several occasions in interviews that she started out to make serious points and was originally 'devastated' to discover that she made people laugh (see Spencer 1995). Certainly, confronted by Sprinkle's performance, my own reaction was to laugh *at* rather than *with* some sections, and this included ostensibly 'serious' sections. There seems to be an ambivalence at play in the reception of these works, so that sometimes it is hard to tell what the joke actually is, if it is *intended* as a joke and as a result who is the author and who is the object of the joke. This ambivalence might be definable as a product of the writerly/feminine form of these pieces and indicate the subversion of phallic authority, producing a *jouissance* and multiplicity of meanings that defies the norms of intelligibility and produce a subversive confusion in terms of the separation of subject and object. Alternatively, Freud suggests that humour is often the return of the repressed in a socially acceptable guise, a defensive reaction that represents both a transgression of the social order and the containment of that transgression. As such it is not impossible that some of the laughter at these shows is at the expense of the performers and represents an implicit rejection of a woman as author(ity) or speaking subject (see Gray 1994: 28–9). In this case, laughter might be evidence of the reinscription of phallic authority and a refusal to take these performers seriously, indicating defensive recuperation of the 'menace' these shows offer to the sense of self as constructed by the patriarchal, social and symbolic order.

Significantly, while in theory the formal qualities of the writerly and feminine appear interchangeable, in practice Suleiman argues that, in a reversal of tradition and in direct contradiction to Cixous and Irigaray, Barthes actually codes his writerly form as both 'positive and *male*' and for him it is the 'readable text' characterised by 'unity, coherence and systematicity' which is now 'coded as negative and feminine' (1990: 38). As a result of this coding, Suleiman argues that when Barthes's reader, who she says is unmistakably a man, abandons himself to the *jouissance* produced by interaction with the writerly text, he takes up the position usually ascribed in psychoanalytical theory to the 'feminine', that is of 'abjection of our society'. For Suleiman, then, Barthes's theory of the writerly text offers an image of a male reader in the 'feminine' position engaging with a 'masculine' text, so that the bliss provoked could be read as a 'homologue of male homosexual intercourse' (39). This of course assumes that the 'feminine' is the only position that is 'abjected' within our culture and explains homosexuality in terms of heterosexual norms, a point I shall return to in the next chapter. For the moment, following on from the logic of this model, Suleiman suggests that the *female* reader of this writerly text who wishes to experience *jouissance* in these terms 'will have to impersonate the male whose jouissance consists in becoming, for the time of his reading, a fragmented and nonunitary subject – in other words, "feminine"', and so she will effectively be 'a woman, impersonating a man impersonating a woman' (39).

In theory at least, this reading is not entirely inconsistent with Cixous's notion of the 'feminine' text, since she asserts that the ability to experience the *jouissance* offered by such works is not related to anatomical sex and also depends on 'a certain homosexuality' in the reader (1981: 97). However, unlike Suleiman's reading of Barthes, this 'homosexuality' is not 'male' but refers to the polymorphous perversity which, according to some readings of Freud, is experienced by both sexes before the Oedipal stage. If Suleiman's analysis is correct, Barthes's ideas represent an appropriation of 'the feminine' through a sort of drag in which women can only participate in the making of any sort of meanings, even those that are multiple, contiguous and open, in a double drag in which the joke is on her. To experience 'feminine' *jouissance* she must first mime the taking on and giving up of the masculine position: in short, she must act out and remark the feminine as not-masculine, or rather as 'castration'.

Whether or not the shows considered in this book can actually be categorised as sharing the same formal qualities and as all having a similar effect can actually only be explored through paying detailed and specific attention to the works themselves. However, to summarise the points I am attempting to make here, whether or not 'openness' of form, contiguity, and ambiguity and plurality of meaning can be claimed and named as feminine, or masculine, or homosexual in the narrow sense of the term, or polymorphously perverse, modernist or postmodernist or feminist, essentialist or social constructionist, normative or subversive, appears to be a matter of contestation in which the same set of characteristics is read as signifying in ideologically opposite ways by different theorists. Of course no form can be guaranteed or insured against appropriation: hence the fact that 'Brechtian' devices now appear seamlessly embedded in predominantly naturalistic, mainstream, theatrical performance. Yet the level of often vehement and diametrically opposed critical disagreement concerning the set of 'open', formal characteristics in question might be said to indicate, in contradiction to Brecht's own assumptions and those of many feminist performance theorists of the last twenty years, that forms cannot be said to carry specific ideologies. Alternatively, it may be that the very qualities of openness and ambivalence of the formal characteristics in question constitute them as radically double in a way that does not apply to other forms, and this doubleness is both the basis of their potential subversiveness and simultaneously the very point of their vulnerability to appropriation by opposing factions. In any case, these formal qualities do appear to be a site of contest, in both theory and practice, that is bound up with power relations in a fashion that problematises but does *not* resolve or transcend the question of the relationship between subject and object, author(ity), artefact and reader/spectator, production and reception. In a similar fashion, although I would like to believe that because the three female practitioners under consideration in this book are all funny, they are therefore challenging phallic authority, I fear that laughter, like the quality of formal openness, is always far more double than such a view would allow. This point is only too apparent when considered in relation to parody, pastiche and irony, when utilised, for example, by postmodern film makers like David Lynch or Quentin Tarrantino, or in the service of British 'new lad' magazines like *Loaded*.

These issues of form, authorship, spectatorship, humour, 'unreadability', intelligibility and ambivalence are all areas that I intend to explore in greater detail in the next chapter, through an examination of some influential theories that use performative metaphors to analyse the social construction of sex and gender. However, there is one final similarity between English, Baker and Sprinkle that will allow for the building of bridges between these concepts and some of the associations and connections I have made above. Linda Williams has described Sprinkle's 'Anya' as 'an imitation not unlike that of a drag queen' (1993: 187). In a far less tentative fashion, British newspaper reviewers have on several occasions compared Bobby Baker and Rose English to popular male to female impersonators. This means that, to some extent, these auteurs/performers of humorous texts have all been read as women, impersonating men, impersonating women. Is this 'intentional' or accidental, a deliberate part of the joke or an effect of an operation whereby, in assuming the position of deciding over meanings, they must inevitably appear 'phallic'? Or do these descriptions indicate a defensive reaction against performances, the formal qualities of which potentially challenge phallologocentrism and function to confront the spectator with the menace of their own unintelligibility?

Notes

1 The debate over the relationship between theatrical performance, performance art and works including 'live' elements by artists from non-theatrical backgrounds in Britain in the late 1980s and early 1990s led to some artists, venues and publications introducing the term 'live art' to refer to certain types of work. However, this intensified argument rather than clarifying confusion. Moreover, the mainstream British press still tend to prefer to use the category 'performance art'.

2 Frida Strindberg launched *The Cave of the Golden Calf* in London in 1912. Her chief aim was apparently to stage the work of her former husband, August Strindberg. Despite the collaboration of Augustus John, Jacob Epstein, Wyndham Lewis and the Italian futurist Marinetti, the club failed to make an impression and rapidly disintegrated.

3 So, for example, works like Holly Hughes's *Dress Suits for Hire* (1989), created with Lois Weaver and Peggy Shaw of Split Britches, which tend to be championed in oppostion to cultural feminist performance by Dolan, have been analysed as demonstrating a 'postmodern' multiple, fragmented subjectivity. However, Hughes's text could equally be discussed in terms of *ecriture feminine*, and the drive at the end of the piece towards a Freudian reverse discourse might even be described as cultural feminist.

4 All quotes from *The Double Wedding* are taken either directly from the show or from the unpublished text, copyright Rose English, 1991.

2

The size of the apparatus: drag, masquerade, mimicry, performativity and Bertolt Brecht

On 23 December 1993 I was watching Ru Paul's *Christmas Ball* on television and noticed that the costume worn by Ru Paul in the opening section of this show was almost identical to that worn by Rose English for both *The Double Wedding* and the first act of *My Mathematics*. This consisted of a tall blonde wig, a skin-tight silver-sequinned fishtail dress, high heels and red elbow-length evening gloves. In both cases the wig and the heels added to the above average height of the performers, and although Ru Paul also wore a pink feather boa, at one point in *The Double Wedding* Rose English sported a stole, garments of roughly the same genre in that, as she put it, they 'signify warmth without giving any'. However, for *The Double Wedding* English's false eyelashes were far longer than Ru Paul's, and by *My Mathematics* they had, according to some reviewers, grown to a length of around four feet. Personally, I think this is something of an exaggeration and the actual length was somewhere between one foot and eighteen inches.

Clearly, both Ru Paul and Rose English wore these costumes with a certain irony. In Ru Paul's case this was produced by the opportunities for comic ambiguity arising from the contrast between his known sex and his performed gender. Strictly speaking this should not be the case with Rose English since she is, presumably, biologically female and was dressed in 'feminine' clothing. Yet in a review of *The Double Wedding* for *The Guardian*, Betty Caplan cited two other shows running as part of the Barclays New Stages Festival programme, by Dogs in Honey and Adventures in Motion Pictures respectively, and went on to assert:

> In this arena then, with gay theatre so obsessed by pastiche, Rose English emerges as undisputed queen, a larger than life figure

> dressed in the manner of a latter day Danny La Rue and prowling around a stage she cannot help dominating by her sheer presence. (Caplan 1991)

It is not entirely clear here, or in the rest of the review, whether this reference to 'gay theatre' is intended to embrace English's work, which normally is not categorised in this fashion. In any case, this syntactical ambiguity lends a double meaning to the description of English as an 'undisputed queen', reinforced by the analogy with the British drag artist Danny La Rue. Claire Armistead, also writing in *The Guardian*, took a similar line in her preview of *My Mathematics*: '[English] loves dressing up but wears her frocks with the irony of a drag queen' (Armistead 1992). On the same piece, for the *Evening Standard* Michael Arditti added: 'Like Ms Dietrich, Ms English dolls herself up in figure hugging silver lamé and then guys her own image' (Arditti 1992). It is not clear whether Ms Dietrich is included in this 'guying' of her own image, but, to summarise, English appeared as an undisputed (drag) queen of gay theatre, dolled up like Danny La Rue and/or Dietrich and 'guying' this image. In this costume, then, despite their consistent use of feminine pronouns, for these three critics Rose English produced exactly the same sort of comic gender ambiguity as might be expected from a performance by Ru Paul.

These comments might be partly accounted for by the fact that the cast of *The Double Wedding* incorporated some fairly well known gay performance practitioners, including Nigel Charnock, and while English does not personally cross-dress in either of the two shows cited, *The Double Wedding* did contain some male to female cross-dressing. Why a similar sort of confusion should arise around Bobby Baker is harder to explain, particularly since she starts *How to Shop* as she 'make[s] a point of doing on any occasion I appear in public, by making it absolutely clear that I am Bobby Baker and I am a woman and I'm also, and this seems to be of great relevance and interest these days, that I am middle aged, I am 42 years old and, to be precise, I am a mother of two and a housewife'. This self-nomination produced cheers from the audience and could be read as a positive affirmation of an identity position normally marginalised and undervalued within our culture. Yet Baker reveals that she actually finds this need to introduce herself 'slightly tedious' but does it 'because mistakes have been made on many occasions and people have expected to see a man'. Of course, in theory these mistakes can be accredited to the ambiguity of the name 'Bobby', but in practice reviewers who having seen Baker's work and should therefore have had the benefit of this clarification have frequently compared Baker, directly and indirectly, to a male to female transvestite performer. When, in his review of *Take a Peek* (1995), Nigel Slater of *The Observer* stated, 'there was more than a whiff of Dame Edna Everage about Bobby Baker's show', he was following a line already taken by Charles Spencer in the *Daily Telegraph* and Susan Melrose in *Hybrid* with *How to Shop*. Spencer started his review, 'Like Dame Edna Everage, Bobby Baker is fast establishing herself as a housewife superstar' and continued this analogy later in the piece with reference to Everage's sidekick Madge (Spencer 1993). In a similar vein, Melrose commented, 'I kept thinking of Dame Edna and my throttled desire to see her get her gear off to show how its put together. Too Brechtian for the 90s?' (Melrose 1993). Yet, unlike Edna Everage, Baker does more or less get her gear off in *How to Shop*, and in *Take a Peek* she also stripped off in order to submerge herself in a bath of chocolate custard. Even more so than with Rose English, then, there should be no legible gap between her apparent sex and the gender she performs. Despite Williams's comment quoted at the end of the last chapter, the same should hold for Annie Sprinkle who, in the course of all her shows, offers seemingly incontrovertible evidence of her biological sex.

Ultimately, as with the issue of form, I do not believe that the ambiguities in relation to the sex and gender which appear to arise around these performers can be properly examined or explained outside the specific contexts of their shows. However, for the moment I want to use these various critical gender confusions as a basis for both exploring and questioning some recent theorisations of sex and gender in relation to drag, mimicry, masquerade and gender performativity. Since the work of Judith Butler has come to dominate this field of enquiry and in *Gender Trouble* (1990) she expounds her ideas through direct reference to drag as a genre of theatrical performance, and since Williams's comment was made in relation to these ideas, this book seems a reasonable starting point. According to Butler, gender can be said to be 'performative', by which she means that gender is a series of mimetic, socially constructed, stylised acts, which operate discursively and as such are only naturalised and appear as authentic expressions of biological sex through a process of constant repetition. For Butler, drag is potentially deconstructive in so far as it can subversively repeat gender so as to 'promote a subversive laughter in the pastiche effects of parodic practices in which the authentic and the real themselves are constituted as effects' (Butler 1990: 146). Rather than representing a 'poor copy' of the signs that denote gender and so reinforcing the naturalness of the 'original', drag can be read as revealing that the original itself is already an 'act'. However, as Butler herself acknowledges, not all drag necessarily produces this sort of 'subversive laughter', and some drag can actually reaffirm and reinforce heterosexual gender norms.

In terms of effect, Ru Paul and Rose English, Bobby Baker and Dame Edna could be embraced by Butler's definition of drag as subversive repetition, in so far as they all appear to produce laughter through parody and pastiche. On the other hand, this ignores the multiple, manifest differences that exists between them, not least that in the shows cited, English, Baker and Sprinkle properly speaking are not *in* drag since they are all wearing 'feminine' clothes. In fact, when in *Tantamount Esperance* English performed in extremely convincing full *male* drag, this impersonation virtually failed to provoke comment, let alone laughter, and the show was generally received by reviewers as a rather solemn, if not pretentious, affair. In the examples cited above, Baker and English only appear to be in 'drag' through reference to male to female impersonators. This would still support Butler's thesis, since the 'drag' could be said to operate retrospectively to illuminate the fact that the 'real thing' is as much 'drag' as the supposedly poor copy. In the case of Bobby Baker, this argument is potentially supported by the insistence of several critics on Dame Edna's 'reality'. Roger Baker, for instance, states, 'Dame Edna is not a drag act', but is a 'totally believable character' (Baker 1994: 222). Marvin Carlson asserts that 'The "reality" of Dame Edna has become so overwhelming as to quite eclipse her male originator' (Carlson 1996: 156). Finally, John Lahr describes Edna as 'amazingly actual … a person soon loses the sense that this is man-as-woman, and accepts her as real' (quoted in Ferris 1993: 11). While such comments, placed alongside those on the female practitioners cited above, could be read as implying that 'femininity' is always already an artificial discursive construct, this remains a one-way street on which the originating 'masculinity', which allows the 'drag' to appear as such in the first place, is 'eclipsed', remains in the shadows and unquestioned. What may in fact be revealed by all these comparisons, as with Suleiman's reading of Barthes, is that 'femininity' is always 'drag', the poor copy, even when performed by a woman, because masculinity is the norm and the original. As such the male 'drag' artist actually appears to be 'the real thing', in the sense that, according to certain theorists, within our culture the position of 'speaking subject' is always implicitly 'masculine'. In terms of this perspective, any woman clearly and publicly playing this role will effectively be perceived as a man in drag.

It may therefore be more appropriate to discuss English, Baker and Sprinkle in relation to theories of 'mimicry' and 'masquerade'. Masquerade, as it is frequently employed by feminist theorists, often refers back to Joan Riviere's Freudian-derived theory of femininity as masquerade. This describes a woman who in some way usurps masculine prerogatives, in Riviere's terms 'has stolen the father's penis' and dons the mask of 'excessive femininity' as a defensive, placatory strategy to avoid punishment. The radical aspect of this theory lies in the fact that Riviere insists that in her view there is no difference between this masquerade and 'real' femininity, 'they are the same thing' (Riviere 1929: 306). The full implications of this assertion become clearer when considered in relation to the work of Jacques Lacan and Luce Irigaray.

For Lacan, the masquerade or 'parade' indicates the involvement of both sexes in a 'comedy' of phallic fetishism in which the masculine position is defined by appearing to 'have' the phallus, while the feminine position is defined as appearing to 'be' the phallus. The 'joke' is that while it is necessary to assume one or other of these gender roles in order to appear as a proper subject, these positions are purely idealised, linguistic constructs which refer to nothing 'real', since no one can 'have' or 'be' the phallus. This is because the phallus itself has no signified; instead it refers only to the 'gap' in language which allows signification to take place but which simultaneously ensures that the sign can never be the thing itself. Lacanian theory explains how the phallus, rather than any other term, has come to stand for the process of signification through reference to the historical and discursive dominance of patriarchal structuring within cultural and symbolic systems, by which the masculine position has come to stand for the norm. There is a metonymic but supposedly phantasmic relationship to anatomy implicit in the masculine and feminine positions, in so far as masculine identity is based on a misrecognition of the penis as the phallus. This phantasy is maintained through a corresponding delusion that the 'lack' of the penis in women symbolises the 'lack', or loss, of the phallus. The male subject's fear of experiencing a similar loss, or lack, through (symbolic) castration is apparently compensated for through a process of fetishisation in which women are perceived as 'being' the phallus. The feminine is, therefore, properly speaking not a position in its own right but is defined purely negatively in relation to, and as other than, the masculine and as an object that is literally and metaphorically to be 'had' by the male subject. While the masculine position is taken up under the threat of symbolic castration, since the feminine already symbolises castration the threat for the woman who fails to play her allotted role in this masquerade is of appearing as 'castrator'. It is retribution for this imaginary act of symbolic violence that Riviere's masquerader seeks to avoid (see Lacan 1977, Grosz 1990 or Butler 1990).

As an extension or rather a reworking of Lacan, Irigaray's concept of mimicry, like the Rivierian masquerade, once again denotes a deliberate assumption of femininity by a woman and an exaggerated playing up of 'being', rather than trying to 'have', the phallus. In this case, this action is offered as an actively offensive rather than defensive strategy, 'so as to make visible by an effect of playful repetition, that which was supposed to remain invisible' (Irigaray 1985b: 46). What is made visible and explicit is the point acknowledged within the Lacanian concept of masquerade, that the cultural symbolic depends on the repudiation of the feminine, and as a result this is a system in which in fact there is only one gender – masculine, one sex – male, and therefore only one sexual economy – in her terms 'hommosexuality' (Irigaray 1985b: 46): hence the critics' comments on English, Baker and Sprinkle constructing them as men in drag. However, both Lacan and Irigaray in different ways leave open the possibility of a repressed feminine sexual economy that exists 'elsewhere' outside the symbolic, although this cannot be theorised because we are always already within the symbolic and have no access to an 'outside', except perhaps through the operation of the unconscious. According to both Irigaray and Hélène Cixous, it is the traces of this excluded 'feminine' economy that may be divined in the multiple and contiguous forms of '*ecriture feminine*'.

All these theories represent speculations on how the norms of heterosexual genders are produced and maintained within our culture. They all posit that gender is socially and culturally determined rather than 'natural' and in recent years have all been employed within projects seeking to develop pragmatic, political strategies for challenging these norms. It is on the level of practice that certain problems start to arise, and these approaches can end up reinforcing that which they wish to critique. Some of these theories are sex specific, either by implication or design. Obviously, in the terms in which these theories are articulated, only women can be described as practising Irigarayan mimicry or Rivierian masquerade. Conversely, in common usage, men have tended to be described as wearing the generic 'drag', while women 'cross-dress', play 'travesty' roles, or wear 'male' or 'butch' drag, the qualifier indicating a divergence from the norm. Some commentators also separate them out in relation to sexuality. For example, Sue Ellen Case in her seminal essay 'Toward a Butch-Femme Aesthetic' (1989) and Carole-Anne Tyler in 'Boys Will Be Girls: The Politics of Gay Drag' (1991) both make a distinction between theoretical and embodied strategies of mimicry and masquerade as deployed by gay and lesbian subjects and those developed and practised by heterosexual feminists. In fact, like Moe Mayer in *The Politics and Poetics of Camp*, Case is extremely critical of the appropriation of what she sees as gay and lesbian subversive practices by heterosexuals. Mayer places such practices under the sign of 'camp' which he defines in relation to Butler's concept of gender as performative, but he goes on to assert that 'There is only one kind [of camp]. And it's queer' (1994: 5). Strictly speaking, the nomination 'queer' does not necessarily exclude those who engage in sexual activity with members of the opposite sex, but it does tend to imply at the very least a theoretical, if not actual, lesbian desire, homosexuality, bisexuality or 'polymorphous perversity'. Following these guidelines, since Baker's self-nomination cited above places her as clearly heterosexual, the 'drag' effect of her work can be discussed in relation to Irigarayan mimicry and both versions of masquerade. Within Sprinkle's shows, the range of her sexual activity identifies her as polymorphously perverse, and she has already on several occasions been discussed through reference to camp and queer theory. Rose English, on the other hand, has never made any sort of direct public reference or statement as to her sexual preference, in or out of performance, and discounting the implications of the critics' comments on *The Double Wedding* and *My Mathematics*, this issue does not appear to be discussed in reviews of her work. Even if the reviewers' characterisation of English as a gay man or drag queen is acknowledged, this may actually suggest a tendency towards Irigarayan 'hommosexuality' on their part, rather than lesbian or queer tendencies in English's performance. Such descriptions could imply a heterosexual woman who, having usurped the position of speaking subject, appears as a masculine figure who desires men. There are aspects of English's work, and particularly her interest in cross-dressing, which could easily be read in relation to queer theory, but the 'open' form of her work also allows for a whole range of other normative interpretations. Outside asking English or her personal acquaintances for enlightenment on this issue, which would be a gross intrusion of privacy, I therefore have no sure means of divining whether the gender confusion her performance produces should be read as heterosexual, Irigarayan mimicry or Rivierian masquerade or as gay, lesbian or queer camp, masquerade or drag.

This points up the problem that if any version of gender mimicry or masquerade is to be effective as a resistant or subversive strategy, at some point or on some level it must be clearly legible as differing from the norm. Moreover, if it is possible to separate out gay, lesbian and straight versions of such strategies, then they must in some way be legible as differing both from the norm and from each other. As Carole-Anne Tyler indicates, it is at this point that these apparently social constructionist theories reveal their dependence on some form of essentialism in relation to either sex or sexuality (Tyler 1991). With male to female and lesbian butch drag, the masquerade can always be made visible as such through reference to the 'actual' sex of the performer, but this may simply reinforce the notion of certain gender attributes 'naturally' being proper to one sex or the other and simultaneously reinforce the 'originality' of heterosexuality as the a priori model for sexuality. With the lesbian femme, the 'difference' is primarily one of sexuality, so that for Sue Ellen Case for example, the distinction between the lesbian femme and 'straight' unsubversive citing of the feminine lies in the fashion in which the femme's sexuality is actively directed at another woman, the butch (Case 1989). In this way, dominant notions concerning sexuality and gender may be challenged but only in and through the presence of the butch. On her own, in terms purely of appearances and outside a clearly marked lesbian context, how is it possible to distinguish the lesbian femme either from the 'norm' or from the heterosexual, feminist mimic? Indeed in both these cases a deliberate assumption of 'excessive femininity' can only be made to signify as other to 'normal' femininity if it is accepted as a given that there is such a thing as an identifiable, definable 'norm' of femininity in the first place. This latter is the very notion which such strategies of mimicry and masquerade supposedly reject and seek to expose as a discursive construct, and yet, as Tyler also points out, these same theories do tend to speak of 'the' feminine, which implies that there is such a thing as 'common femininity' (1991: 58). In fact, as she goes on to argue, to assume that any type of gender mimicry or masquerade can be employed as a deliberate and conscious strategy of subversion is to imply that there is some sort of fixed and stable identity category, from which 'one' may choose to put on a mask and in contrast to which the mask can be rendered legible as such in a fashion that will be transparent and decodable by others.

> But if all identities are alienated and fictional, then the distinction between parody, mimicry, or camp, and imitation, masquerade or playing it straight is no longer self-evident. What makes one credible and the other incredible when both are fictions? The answer, it seems, are the author's intentions: parody is legible in the drama of gender performance if someone meant to script it, intending it to be there. Any potential in-difference or confusion of the two is eliminated by a focus in the theories on production rather than reception or perception. (Tyler 1991: 54)

For Tyler, this focus on production over reception and perception within theories of mimicry and masquerade operates to conceal the manner in which the legibility of such acts is often dependent on differences other than those of gender, sex and sexuality. She argues that actually some women do 'have' the phallus in our culture because the phallus is not just the insignia of sexual difference but of all other signs of power and privilege and as such stands 'in a metaphoric and metonymic relation not only to "penis" but also to "white" and "bourgeois" – the signs of a "proper" racial and class identity' (58). As a result, Tyler reads complex processes of narcissism, fetishism, identification and dis-identification related to class, race and ethnicity, as *well* as to masculinity and femininity, in a number of examples of drag and queer parody. These are aspects of these genres of performance that tend to be ignored when sexual difference or differences of sexuality are privileged as a primary focus. So, for example, the perception of Sprinkle as 'not unlike a drag queen' may be bound up more with Sprinkle's class status as a former sex worker than with her performance of sex or sexuality. Equally, the 'comic ambiguity' I identify as pertaining to Ru Paul's performance may well have a double edge, in so far as it may have as much to do with his race as his sex in a culture where, as well as 'masculine', the normative speaking subject tends to be 'white'.

Yet oddly and paradoxically enough, particularly considering her comment on critics who speak of 'the' feminine as a single concept, it is noticeable that Tyler treats both 'feminists' and their brand of 'mimicry' as if there is one common brand of feminism and one mode of feminist mimicry. In Tyler's judgement, feminist mimicry actually consists of 'white and middle class' women appropriating what they perceive as 'excessive', 'bad taste', 'lower class style', thereby indirectly affirming white, middle class style as the cultural norm for 'proper' femininity (1991: 57). As such, the mimic is guaranteeing her own 'having' of the phallus, 'flaunting or camping up lack', by 'fetishistically projecting it on to the class, ethnic, or racial other, from whom she distances herself through dis-identification which takes the form of an apparent identification' (57). This analysis is very similar to that which she offers in discussing drag and lesbian masquerade, but whereas these genres of impersonation are explored in detail, her argument concerning feminist mimicry is supported by only a generalised reference to Dolly Parton rather than to a self-confessed practitioner of such mimicry. She asserts that it is only from a white, middle class perspective that Dolly Parton looks like a female impersonator; 'from a working class point of view, she could be the epitome of genuine womanliness' (57) – except, of course, Parton is an extremely famous singer and film star, whose plastic surgery and acknowledged fondness for wearing large wigs and extravagant 'theatrical' costumes have regularly made headlines in the popular media, all of which constitutes intertextual knowledge that could be expected to colour most people's judgement of the 'authenticity' of her womanliness.

This aside, if Bobby Baker, who is white, heterosexual and middle class, can actually be said to practise 'feminist mimicry', since she mimics herself, it is her *own* style of femininity that is being mimicked. In fact, in Britain it is the Australian Dame Edna who represents a notion of a bad taste, lower class, ethnic, 'other' style of femininity, and so on the level of reception and perception it may be that, in identifying Baker with Everage, the reviewers are actually dis-identifying from Baker's performance. In short, the comparison between them may be a way of implicitly reasserting the naturalness of a norm of femininity that Baker has somehow managed to destabilise by unconsciously suggesting that Baker cannot possibly be the 'real thing'. As such, Baker could be said to be performing the form of 'self-criticism' that Tyler suggests as a means of 'unveiling phallic impostures', revealing that we are all 'acting' in support of a symbolic which is 'really a white, bourgeois and masculine, fetishistic imaginary'. In these terms, Baker foregrounds the 'self-difference', the 'mis-recognitions' and fantasies that found her subjectivity, revealing her own 'having' of the phallus as a white, middle class woman to be an imposture. Yet this notion of 'self-criticism', performed by women who are still at various times socially and legally treated as a subordinate group, may simply confirm them as 'castrated' and reinforce the white, heterosexual *male* phantasy of 'having' the phallus. Similarly, it is not clear just how such 'self-criticism' may be useful to those who, by dint of race, sexuality, class or age, find themselves violently and forcibly reminded of their 'lack' and 'impostures' on a daily basis. The example of such self-criticism offered by Tyler is taken from a novel which features a working class 'hustler'. For this character the recognition of his own role in 'the comedy of sexual relations' brings a 'painful' awareness of lack, in our 'cold cold world', which he rapidly suppresses, leaving him with a vague sense of possibilities and the feeling that 'heaven is unfairly barred to some' (1991: 63). In short, no one is laughing and the 'comedy' turns out to be a Greek tragedy after all, in which we are all fated to incompleteness and lack, the awareness of which can be born only by 'blinding' ourselves to the truth. It is also significant that the consciousness of lack is invoked in terms of a 'barred heaven', since, as Judith Butler among others has pointed out, the psychoanalytical description of a subject's entry into language is presented by both Freud and Lacan as a tragic narrative of the loss of wholeness and 'bliss', very similar to the biblical version of the 'fall of man' (Butler 1990: 56–7).

While Tyler defines the phallus in terms of numerous other signs of power and identifies multiple and fluid identifications and dis-identifications in the examples of drag, masquerade and mimicry which she cites within her argument, the signifier 'phallus' still retains the fixed position of guaranteeing all meanings. Tyler then appears to accept the Lacanian claim for the phallus as privileged signifier, which guarantees signification but which remains unaffected by, and therefore to some degree 'outside', the process for which it stands. As a result, and despite her emphasis on reception and perception, all the examples she offers are treated as 'readerly', always already legible in a manner that does indeed seem 'pre-scripted' by some author(ity), since, however different, they all ultimately only demonstrate some variation of appearing to 'have' or 'be' the phallus and of fetishism as a means of compensating for lack. To reduce all notions of 'power' to a single term represents a metanarrative that can make that power seem unassailable and unalterable in a fashion that denies the possibility of agency and indeed responsibility. Equally, discussing inequalities of race and class in a language derived from a psychoanalytical theory can also detract from the analysis of their historical construction, so that they appear as linguistic 'fictions' which are nevertheless sadly unalterable 'facts', in the same way that the relationship between the phallus and the penis is presented by Lacan as both a fiction and a (sadly?) unalterable 'fact'. As he puts it, the dominance of the penis in 'the shaping of the body image [...] is a fact and cannot be put down to cultural influences alone' (quoted in Grosz 1990: 123). It is hardly surprising, then, that however much theorists insist on the 'neutrality' or transferability of the phallus, it will keep slipping out of control and signifying primarily in relation to the penis. Therefore, although Tyler asserts the importance of considering a range of differences in discussing mimicry and masquerade, I am not sure that describing these differences in a vocabulary which inevitably reinscribes both the primacy of sexual difference and of masculinity is not something of a contradiction.

Ellie Ragland Sullivan has asserted that 'Lacan is describing first causes, not approving them' (quoted in Grosz 1990: 123), and psychoanalytical theory has proved very useful to many feminist academics in offering an account of the production of sexed identities. Yet Lacan's description is 'perspectival': for instance, the 'phallus' is chosen as the insignia of power because 'it is the most tangible element in the real of sexual copulation', an assertion that might be contested by all sorts of people (quoted in Grosz 1990: 125).

Equally, Linda Kintz has suggested that the description of the subject's entry into signification, interpreted by Lacan as a tragic narrative of loss and inevitable isolation, could actually be read as evidence of our sociability and inevitable mutual dependence (Kintz 1992: 111). Indeed, both Lacan and Freud can be said to focus on the processes of production, rather than reception and perception, in a manner which implicitly reinscribes some sort of notion of 'intentionality' to a self-reproducing patriarchal authority. Working backwards and interpreting the past through their own particular understanding of the present, they inevitably find and foreground narratives of first causes and origins that demonstrate the ubiquity of the same old story. As Judith Butler puts it in *Bodies that Matter*, within Lacanian theory 'the phallus governs the description of its own genesis and, accordingly, wards off a genealogy that might confer on it a derivative or projected character' (1993: 82).

In this book Butler takes up the argument she developed in *Gender Trouble* but focuses on the problematic of the relationship between sex and gender in order to address what Tyler describes as the issue of 'hidden essentialism' within theories that assert that all identity is socially constructed. To some extent her thesis is not dissimilar to Tyler's, in so far as she stresses the function of the phallus in instituting the norms of race and class as well as sex and sexuality. As a result, she too works from within psychoanalytical theory and so tends to employ a vocabulary that privileges sexual difference on the principle that 'Sex is … one of the norms by which "one" becomes viable at all, that which qualifies a body for life within the domain of cultural intelligibility' (1993: 2). She also suggests, in line with Freud and Lacan, that these positions are not assumed voluntarily or as an act of will but under the threat of being outside that domain. However, she goes on to reiterate the point she made in *Gender Trouble* that within psychoanalytical theory the apparent 'primacy' of sexual difference is established through the 'dissembling' of the historical nature of 'sex' as a discourse, thereby ensuring this primacy and at the same time apparently rendering it 'impervious to historical variability and possibility' (Butler 1990: 66). Moreover, where Tyler tends to stress the tragic dimensions of a masquerade, with which we must comply and which is always already fated to fail in advance because our phallic impostures represent an identification with unrealisable ideals, Butler re-reads this inevitable failure in positive terms and preserves some notion of 'agency'. Drawing on Foucault, Butler reads the 'power' of the phallus as productive in so far as a prohibitive law, 'by underscoring a given practice in discourse, produces the occasion for a public contest that may inadvertently enable, refigure, and proliferate the very social phenomenon it seeks to restrict' (1993: 109). Like most other theories aimed at the subversion of identity norms, Butler plays on the distinction between the general 'law' or rule and the individual utterance or performance of that law. Yet, rather than reinforcing a notion of 'author's intentions', Butler foregrounds the process of signification which outwits all authorial intentions, including the authority of the phallus. Butler pursues this by arguing that the 'power' and authority of the phallus is performative, in so far as it is the claiming of the position of privileged signifier for the phallus that produces and effects this privilege (1993: 83).

Butler draws on J.L. Austin's theory of the performative in linguistic theory, in which a performative is said to be a discursive practice which enacts or produces what it names. Butler gives the biblical example 'let there be light' (1993: 13). The other classic example is 'I pronounce you man and wife'. Through reference to Derrida, Butler then reformulates Austin's concept of performativity as 'citation', based on the principle that all intelligibility is a matter of 'iterability', or rather of repetition. Butler points out that a performative utterance or act does not bring something into being for the first time and does not imply one single and definitive citation; rather it is part of a continuing process of the reiteration and reinscription of an authority (12–13). However, a performative tends to have the *appearance* of issuing from the authority of the subject who utters it, disguising the way in which this subject only reproduces that authority in so far as they are 'quoting' an already established set of conventions. This, then, is a sort of quoting which operates to conceal its own status as quotation (Butler 1993: 13). As such it is a reinvention and reinscription of an authority, the source or 'first cause' of which is disguised and dissembled because it is indefinitely 'deferred' backwards through previous citations to 'an irrecoverable past'. As a result, as Butler puts it, 'The pointing to a ground which is never recovered becomes authority's groundless ground' (108). With specific reference to Lacanian theory, Butler then argues that gender can be said to stand in a performative relation to sex. Indeed 'sex' itself may be said to be performative on the basis that while gender may be the social construction of 'sex', we actually have no access to 'sex' except through this construction (5). Butler goes on to state that 'there is no reference to a pure body which is not at the same time a further formation of that body' (10). Within Lacanian theory, in order to become 'intelligible' as a subject, 'one is said to assume a "sex"', a process achieved through the identification with one or other of the sexed positions within language (Butler 1993: 12). This implies not only that these positions exist in the symbolic domain prior to their assumption by individuals but also that there is already a 'one' who can effect this assumption, or rather that the body has already been marked, 'staging in advance which symbolic position will mark it' (98). This first mark of 'sex' is then the irrecoverable groundless ground of the symbolic 'sexed positions', since paradoxically it is only retrospectively through the second or double mark that the existence of the first mark can be affirmed. This is because there is no recourse to the 'outside' of the symbolic from within the symbolic, so that any description of the body *before* the symbolic can only take place in terms of the symbolic and is therefore always already a fiction, or a social construct, produced under the authority of the phallus. In short, as Butler states,

> Although Lacan claims that the symbolic law has a semi-autonomous status prior to the assumption or accession of sexed positions by a subject, these normative positions, i.e., the 'sexes' are only known through the approximations that they occasion. The very force and necessity of these norms ('sex' as symbolic function is to be understood as a kind of commandment or injunction) is thus functionally *dependent on* the approximation and citation of the law; the law without its approximation is no law, or rather, it remains a governing law only for those who would affirm it on the basis of religious faith. (Butler 1993: 14)

To put it simply, it is the continuing and continual citation of the sexed positions within the symbolic which establishes that the phallic law that governs the symbolic exists, rather than the phallic law which establishes the existence of sexed positions. This means that the privileged position of the phallus is authorised by reference to its own effects and so is performatively produced in an apparently self-reproducing, closed system. However, as Derridean deconstruction has indicated, for a system to be 'closed' and therefore to refer only to itself, it must have already marked what is 'outside' itself, 'inside' itself, or as Butler puts it, 'A constitutive or relative outside is, of course, composed of a set of exclusions that are nevertheless *internal* to that system as its own nonthematisable necessity. It emerges within the system as incoherence, disruption, a threat to its own systematicity' (1993: 39). Equally, defining an intelligible subject, by implication, simultaneously involves the definition of an unintelligible non-subject, or the 'abject', to use Julia Kristeva's term (see Kristeva 1982). Indeed, Butler indicates that since enacting an identification with one or other of the sexed positions is carried out under threat, the phallic law must have already taken account of, and in fact defined in advance, the existence of other possible types of identification which could be made but must be repudiated as part of the process of becoming a 'proper subject'. Like Tyler, Butler suggests that identifications within the symbolic are always 'ambivalent' in that they always include a dis-identification from some other, but Butler then turns this round to suggest that a dis-identification is always at some point an identification that has been made and given up. So while the law of the symbolic attempts to regulate identificatory practices, this very process of regulation implies and even generates the possibility of other, improper identifications. Furthermore, if some of these 'other' identifications had not at some time been made, there would be no need for a 'law', and if there were not those already living outside the domain of proper subjects, the threat of the law would not be effective. The possibility of an improper citation of the sexed positions is then both recognised and written into the phallic law, and the need to constantly delineate and secure the boundary between the inside and the outside, proper and improper, subject and abject, suggests that without regulation they might become confused. However, ultimately it is the dependence of this law on its approximation or citation, the need for constant repetition and reinscription of the law through its effects, which produces the possibility of a displacement or resignification of this law through subversive repetition.

In this fashion, Butler performs a deconstruction of psychoanalytical theory, working from within to highlight the paradoxes and contradictions on which the system depends. She achieves this by foregrounding the operation known as *différance* within the process of signification, whereby all intelligibility depends on repetition but at the same time repetition constantly produces new meanings in a chain of signification through which the production of final meanings is infinitely deferred. She then shows how, of necess its own terms, the phallus as insignia of power must alway be *inside* this process of signification, demonstrating how i is produced through the operation of performativity. Fin she indicates the ways in which the dependency of the phallus on its effects, which must be constantly repeated, opens up the possibility of its resignification 'in ways and places that exceed its proper place' (1993: 89).

In terms of thinking about this theory in relation to practice, Butler constantly underlines certain points. Sex is one of the norms that qualify a body for subjecthood, and so the assumption of a sexed position is not an act of will, nor is it a single act, nor can sex be put on and taken off like a set of clothes. The strategy she proposes works on the weakness within norm and primarily the principle that to remain a norm it must be reiterated. However, there is no way of guaranteeing in advance that an improper repetition of the norm will not be recuperated and the norm reinforced, and in fact any such improper citations may simply be perceived as poor copies of the norm. Equally, if sex is one of the norms that qualifies a body for life within the domain of cultural intelligibility, to improperly cite the sexed positions may be to risk unintelligibility, to become 'unreadable' and so be 'denied existence'. Even so, for Butler, a notion of political agency can be posited in terms of 'performativity rethought as the force of citationality', which operates by accepting that it 'is necessary to learn a double movement' which is one of 'being constituted in and by a signifier', and therefore being compelled to 'cite or repeat or mime the signifier', in order to provisionally institute an identity but at the same time open up this identity category as 'a permanent site of political contest' (1993: 220–2). This means that any invocation of an identity category is performed in such a way as to foreground the processes of production, the exclusions, dis-identifications and abjections on which that category is based. The idea is not to name or try to include all these excluded 'others' within the category but to demonstrate the category's incapacity to include or summarise the field of social relations, hence creating a space for future rearticulations and resignifications (see Butler 1993: 220–3).

In the next three chapters, I am going to examine the various ways in which, in terms of perception and reception, the drag effect in the work of Baker, Sprinkle and English might be read as the product of this sort of double movement, with reference not only to Butler but also to many other theorists, including those cited in this chapter. I am going to suggest that all three stage the identity category 'woman' but in some way simultaneously open it up as a site of contest, revealing some of the identifications that must be repudiated in order for 'proper' female subjectivity to be assumed. I will argue that, for the audience, this produces moments of unintelligibility, unreadability or rather, in Butler's terms, 'a hiatus in iterability' but that this is no guarantee of sexual political efficacy, since the 'doubleness' of these performances always contains the possibility of recuperation. It may be, then, for example, that the reviewers' construction of these female performers as men, masquerading as women, actually represents a recognition that a subversion has taken place. Equally, these reviews might represent the attempt to defuse this threat by rendering the performers' identity 'readable' in terms of the dominant norm, i.e. masculine subjectivity. In sum, the threat posed by an identification with this unintelligibility may provoke a dis-identification as a defensive reaction. Similarly, some of the laughter the shows produce might be in response to the way that the performance of a double movement reveals the play of paradox and contradiction in the construction of subjectivity. In this sense, these performances may be said to exploit the comic principle of '*double entendre*', which is always contextual and works on the weakness of the norm to restage apparently 'innocent' acts or utterances to allow 'other', opposite meanings to be made apparent within and through each other. On the other hand, this laughter might signify the dismissal of the show as simply non-sense and not worth taking seriously.

However, in pursuing this thesis I wish to avoid adding to the tendency to confuse and conflate performance and performativity that developed in the wake of Butler's use of drag to exemplify the performativity of gender in *Gender Trouble*. For some, the use of this example was taken as an indication that the subversion of the hegemonic norms is a matter of choice of clothing and of 'acting' in the theatrical sense and therefore very much an issue of 'author's intentions'. In *Bodies that Matter*, Butler responds to such oversimplifications by making it clear that performativity refers to a *process*, 'a reiteration of a norm or set of norms', while, in her view, performance is a 'bounded act' (1993: 12 and 234 respectively). If a performative 'acquires an act like status in the present', it is due to the fashion in which 'it conceals or dissimulates the conventions of which it is a repetition' (12). As such, 'performance is distinguished from performativity in so far as the latter consists in a reiteration of norms which precede, constrain and exceed the performer and in that sense cannot be taken as the fabrication of the performer's "will" or "choice" ' (234). For Butler, then, the *apparent* theatricality of a performative act or utterance is produced 'to the extent that its historicity remains dissimulated (and conversely, its theatricality gains a certain inevitability given the impossibility of a full disclosure of its historicity)' (12). In short, if I understand Butler correctly, a performative act only appears as theatrical in that it seems to arise from the authority or will of the actor, and in so far as the process of citation on which it depends makes it impossible to trace the existence of an 'original' or 'real' historical referent. As will become clear, for me, these statements deepen rather than clarify any possible confusion between performance and performativity, a situation that is not helped by the examples offered by Butler in *Bodies that Matter*. Like many other theorists in this area, Butler explores the notion of gender performativity primarily through reference to literature, to theatrical performances or to works like *Paris is Burning*. Although a documentary, this latter is still a film, an artefact in which 'everyday reality' has already been narrativised and rendered theatrical through the mediating lens of the camera. Moreover, in concluding *Bodies that Matter* and focusing on 'queer' citations of identity norms, Butler again asserts the difference between performance and performativity but then seems to reopen the possibility of confusion. She indicates that when the subject who is named as queer 'takes up this term as the discursive basis for an opposition', a kind of citation 'will emerge as *theatrical* to the extent that it *mimes and renders hyperbolic* the discursive convention that it also *reverses*' (1993: 232). The problem is that all the examples Butler gives of this queer performativity have at some time been defined and analysed *as* theatrical performances by theatre studies academics and others (233). In justification of her choice of these examples, Butler states that 'to oppose the theatrical to the political in contemporary queer politics is, I would argue, an impossibility' (232). As a theatre studies lecturer, I am rather surprised at the implication that there may be people who do try to oppose the political and the theatrical in any sort of politics, since a connection between the two was established as far back as Ancient Greece, most particularly of course in relation to comic forms. This connection was recognised by Plato's banishment of theatre from his ideal Republic, on the principle that it was 'dangerous'.

For all sorts of reasons, I think some confusion between theatrical performance and performativity may to a certain extent be inevitable. As Andrew Parker and Eve Kosofsky Sedgwick have pointed out, while Austin's notion of performativity 'separated the actor's citational practices from ordinary speech-act performances', Derrida, who (according to Susan Bordo, alongside Erving Goffman[1]) is one of Butler's chief sources for her reformulation of performativity, 'regarded both as structured by a generalised iterability, a pervasive theatricality common to stage and world alike' (Parker and Sedgwick 1995: 4). It is important to note, however, that this is an 'alikeness' common to stage and world which does not necessarily erase the difference between them. I suspect that what is actually being 'opposed' by those who might wish to separate the theatrical and the political is a too speedy, reductive, overly theoretical assumption of a collapse of the oppositions between the social and the cultural, and the real and the mimetic, that seem to occur in some postmodern theory. This sort of thinking, with its tendency to emphasise the 'free play' of signification, at best can produce the sort of Utopianism that seems divorced from the daily 'reality' of inequality and social injustice that still governs the lives of so many 'postmodern' subjects. Alternatively, for theorists like Baudrillard, this collapse, which for him appears to have definitely occurred, is ascribed to the triumph of post-industrial capitalism as a political system. Yet actually what he describes is a *reversal* of the traditional hierarchy of the real and the mimetic, with the latter becoming the first and prior term. His perspective is once again, like Lacan's, simultaneously socially constructivist and tragic, a vision of a world where all value has been reduced to the symbolic exchange of signifiers and as a result is fated to 'indifference' and equivalence, or rather the loss of all value. Yet, oddly, Baudrillard himself somehow appears to remain 'outside' this system, the lone voice of an Old Testament prophet who can perceive the meta-truth, while the disaffected masses continue to worship brazen idols. Of course, Baudrillard may be being deliberately provocative, ironic even. However, once again the limits and conditions of intelligibility appear to have been decided in advance through reference to an authority, in this case late industrial capitalism, whose power is evident in its effects, and once again 'power' is reduced to a single, monolithic term and agency is denied (see Baudrillard 1988 and 1993).

What Butler and Derrida put into question is not so much whether any distinction can be made between the 'real' and the 'mimetic', but the basis of any authority which attempts to definitely decide on this difference for everybody, and once and for all. As such, it may be that the process of Butler's double movement necessitates a *temporary* reversal, in which the mimetic must be privileged in order to open up to contestation dominant notions of 'the' real on which that authority depends. A temporary reversal, however, is not the same as a collapse and is only the first stage of a deconstruction, not the end point. Nothing is to be gained if 'the' mimetic simply replaces 'the' real and is perceived as a singular stable term that can operate as a universal touchstone for measuring the self-evident 'truth' of the fundamental fictionality and theatricality of all human experience.

In my view, much of the potentially unconstructive confusion and the potentially reductive collapse of oppositions that occur in discussions of performativity, or mimicry or masquerade as strategies of resistance, arises because, as Cindy Patton points out, too often an emphasis is placed on the performer at the expense of location or 'staging' and of the effects of staging on reception and perception (Patton 1995: 182). This can reinforce the idea that the legibility of these acts as subversive strategies is a matter of author's intentions and can also dissemble the historicity and specificity of the strategies in themselves. Such strategies are not in fact produced or performed from out of some generalised place called 'the symbolic', which is everywhere and nowhere at once, but are very much perspectival and contingent. In practice, for instance, Butler's own theories are produced as a mode of '*resistant reading*' and articulated within, through and against distinct social institutions and therefore within, through and against specific discursive modes and metanarratives, such as psychoanalytical theory, philosophy, literature, feminism, identity politics and linguistics. This means that Butler's notion of a double movement as it stands is very much a matter of 'interpretation', or rather reception and perception. Hence the fact that 'author's' or rather 'reader's intentions' have not entirely vanished from her theories, and hence the fact that these theories do not easily translate into a blueprint for practice outside the contexts in which they are produced. A confusion arises when such strategies, even as reading practices, are simply transferred across into other sorts of institutions or domains and applied to other discursive modes without taking account of the change of location. For instance, when such strategies are applied to, or exemplified through reference to, theatrical performances or to the citation of theatrical conventions outside performance, the way in which these acts are signified in relation to *theatre* as institution is often overlooked, if not completely ignored. A challenge to a particular articulation of authority within one sphere or institution, or even within different spheres within the same institution, does not necessarily produce or effect its contestation in another. 'Authority', or 'power', is not singular and is always being reinstated and reinterpreted in a multitude of different ways across and within different institutions and as such must always be disputed in its own terms, on its own groundless ground. If subversion or resistance is always legible in the same fashion, everywhere, in the past and in the future, it has already been appropriated to some single, pre-existing 'outside' authority, or rather to 'author's intentions'. And if the subversion of authority or dominant norms is not simply a matter of 'author's intentions' but is rather one of a process of interpretation that opens up contestation (which, in order to be said to occur, must in some way be taken up), it must to a large extent be contingent on the historical, material and discursive location of the act in question.

The reason theatre as an institution is so attractive and yet so problematic to theorists of performativity is because it has traditionally been perceived as both quoting the 'reality effects' they describe as being performatively produced and as simultaneously differing from those 'reality effects' – which is, of course, exactly the effect they seek to achieve as a strategy for subverting identity in the realm of the social. However, in order to be intelligible as such, a theatrical performance depends on the legible presence of the quotation marks, which, as described by Butler, the process of performativity as citation operates to conceal in 'everyday life'. In short, to state the obvious, any sort of act or 'movement' within the theatrical frame or otherwise is already marked *as* double, already in quotation marks. This marking places a performance as belonging to a particular realm of discourse, which is governed by laws and conventions that may be similar to, but are not exactly the same as, those that govern other spheres. The difference between the theatrical and the social may then only be a matter of the legibility or otherwise of quotation marks, but these quotation marks make all the difference. To further complicate matters, this marking is actually achieved through the citation of a set of institutional, theatrical conventions, established through repetition and simultaneously perceived as both not reality and not, not reality – or rather as a stylised manner of reflecting reality. The *apparent* reference to 'reality' within these effects, then, lies in the dissembling of the historical and discursive nature of the theatrical conventions of which they are a repetition and the indefinite deferral of the source or ground of the 'reality' which these conventions supposedly reiterate and reinvent. Therefore, the presence of these quotation marks, without which a theatrical performance cannot be said to take place, are themselves performatively produced, through the citation of specific *theatrical* conventions which precede, constrain and exceed the performance and gives it the *appearance* of arising from the performer's or author's will and of being a 'bounded act'. In short, the intelligibility of any given performance depends on the manner in which it is specifically staged or located within, through and against the history of theatre as a discursive institution, in a fashion that is beyond 'author's intentions'.

Following Butler's logic, the need for performance to establish its difference from 'reality' through the continual citation of these conventions produces the possibility, if not the inevitability, of 'improper citations' of this difference. This is evident in the historical variations within theatrical conventions and indeed the historical variation in the perception of the relationship between these conventions and the 'reality' to which they supposedly refer. Indeed, a tendency to improperly cite this difference and therefore open it up to contestation has always been a feature of performance practice and the source of its 'danger'. However, while, in order to remain legible to an audience as theatre, a performance must cite this difference, once remarked, this difference may then be confused. Producing just such a confusion has been the aim of many modernist and postmodernist practitioners, but the initial marking can never be fully erased if the performance is to remain intelligible as such. Therefore, any discussion of performance and performativity must take into account both this difference and the specific performativity of performance, because paradoxically the possibility of improperly citing this difference in performance is due to the operation of performativity as citation.

It is not surprising, however, that at the Queer Up North conference that took place alongside the festival in Manchester, 1994, Alan Sinfield suggested that many of the approaches discussed in this chapter and particularly the concept of performativity could be best understood in terms of action through Brecht's concept of alienation, or defamiliarisation. In a similar vein, describing what she terms an 'Irigarayan double gesture' within feminist theory, Rebecca Schneider asserts that, 'Like a Brechtian "not, but" this feminist "both/and" makes room for critical enquiry, political agency, and discursive mobility' (Schneider 1997: 36). In theory, these suggestions are useful, but once again, in practice, it is important to guard against the possibility of 'like' being taken as equivalence in a reductive fashion. This Brechtian 'not, but' is one of a series of exercises intended to promote an acting style that marks a distance between actor and character, which allows the performer to be seen as quoting or demonstrating the character instead of producing the illusion of 'being' the character. This should, theoretically, result in preventing the audience from an empathic identification with that character. This technique is intended to produce alienation, or defamiliarisation, allowing the audience to perceive the contradictions within the character as a 'type' operating within a field of social relations which influence but do not predetermine the choices the character makes. As Josette Feral indicates, the idea is to 'make strange' not only the stylised theatrical conventions his theatre cites but also the 'primary extra theatrical phenomenon' which these stylised conventions represent (Feral 1987: 468). Brechtian performance, then, aims to indicate that it is possible to act otherwise within a social reality that is altering and alterable (e.g., see Brecht 1987: 86, 110, 137, 190). So far so good. The three shows considered in this book, like most, if not all, postmodern experimental practice, can most definitely be said to utilise various forms of alienation or defamiliarisation. However, as many critics, including Feral, have pointed out, Brecht's theory implicitly places both the performer and the author (Brecht) 'outside' the fiction in a position of 'mastery', implying the existence of a stable subject position from which to quote the character and indeed from which to represent 'social reality'. The audience is then presumed to identify with the author or actor, who are constructed as knowledgeable, objective observers of social reality for whom the contradictions have actually already been resolved (e.g., see Brecht 1987: 93). In short, Brecht sought to contest and alter the dominant false perception of 'reality', to replace it with the 'truth', which is the truth of class struggle. As a result, although Brecht asserts that his theatre shows 'this particular individual at this particular moment', the primary difference between individuals is always, already assumed to be class difference (Brecht 1987: 195). Brecht therefore assumes in advance an audience to whom the implications of his theatre will be transparent. Since, according to Brecht, this audience is inherently rational, they may be temporarily 'split' and caught up in contradiction but will inevitably achieve a state of synthesis or 'wholeness' through grasping the fundamental truth of social reality when it is represented to them in the correct scientific fashion. Brecht's theatre theory, then, reinscribes notions of an ideal, stable, universal subjectivity and 'author's intentions'. He also works backwards, presupposing in advance a self-evident truth, its perception by a rational audience and their 'natural' reaction, which will be to recognise and react so as to bring about the inevitable downfall of the forces of class oppression (e.g., Brecht 1987: 110–12). Butler, on the other hand, does not offer a notion of teleological progress or of a synthesis and 'wholeness' but rather of permanent struggle over meanings, permanent political contest. In terms of identity, Butler's 'double movement' *is* like the Brechtian 'not, but' – but it is a not, but infinitely recurring.

As theorists like Elizabeth Wright and Elin Diamond have demonstrated, it is possible to construct a 'postmodern Brecht' and therefore bring him closer to Butler (Diamond 1988 and 1995, Wright 1989).[2] For me, one of the objections to such readings lies in the fact that in practice they tend to reinforce the reification of Brechtian theory as the 'master' discourse for political theatre that occurred in the 1970s and 1980s in Britain. This reification tended to be based on the assumption that the relation between Brechtian theory and practice was seamless and coherent and that his notion of epic theatre functioned in terms of audience response in the way he described. These sorts of theoretical presuppositions generated a privileging of a particular set of theatrical conventions as properly political, establishing a dominant discourse which effectively, for at least a decade if not more, foreclosed the domain of intelligibility for social and political dissent within theatre practice. Brechtian conventions continued to be perceived in this manner even when it became clear that they could be 'improperly' cited in ways and places where they might be read as signifying as normative, if not reactionary. Ironically, this privileged position was only achieved by dissembling the way in which Brecht staged his theory and practice within, through and against specific historical, theatrical, social and political institutions. In fact, the construction of a postmodern Brecht is facilitated by the contradictions, paradoxes and gaps within his theories and between his own theories and practices, which render his works 'writerly' and therefore open to reinterpretation. This reinterpretation is also possible, as Brecht so often stressed, because of both the provisional and historically located nature of his ideas and the fashion in which they restaged and recontextualised pre-existing theatrical conventions. So although Brecht constantly stressed the 'newness' of his epic theatre form, he acknowledged the influence of a whole range of forms, including Chinese theatre and many of the popular forms that Marvin Carlson refers to as antecedents of postmodern performance. He also compared it stylistically and in terms of its didacticism to old Asiatic theatre, medieval mystery plays, the classical Spanish theatre and also the theatre of the Jesuits (Brecht 1987: 75–6). Brecht's theatre, then, most certainly relied for its intelligibility on the manner in which it was staged, within and through existing theatre as a discursive institution in a fashion beyond and potentially undermining of his authorial intentions – which is why there are gaps and contradictions between his theory and practice.

To bring Brecht and Butler together in a useful fashion, it is, then, first necessary to take account of the ways in which they differ as well as repeat each other, and to acknowledge and preserve the difference between these discourses and the realms in which they operate, as well as any intersection. There is no *one* theory, strategy or form that can ensure, provoke or even explicate how subversion may be achieved or fail to be achieved in any given situation in any given sphere. To imply that there is, is to reinstate a notion of author's intentions and to ignore the significance of staging, deciding in advance on the terms and conditions of any future subversion or contestation.

In the next chapter I am going to explore the performance of identity in Rose English's *The Double Wedding*, with reference to Butler's notion of a 'double movement'. However, I am going to achieve this by analysing in the first instance the fashion in which this show improperly cites specifically *theatrical* conventions, so as to foreground the performativity of performance. I will therefore be arguing that any subversion of identity that does or does not take place within the show is not a matter of English's individual performance or necessarily of authorial intentions, but depends entirely on the very particular staging of the piece within, through and against theatre as a discursive institution and as such is very much a matter of reception and perception. In doing so, I am going to suggest that this show plays on the borders of intelligibility in radically paradoxical fashion that resists appropriation to any single theoretical position, including Judith Butler's or any other approach which I might offer up.

Notes

1 See S. Bordo (1995) *Unbearable Weight*, p. 289, and E. Goffman (1959) *The Presentation of Self in Everyday Life*.

2 According to Diamond,

> The idea of the *Verfremdungseffekt* was to drive a wedge not just between actor and character, but between the historical subject and the actor's function. While the critical actor is presumed to have superior knowledge in relation to the character the subject herself remains as skeptical and uncertain as the audience to whom the play is addressed. She disappears neither into a representation of the character nor into a representation of the actor: each remains processual, contingent, incomplete. (Diamond 1995: 160)

I hesitate to argue with as distinguished a Brecht scholar as Diamond, but this does seem to be very much a perspectival, re-presentation of Brecht, and I have struggled and failed to find references that clearly and directly support this claim within the Brechtian theory available to me.

1 The Lido scene in *The Double Wedding*.

3

Undecidable doublings: the performativity of performance in Rose English's *The Double Wedding*

> The scene illustrates but the idea, not any actual action, in a hymen (out of which flows Dream), tainted with vice yet sacred, between desire and fulfilment, perpetration and remembrance: here anticipating, there recalling, in the future, in the past, *under the false appearance of the present*. That is how the Mime operates, whose act is confined to a perpetual allusion without breaking the ice or the mirror: he thus sets up a medium, a pure medium of fiction. (Mallarmé, quoted in Derrida 1981: 175)

Part one: describing the Wedding

The Double Wedding was performed in 1991 at the Royal Court Theatre Upstairs as part of the Barclays New Stages Festival. The show was divided into acts and scenes but might equally be described as having consisted of a series of 'episodes' or 'turns'. These 'turns' included mock hypnotism, ballet and other dance forms, acrobatics, ice skating, comic interchanges, singing, chanting and music, and were interwoven with dialogues and monologues concerned either with the general nature of performance or with the specific nature of *The Double Wedding* itself. Although no filmed material appeared in the show, there were numerous allusions to the cinema in Act one. In short, as one of the characters indicated, the show evinced 'an addiction to a multimedia format', and the tone and style of the performance constantly shifted across a range of registers from irony to comedy to moments of apparent seriousness, from 'realistic' acting to melodrama via variety and farce. For the most part, the show evoked laughter and audience response to sequences that at face value might not appear particularly funny, suggesting that much of the piece was received as parody.

The set consisted of two sets of steps and a cylindrical 'vortex' curtain, centre stage, all faced with black-sequinned material. In addition to the lighting rig, six visible hanging globe lights illuminated the stage in Act one and were replaced by two mirror balls in the second act. The style of the costumes, varied from plus fours, to dinner jackets, to showgirl outfits and classical ballet costumes but most of them were also covered in sequins of various colours or were made of reflective material.

The Double Wedding appeared to be an attempt to recall and recreate a show called 'The Double Wedding' that had supposedly happened in the past. This reconstruction, however, was fraught with paradox and contradiction. The cast, who all claimed to have been in the 'original', were described as an 'ensemble made up of solo performers'. Apart from a character known as the Cantor, they were also all either doubling, that is playing more than one part, sometimes simultaneously, or doubled, as in part of a couple. Rose English, the writer and director of this piece, played 'Rose', the writer and director of this 're-production' within the fictional world of the piece. She also introduced herself as both the Hostess and the Hermit, 'a very private sort of person in the privacy of my own show', and was coupled with the Consort, later known as the Figment, whom she 'pursued' in Act two.[1] Similarly, the couple known as the first and second Cameramen were also referred to as 'Harry' and 'Otto', while the Dew/Fake Adagio, often referred to as Nigel, was coupled with the Dawn/Fake Adagio. This pair was linked with another couple, the True Adagio, a pair of ice skaters who did not appear until the final moments of the show but whose performance was prefigured at times by Rose/Hostess/Hermit and the Consort/Figment and at others by the Fake Adagio. The first Hypnotist remained known by this function, whilst the second Hypnotist was also 'Roddy', and there were two further non-speaking couples – the Nebula, who were aerialists, and the Viscera, who were dancers, all four also functioning as stage hands. Most characters, then, had names that suggested an allegorical function within the show, some were also addressed by their 'real' or proper names, others by proper names that were not theirs. For example, while 'Nigel' and 'Roddy' were the names of the performers playing these parts, 'Harry' and 'Otto' were fictional inventions.[2] However, although there was variation in terms of mood and modes of expression and address, there was never any distinct change in characterisation between any of the different personas played by any one individual. So although English declared in Act two that she was playing the friendly Hermit in Act one and is now playing the Hostess, there was never any practical distinction between the portrayal of these characters or 'Rose', who spoke to the audience and was addressed by other cast members as the author and director of the piece.

In a similar fashion, the distinction between the original production and this present one became increasingly confused as the show progressed. In the first act English used a glittery 'magic wand' to hypnotise each member of the cast in turn and, suspending them across her knees, asked, 'What is The Double Wedding?' This was supposed, as English put it, to help 'solve the mystery of our identity' but elicited contradictory information. Although they all affirmed the existence of an 'original' version, it was difficult to distinguish this original from the various, previous remakes they mentioned, which included one in which the dancers only talked about dancing and one which might have been a film. There was a general agreement, then, that it 'all seemed so new' but we would 'do it differently today', yet as this present show continued, the exact things that they identified as needing to be done differently were repeated. Particular props, such as the glittery pipes that featured heavily in the 'original' version, still proliferated, the Hypnotists still wore capes which still did not fit, the Dawn/Fake Adagio still bent over backwards, the famous Lido scene still occurred (twice) and the Consort/Figment still did not feature strongly until Act two, in which he did a lot of dancing. Conversely, the reproduction of a scene between the two Hypnotists became sidetracked by an argument over which side of the stage each one had occupied in the 'original' show, so that we never actually got to see their act. A section in Act one, described by Rose as the 'great deconstruction scene', apparently consisted of the cast reconstructing this scene as it was done in the original production of 1991, but she also told us that previously this scene was entirely text based, whereas what was now shown was predominantly non-verbal. There are a number of paradoxes here, not least that this *was* the production of 1991 and there were no previous stage productions of this particular show of that year, or any other. Although there *is* a film entitled *The Double Wedding* dating from the 1940s, it appears to have no connection with this piece. Moreover, what was shown in the 'deconstruction' scene consisted of fragments of action and snatches of song that appeared in their 'proper', complete form in Act two. Therefore, although English defined this as a re-creation, it could equally be regarded as a rehearsal or a preview of something yet to appear, in a similar fashion to the various prefigurations of the True Adagio. In the final scenes, all the characters spoke of going to the Double Wedding but then all refused to marry one another. Yet this was followed by the performance of a celebratory, circular 'Greek' wedding dance, which climaxed with the appearance of the True Adagio skating on a miniature ice rink.

The simple answer to the question 'What is The Double Wedding?' is that it is a piece of theatre, and so, according to the classical Aristotelian definition, it should therefore be an imitation of a pre-existing action or a reflection of reality, its meaning being guaranteed through reference 'outside' itself. However, since *The Double Wedding* is a show that attempts to reproduce an earlier version of itself which does not exist, there is apparently no 'outside' prior action or reality being imitated. *The Double Wedding* therefore appears to be a self-reflexive show which refers only to the idea of itself. Yet if this were the case, it would be producing and enacting itself as its own original, and, since all intelligibility depends on repetition, not only would it no longer be recognisable as a piece of theatre, but it would be completely unintelligible. In fact, *The Double Wedding* does not only refer to the idea of itself, but it constantly refers to the idea of itself *as a piece of theatre*, or rather as this piece of theatre which is in the process of being performed. As such it must be citing already established conventions for performing; in this way the show is remarked as mimetic without referring to any actual or originating action or idea, and to quote Jacques Derrida on the passage from Mallarmé's 'Mimique', cited above:

> We are faced then with mimicry imitating nothing, faced, so to speak, with a double that doubles no simple, a double that nothing anticipates nothing that itself is not already double. There is no simple reference [...]. This speculum reflects no reality; it produces mere 'reality effects'. (1981: 206)

For example, in Act one, the two Cameramen, flourishing oversize quill pens, 'acted' reading and writing and looking at each other in an exaggerated and theatrical manner while simultaneously asking each other if, while 'acting' reading, writing and looking at each other on stage, they ever really do these things or whether they just 'act' them. The scene ended with 'Otto' bemoaning the fact that realism 'promises so much but delivers so little'. So far, so Brechtian – but their actions signally failed to deliver or refer to the 'real' in a fashion that differs from the Brechtian paradigm. In the first place, within the diegetic world of this piece, these actors were supposedly quoting the characters they performed in a wholly fictional, previous production of this show, and therefore, rather than commenting on 'social types' or behaviour, they were literally mimicking nothing that had ever taken place, even in theatrical fiction. In the second place, they were simply commenting on what they were in the *process* of doing in this version of the show, which was mimicking certain established 'realistic' conventions that performers employ for 'acting' reading, writing and looking at each other on stage. As a result, they were not imitating reality; they were imitating the stylised codes for representing reality, or producing reality effects.

This produces a problem for the interpreter. The status of *The Double Wedding* as a false quotation of itself means that, like a performative utterance, it gives the *appearance* of producing itself through reference to its own authority, dissembling the fashion in which its intelligibility depends entirely on the process of 'iterability', or rather on performativity as a process of citation within theatre as a historical institution. As such, this show constitutes, in Derrida's terms, a structure that is 'open and closed at the same time' and which, in apparently referring 'back only to itself', potentially refers, '*at the same time*, indefinitely and systematically to some other writing' (Derrida 1981: 202). In short, any attempt to track down the origins of these reality effects and hence provide some sort of meaning for the show potentially opens up a journey back through the history of theatre. This problem is compounded by the show's multimedia format where conventions are drawn from a whole ranges of genres, including mainstream theatre, dance, ballet and opera, cabaret, melodrama, music hall, variety, circus and even film. Moreover, recognition of the conventions being cited depends entirely on the individual spectator's pre-existing knowledge of theatre practices. All of this makes it impossible to offer a single, authoritative interpretation of this piece, and so, to a large extent, as with Mallarmé's 'Mimique' above, it is only possible to describe how the show 'operates'.

In fact, *The Double Wedding* could be described as starting in Plato's cave – for where else do hermits live? In Act one, English asked the audience to imagine 'so far back the dust was only just beginning to settle and we were all enthralled, we were in the thrall of some immense and powerful image'. In Plato's allegory of the cave, 'humanity' is represented as entranced, hypnotised, by the false play of shadows on the wall of the cave, caused by firelight, their backs turned from the real and 'true' light of the sun. Plato often appears as the 'villain' in contemporary theory in so far as he is often accredited with establishing the hierarchical binary system that is said still to inform the structure of Western language and thought. The allegory of the cave which represents the lure of illusory worldly pleasures, like much of Plato's writings, has been deconstructed by many poststructuralist philosophers, including Derrida, Irigaray and Judith Butler. Somewhat surprisingly then, this production appears to reinscribe the Platonic separation of mind and body (the Nebula and the Viscera), as well as Plato's method of identifying the 'truth', based on the establishment of both a temporal order and a numerical discernibly between one and two (first and second Cameramen and Hypnotists), single and double, original and copy (True and Fake Adagio). For Plato, all things had a true, ideal original, preceding and separate to human existence and perception, and in a Platonic fashion the characters in this show constantly referred back to an 'ideal', a 'real' or original '*The Double Wedding*' (see Derrida 1981: 191). This is referred to as a 'great form', supposedly already in existence, which, when revealed, will satisfy their own and the audience's longing to be 'one' with 'The Wedding', presumably abandoning 'false' mimetic pleasures in favour of a higher metaphysical truth. English's hypnotism of the cast might then be read as mirroring Plato's disapproval of the 'hypnotic' effect of the mimetic arts on the principle that they put 'true' memory to sleep and prevented discovery of the metaphysical essence of existence (see Derrida 1981: 110). However, the very same act could be interpreted as a reference to Artaud's designation of 'acting in a trance', as a crucial feature of the 'Theatre of Cruelty' in *The Theatre and Its Double* (see Artaud 1958: 53–67).

Indeed, in Act one, English spoke of once having debated the meaning of the term '*gesamtkuntswerk*' (integrated work of art) with the second Hypnotist, a term chiefly associated with Wagner, who influenced Nietzsche, many of whose ideas are repeated by Artaud.

As both Hermit and Hostess, English might actually stand for the Nietzschian philosopher/artist (see Megill 1987: 36). The 'doubleness' of this figure represented a rejection of the hierarchical binary oppositions between life and art, the real and the mimetic, mind and body, established by the Platonic tradition of dialectical thought. While Plato asserted that Socratic dialectical logic offered a direct means of revealing and experiencing the 'truth' of existence, for Nietzsche there could be no unmediated acesss to 'truth' or reality, so that such thinking merely represented another form of 'illusion'. In *The Birth of Tragedy*, Nietzsche challenged the hegemony of the Platonic binary oppositions through a reversal, championing an aesthetic, irrational, pre-Socratic, 'Dionysiac' mode of thought, as representing the acceptance of the fundamentally illusory nature of all human perception and experience. In *Thus Spake Zarathustra*, Nietzsche went further and attempted to transcend the Platonic binaries, seeking to create a 'new' poetic, performative language which would, as Alan Megill puts it, 'constitute a new system of interpretation [of reality] that by virtue of its existence will bring into being the new reality corresponding to it' (Megill 1987: 97). In a similar fashion, in *The Theatre and Its Double*, Artaud also privileged the poetic, the mimetic and the Dionysiac over Platonic logic and truth, seeking to develop a new theatre form which would performatively alter reality, having 'the power to influence the aspect and formation of things' so that 'between life and the theater there will be no distinct division, but instead a continuity' (Artaud 1958: 79 and 126). There were numerous aspects of *The Double Wedding* that favoured a Nietzschian and/or Artaudian reading for the show – not least the title, the emphasis on the beautiful, fleeting and illusory nature of the piece and on non-verbal forms of expression, plus several references to the 'void' and 'veil', terms fairly central to both writers.[3] The show was also described in chemical terms as 'volatile' and a 'matter of liquid and gas', and as author/director/Hostess/Hermit, English played out the sort of multiple role represented by ancient alchemists.[4] Alchemy was an important model for both Nietzsche and Artaud, since its earliest devotees preceded Plato and it also combined art, science, religion, philosophy and magic. Further, an 'alchemical wedding', in which opposites are confused and transmuted into a new element by means of a mythical 'philosophers' stone', attempted to reproduce and simultaneously transform the workings of nature. We are told it is English's 'obstinate' refusal of fiction, her belief that acting is 'basically lying' and therefore her insistence on upholding an idea of truth and reinscribing the Platonic opposition between the single and the double, original and copy, that is preventing '*The Double Wedding*' from appearing. Eventually, it is her pursuit of the figment, standing perhaps for the philosophers' stone, and her acceptance of the *fiction* that allows the True Adagio to be unveiled, an act that has already been mimicked in advance several times. As such, *The Double Wedding* might be said to represent an attempt to transcend Platonic dialectics and, in an Artaudian fashion, to effect a transformation of reality through the mimetic or double, bringing the idea of itself into being as something that is both 'original' and yet wholly theatrical.

To complicate matters, also in Act one, the second Hypnotist cited the name Walter Benjamin, the Cameramen had a discussion concerning the relative artistic and technical merits of kinescope and vista vision, Nigel attempted to demonstrate screen acting on stage and the Cantor sang a song asking, 'Why can't a film be like a show and why can't a show be more like a film?' Conceptually and in the specificity of the vocabulary employed, all of this appeared to be referring to Benjamin's essay, 'The Work of Art in the Age of Mechanical Reproduction' (Benjamin 1992). In this essay, while continuing to ascribe to a form of dialectical logic that owes much to Plato and Socrates, Benjamin, too, appears to reverse the Platonic temporal and numerical order of truth. He argues that historical variation in the modes of reflecting reality, in artistic practices indicates alterations in the perception of that reality, and since all experience of reality is mediated through perception, the development of new forms of art can in turn produce a transformation of reality. He concludes that, due to their processes of production, certain 'new' forms, such as photography and cinema, can show things in a way they have never been perceived before and therefore have potential for producing a politically radical alteration of reality. Put in this fashion, Benjamin's and Nietzsche's ideas seem very similar, and indeed they both owe much to the same German philosophic tradition. Yet they operate on virtually opposite assumptions concerning the nature of the 'new' reality they predict as emerging, not least because Benjamin's 'new' reality already exists in the world of the social and simply needs to be unveiled, whilst Nietzche's exists only in the realm of aesthetic possibility.

Further, in 'The Work of Art', Benjamin insists that he is arguing not for 'art for art's sake', nor the aestheticisation of politics – positions usually associated with Nietzsche – but rather for the politicisation of art. The former he associates negatively with Fascism, and Nietzsche's and Wagner's ideas were famously appropriated for Fascism under Hitler, while for Benjamin the latter represents a 'positive' aim of Communism, which rather overlooks the way that certain forms of Communism had already turned out not to be so dissimilar from Fascism (Benjamin 1992: 235).

It is less contentious to relate Benjamin to Brecht, who is cited twice in the footnotes of 'The Work of Art', and despite his focus on film, Benjamin's analysis echoes much of Brecht's writing on epic theatre, in terms of the description of its formal qualities, its presumed effect on the spectator and its resultant power to alter perception and transform, or rather reveal, 'reality'. It is not surprising, then, that, despite my comment above, much of *The Double Wedding* can also be read through reference to Brecht as well as Artaud, and the hypnotism in Act one interpreted as referring to Brecht's denouncing of naturalistic acting by 'means of hypnosis where the actors go into a trance and take the audience with them' (Brecht 1987: 26). The foregrounding of the apparatus of theatrical production, the show's episodic structure, the way in which the songs tended to comment on the action and pose dialectical questions, even the 'visible' light sources in Act one, are all classic epic theatre devices. The manner in which performers offered critical comments on the meaning or lack of meaning of the show and criticised each other's performances, frequently using direct audience address, all recall Brecht's ideas for achieving alienation, distanciation or defamiliarisation. Act one also contained a 'pipe dance', in which the cast struck attitudes of 'thinking while smoking' that could be a literal, if parodic, repetition of Brecht's desire for his audience to take up an 'attitude of smoking and thinking', because he says 'it is impossible to try to carry away any man who is smoking' (Brecht 1987: 44). Interestingly, in the essay 'The Modern Theatre is the Epic Theatre', in which he makes this comment, he explains his concept of epic opera in terms of how it differs from Wagner's and cites the same term, '*gesamtkuntswerk*', quoted in *The Double Wedding* that originally led me to Artaud, via Nietzsche and Wagner. And actually the attitudes struck in the pipe dance could equally be read as a similarly parodic enactment of Artaud's call for a concrete language for the theatre, 'somewhere between gesture and thought' (Artaud 1958: 78). Further, *both* Artaud and Brecht, for completely opposite reasons, could be said, like *The Double Wedding*, to be 'addicted to a multimedia format'.

It is possible therefore to produce three opposing, yet interconnected, readings for *The Double Wedding*, one Platonic and 'classical' in which the show represents a search for a pre-existing truth beyond the mimetic, one Benjaminian/Brechtian in which the show attempts to defamiliarise 'reality' in order to bring about a social and political transformation, and a Nietzschian/Artaudian formalist reading in which the Platonic distinction between art and life is reversed, confused and transcended. The co-existence of these contradictory readings is possible because the ideas developed by Plato and Nietzsche, Nietzsche and Benjamin, Brecht and Artaud are only apparently 'opposite' and are actually closely related. This is because they all define their ideas either in relation or in opposition to one another, or in relation or opposition to the same sources and authorities, and so at some point they all repeat, as well as differ from, one another. As Derrida indicates in *Dissemination*, even Plato must define his ideas in relation to and therefore through that which he wishes to critique and as a result becomes caught up in the paradox of privileging 'true' speech over the mimetic form of writing, *in* writing and while using writing as a metaphor for the truth (Derrida 1981).

In terms of the background presumptions that inform *The Double Wedding*, there is plenty of evidence to suggest that the show is concerned with the role of theatre in the perception and construction of 'reality'. Yet, whether the show is intended to reinforce, critique, deconstruct or parody all or any single one of the perspectives discussed so far remains uncertain. This ambiguity is only deepened by allusions in the piece that appear to refer to postmodern and poststructuralist conventions and ideas, a change of emphasis that occurred between Acts one and two, when significantly the single, globe light sources were replaced by the fragmentary illumination thrown by rotating mirror balls. The general structure of the show would allow it to be described as a simulacrum of a simulacrum. Morever, a reference English made at the start of Act two to living in the age of the 'hyperreal', a term chiefly associated with Baudrillard, would seem to weigh the scales in favour of a 'political' reading, since his writings condemn the 'aestheticisation of the political' under late industrial capitalism. Yet, Baudrillard also draws heavily on Nietzschian-influenced post-structuralist linguistics and has been described as the most Nietzschian of the postmodern philosophers. Even so, there are significant differences between Nietzsche and Baudrillard. Both perceived a crisis in the social arising from the loss of belief in pre-existing truths, or fixed referents such as God or Reason, and a subsequent collapse of existing value systems or metanarratives. However, in reaction to this crisis Nietzsche posited a concept of 'active nihilism', a 'dancing on the void', remarking this collapse as an opportunity to become 'artists of our own existence' (see Megill 1987: 33–4). Conversely, Baudrillard seems to imply that for the postmodern subject only a passive, fatalistic response to this crisis is possible or at best a return to universal truths (see final pages of Baudrillard 1993).

A similar difference, indeed one that is produced through the various ways they interpret the same sources, exists between Baudrillard and Derrida who can be said to be cited in *The Double Wedding* in so far as there are three, not particularly positive references to 'deconstruction' in the show. This negativity is rather unfortunate, since so far I have actually been reading *The Double Wedding* through Derrida's essay 'The Double Session', in which he considers two pieces of writing, one by Plato and the other by Mallarmé, an author, incidentally, Benjamin criticises in 'The Work of Art' as a practitioner of 'art for art's sake'. Derrida has also written elsewhere on Artaud; in 'The Double Session' he uses a quote in which Artaud makes reference to alchemy, and the essay ends with the citation of Nietzsche and Wagner (see Derrida 1978 and 1981: 285–6). It is worth indicating that Alan Megill notes Artaud as an influence on Foucault, one of the sources Butler acknowledges for her own writing.

For Derrida, Mallarmé's 'Mimique' represents a repetition, a reversal and a displacement of the Platonic concept of mimesis by reason of its formal structure, which as I have already indicated is very similar to that of *The Double Wedding*. Both Derrida and Baudrillard, drawing on, among others, Nietzsche and Saussure, agree that our perception of the world and indeed our very subjectivity is created in, by and through linguistic, or rather symbolic, signifying systems. Both agree that this means that there can be no direct access to 'the' real or to absolute, a priori truths or universal meanings and that the erosion of such concepts means that the process of signification within these systems can now be perceived as being governed by 'pure difference' or, for Derrida, '*différance*'. Within this perception, Derrida sees the political possibilities for 'remaking' the world, while Baudrillard sees it only as producing an evacuation of the political through relativism and indifference, with meanings proliferating to the extent that they implode into a 'black hole' which absorbs all meaning and produces a 'social void' (see Baudrillard in Kellner 1989: 85). This very concept of 'pure difference' could be said to be mimed within *The Double Wedding*, and indeed my reading so far consists of an attempt to demonstrate that the form of the show as a whole does exactly that. In Act two, we are told that it is the pursuit of the figment, played by a dancer, which will allow The Double Wedding to appear, and the climax of the piece, the moment of 'truth', is marked by the ice dance of True Adagio, a performance already prefigured by earlier dances. 'Dancing' is a favoured metaphor for Derrida and his followers, to suggest the 'double movement' (of repetition and difference) of the signifier (see Derrida 1981: 239–44, Derrida and McDonald 1982: 68). Also, the term 'figment' means no-thing that exists except in the imagination, just as an adagio refers not to a 'thing' but is a musical term for a 'movement'. The dancing of the figment and of the True Adagio, as well as the final circle dance, could then be said to mark the 'appearance' of '*The Double Wedding*', as a quotation of itself, inside itself. Like the whole show, they refer to no-thing except the process of referring back to the past and forward to future meanings, the double movement or 'spinning' of the signifier by which meanings proliferate and final meaning is constantly deferred, so that ultimately no-thing or meaning is ever made present.

The problem is that if these dances do indeed represent a quoting of '*The Double Wedding*', within *The Double Wedding* as referring only to this process of signification, this itself renders it impossible to decide whether these 'dances' are 'positive' citations of a Nietzschian/Artaudian dancing on the void, a Benjaminian/Brechtian critique of aestheticism, a Derridean celebration of the 'choreographies of pure difference' or a Baudrillardian vision of contemporary society as a 'brothel of substitution and commutation' (Derrida in Elam 1994: 58 and Baudrillard in Kellner 1989: 64). This is because the effect of this process, which is one of infinite deferral through infinite referral, is such that these names only represent a tiny fragment of the possible intertextual references (and hence ways of interpreting the show) opened up by the citation of 'Benjamin', '*gesamtkuntswerk*', 'void', 'deconstruction', 'veil', 'adagio', 'the hyperreal', and so on. Furthermore, for the sake of brevity and sanity, I am being forced to ignore whole sections of the piece that might generate other references, but it is clear, for instance, that striking similarities might also be found between *The Double Wedding* and, say, Shakespeare's *The Tempest* or Pirandello's *Six Characters in Search of an Author*, the long list of Pierrot performances, cited by Derrida in 'The Double Session' or even Sophocles' *Oedipus Rex*. In many ways, *The Double Wedding* mirrors the narrative structure of this latter text, based on the Ancient Greek myth which features so significantly in Freudian theory, which might in turn promote a psychoanalytical reading of the show. In Lacanian terms, the search for identity, unity and wholeness within *The Double Wedding*, by subjects whose names and relationships mark them as 'split' or double, could stand for the fetishistic and narcissistic attempt to disavow lack through art. As author and director, English may be said to have usurped the masculine position, stolen the 'phallus', become the castrator or phallic woman and hence 'man in drag'. Her final acceptance of the 'fiction' at the end of the show could stand for the recognition of her own phallic impostures and the unattainability of wholeness or 'oneness' from inside the symbolic system. Of course, Lacanian psychoanalysis reworks Freudian theory, drawing on, among other sources, Nietzsche and Saussure, and Freud's work is cited by Benjamin in 'The Work of Art', as reflecting a change in the perception of reality (Benjamin 1992: 229). In drawing on Ancient Greek myths, Freud repeated and reinforced many of the implicit assumptions held by Aristotle and Plato and expressed through a series of hierarchical binary oppositions. Platonic dialectics repeated and differed from ideas propounded by Socrates, who produced his ideas in reaction to concepts developed by earlier thinkers, including some ancient alchemists – and so on

The Double Wedding, then, poses the same question concerning itself as a piece of theatre as that put by Butler in relation to the 'origins' of the sexed positions: 'Is there an original authority, or is it rather in the very practice of citation, potentially infinite in its regression, that the ground of authority is constituted as perpetual deferral' (Butler 1993: 108). As such, in Derrida's terms, it is a piece that 'does not show "things in themselves", nor does it represent them; it shows a representation, shows itself to be a fiction, it is less engaged in setting forth things or the image of things than it is in setting up a machine' (Derrida 1981: 238). To put it another way, the piece could be said to deliberately foreground the process of performativity as citation in theatre as a discursive institution, opening up the whole shifting and unstable history of the construction of the difference between the real and the mimetic, on which this institution as a whole depends for its intelligibility. In opening up the history of the construction of this difference, it opens up the history of 'representation' and thereby of the relationship between the aesthetic and the political, philosophy and literature, the social and the cultural, science and the humanities, sex and gender, modern and postmodern etc. etc.

Alternatively, this show does *absolutely none of this* because, although I have been confidently identifying references and supporting them with other 'evidence' from the production, all of the above is entirely a matter of my own retrospective, intertextual interpretation. Not only is it extremely unlikely that anyone, other than perhaps a philosopher of the status of Butler or Derrida, would interpret the show in this manner at the time of viewing, but Bert O. States might argue that my reading is for the most part a matter of illusory transitivity, finding 'family resemblances between things that gradually become more different than they are alike' (States 1996: 2–3). It may be most telling that, although Brecht insisted his shows should be 'fun', the work of several of the other authors I cite have been described as playful or witty and both Baudrillard and Derrida are said to employ parody, frankly I have never heard of any of their works producing gales of laughter, whereas *The Double Wedding* did. Yet illusory transitivity is an effect of pure difference, and, as I have indicated above, the nature of some of the references in the piece and audience response suggests that some, if not all, of this laughter was provoked by parody. Parody depends upon an intertextual recognition of the 'original' from which the parody differs. In this case this 'original' cannot be the 'original' show, because it does not exist. Therefore the parody *must be* of existing theatrical conventions, so the show could be a parody of Brechtian, Artaudian, or naturalistic or postmodern theatre, and indeed the 'great deconstruction scene' certainly seemed to be taken as a parody of experimental, deconstructive, performance (art?). Yet this does not necessarily clarify the ultimate 'meaning' of the show since, as Chuck Kleinhans points out, almost any text can be *received* as parody. Moreover, he also identifies parody as having been variously perceived as intrinsically apolitical, politically subversive and simply as an inherent aspect of all contemporary art (Kleinhans 1994: 196–9). Therefore, describing *The Double Wedding* as a parody still leaves the issue of author's intentions and its 'meaning' wide open as a matter of interpretation.

Part two: the mystery of our identity

The structure of *The Double Wedding* could be said to operate as a 'hymen', in the same 'undecidable' fashion Derrida ascribes to this term in the passage from Mallarmé's 'Mimique', cited at the head of this chapter. This does not provide a 'meaning' for the piece, nor does it necessarily weigh the balance in favour of a Derridean reading since this concept reworks some of Nietzsche's ideas and Baudrillard has also used this term in a fashion that repeats and differs from Derrida.[5] For both Baudrillard and Derrida, 'undecidables' are words that have double or opposite meanings but resist synthesis or reduction to one meaning or the other, so that 'hymen' can either signify a wedding or that which signifies virginity. As such, undecidables undermine any attempt at authoritative interpretation, since whichever meaning is privileged in a given text, the opposite meaning remains as a potential internal contradiction.

However, as Derrida points out, undecidability is less a quality of the term itself but more to do with structure or syntax. In the case of 'Mimique', the undecidability of 'hymen' occurs through its relation to the word 'between' (*entre*),[6] which itself has no meaning except in relation to the word 'hymen' (Derrida 1981: 220–1). This relationship remarks the hymen, where the scene takes place in 'Mimique', as '*between*' opposites, 'between desire and fulfilment, between perpetration and remembrance, between past and present', in a fashion that makes it impossible to definitely decide on one or the other of its meanings and hence on a single meaning for the piece. As a membrane this hymen separates these opposites, but as a marriage or union it brings them together, therefore creating both a difference and a confusion of identity. According to Derrida, this means that in Mallarmé's text, 'It is not only the difference (between desire and fulfilment) that is abolished but also the difference between difference and nondifference.' As such, this hymen suspends 'the decidable exteriority of differing terms', or rather 'thanks to the confusion and continuity of the hymen ... difference inscribes itself without any decidable poles, without any independent irreversible terms' (Derrida 1981: 209–10). This is because in 'The Double Session' Derrida interprets this hymen, where in 'Mimique' the 'scene' takes place as operating as the *space* of representation in a multiple sense, which in itself contains and confuses opposites. On the one hand, it stands for the 'membrane' or the 'material', as in scene, page, stage, screen, signifier, the medium or form, which is 'blank', or rather has no meaning in itself, but which must be present for things or meanings to appear while simultaneously preventing direct access to these things or meanings, except as already mimetic. Since the thing or meaning cannot appear 'outside' such mediums or forms, the difference between the thing or meaning and the material, medium or form, the signifier and signified, the single and the double, is itself effectively undecidable. Yet this hymen also stands for the 'space' of representation in terms of that which must be 'absent' for things or meanings to appear, where the structure of signification means that the meaning of a given signifier is always produced through relation to other absent signifiers from which they differ. This is most clear in relation to binary oppositions where each term obviously depends for its meaning on that which it is not, so that without the term 'feminine', 'masculine' would not make sense, and vice versa. Finally, this 'hymen' is also the space or interval between two repetitions of a thing, meaning or signifier, in which repetition must be based on difference, since to be an *exact* repetition, it would have to be the original. As such, this is the space of substitution, in which repetitions gradually become more different than they are alike and where each repetition produces a new meaning, so that a continual displacement of the 'original' takes place through the production and proliferation of an excess of supplementary meanings. None of this indicates the *meaning* of the term 'hymen' in Mallarmé's 'Mimique' or of 'Mimique' as a whole. It simply describes how this term *operates* within the structure of this piece of writing, since its 'undecidability' is dependent on that structure and this undecidability prevents the production of a single meaning, for either the term or the piece as a whole. Yet, paradoxically, Derrida does in a sense provide an interpretation for both the hymen and 'Mimique' as a whole, in so far as he suggests that 'Mimique' can be read as a piece of writing that refers to no-thing except the 'act' or process of reading and writing and therefore to how these processes operate.

In a similar fashion, *The Double Wedding* can be read as a piece of performance that refers to no-thing, except the 'act' or process of performing and of interpreting performance. Equally both meanings of the term 'hymen' appeared in *The Double Wedding*. Obviously, a wedding is cited not only in the title but in the ceremony at the end of the show, and in Act one, describing the show, the first Hypnotist said:

> It's a fine line between excess and absence. It's a fine line between the two. It's like a membrane. It's like a thin film on the surface that has to be there for the shadow to reveal itself. Without the surface the shadow would never be revealed [...] and when the shadow and its double meet, we have The Double Wedding.

In the final scene, English said good-bye to the rest of the cast, stating that she was going 'for ever and ever', but she did not leave. At this moment she said:

> This is the membrane. This is the surface that has to be there for the shadow to reveal itself. There was the wedding and there was its shadow, this is the fine line between absence and excess. Once I'm through the membrane I will no longer be refusing the fiction will I?

This 'surface' can only be revealed at the end of the performance because the whole show is *The Double Wedding*, and so it cannot be perceived in its entirety until it is over. Like the hymen in 'Mimique', *The Double Wedding* takes place *between* past and present, in so far as it is repetition in the present of a past version of itself, and between the present and the future, because it is always in the process of becoming or having been but never actually 'is' *The Double Wedding*. In fact, since the original *The Double Wedding* never existed 'anywhere, not even in theatrical fiction', it cannot be made 'present' (see Derrida 1981: 200). Even if an original *had* existed, it would still be 'absent' because we are told that this present production differs significantly from the show(s) it supposedly copies. This means that effectively there is simultaneously a difference and no difference between the fictional original and this copy which the original needs to appear. At the same time the status of the show as a false quotation of itself produces a suspension of reference to anything other than to the idea of itself as a piece of theatre, or rather as this piece of theatre which is in the process of being performed. As a result its intelligibility is wholly dependent on the fashion in which it repeats existing conventions for performance, which are themselves established by virtue of performativity as a process of citation, potentially infinite in its deferral. Therefore, while no-thing is actually performed, the show operates as a blank surface, on which, intertextually, the whole history of the 'idea' of performance may be read. As such, *The Double Wedding* acts as a membrane that brings together opposing ideas from this history, which become confused and impossible to differentiate because they all both repeat and differ from one another, just as *The Double Wedding*, in bringing these ideas together, repeats and differs from any single one of them, and so it can neither be separated from them nor fully explained through reference to any one of them.

Since the history of theatre is still in progress, supplementary ideas about theatre which will repeat and differ from all that can already be read as being cited within *The Double Wedding* will continue to proliferate. As such, at the end of the show the membrane separating the difference between the real and the mimetic is remarked because the close of the piece brings a return to reality, but it is also confused because *The Double Wedding* is not 'finished' and reference to reality is infinitely deferred. The meaning of *The Double Wedding* remains between the past and the future, and it is and always will be impossible to decide on a *single*, definite meaning for the show in the present. In sum, meaning is not absent in this show, since it remains legible as a piece of theatre, nor does it contain an excess of meanings, since these meanings only appear by reason of the fact that it appears to refer to nothing but itself. It is therefore like Derrida's reading of Mallarmé's hymen – meaningless and enveloping an excess of meanings at the same time. As English said in the show, 'sometimes things are so simple that it becomes dense and sometimes it is so dense with complexity that it becomes merely empty', or again, with reference to the set and costumes, 'never has the sequin been required to signify so much and so little at the same time'. Black sequins, of course, contain and confuse opposites, in so much as they are dark but also operate as a surface which reflects the light. To put it another way, *The Double Wedding* remarks the necessity of making meanings through a process of deciding on differences, even while it remarks the impossibility of finally deciding on differences because apparent opposites are actually interdependent and therefore 'without any decidable poles, without any independent irreversible terms' (Derrida 1981: 210). So, if the show is a parody of anything, it may be a parody of the very idea of definitely deciding on meanings and distinguishing between opposites, such as original and copy, real and mimetic, single and double. And since parody is of necessity a matter of making such decisions, it is also a parody of the very 'idea' of parody itself.

Derrida's interpretation of 'hymen' in 'The Double Session' can also be read as performing a series of repetitions, reversals and displacements of the Lacanian phallus, although this is once again purely an intertextual reading since there is no direct reference to Lacan in this work. In this essay, the hymen stands for both the space or gap in language, and the sliding of the signifier over the signified, thereby repeating the role of the phallus as identified by Lacan. Yet, unlike the phallus, the hymen is not a privileged signifier, since its meaning, or rather lack of meaning, and its effects cannot be decided in advance or once and for all because they are produced by syntax. However, just as the privileged position for the phallus is produced through reference to the phallus, the *un*-privileged position of the hymen in 'Mimique', as Derrida demonstrates, is produced by the effect of the hymen, whereby 'hymen' can itself be substituted by other terms. Derrida's reversal then opens up to contestation the idea that the meaning or lack of meaning of the phallus, and therefore, since the phallus is the signifier of signifiers, anything else, can be decided in advance, out of context and for once and for all. This is achieved by foregrounding the dependency of the phallus on the membrane, veil, surface, space or rather the structures of representation, which it supposedly governs and yet without which phallic authority cannot operate. Indeed Lacan has remarked that the phallus 'only operates when veiled' (Lacan 1977: 288). Therefore, the hymen puts into question the position of the phallus as a single, independent and irreversible term, which remarks the difference between opposites, is somehow 'outside' the process of signification and as such is not subject to displacement and reinscription – all of which is implicit in Lacan's claim for the phallus as a privileged signifier. However, since the hymen contests the phallus within the phallus's own terms, and the hymen remains in part dependent for its meaning on the absent phallus, which it both repeats and differs from, the phallus continues to haunt this reading of the hymen as an internal contradiction. As a result, the hymen only subverts phallic authority in so far as it performs the sort of 'double movement' described by Judith Butler, and whether or not the authority of the Lacanian phallus is reinforced or subverted by the Derridean hymen is quite literally a matter of interpretation, or rather a (phallic) decision on meaning. Whether or not the hymen contests the privileged position of the phallus then remains 'open', yet this very openness represents but does not guarantee the possibility and condition of contestation. In fact Derrida's use of the term 'hymen', which relates to the female body, has been heavily criticised by feminist writers as potentially reinforcing the notion of the feminine as passive surface, matter or no-thing on which the masculine phallus inscribes meanings. Yet, not only does the hymen foreground the masculine phallus's dependency on this feminine space or material, but the hymen's other meaning as 'marriage' signifies a 'masculine' patriarchal institution, or rather the active process for the reinscription of 'phallic' authority. The hymen is therefore always double, neither passive nor active, feminine nor masculine, matter nor idea, space nor process – it is both at once.

If *The Double Wedding* does operate as a double hymen, in a similar fashion to that described in 'Mimique' in which opposites are both remarked and confused, this might explain why English, a woman dressed in 'feminine' clothes, was perceived as like a 'man in drag'. This effect is not entirely a matter of the specific quality of English's own performance, since it extends to other performers, so that Betty Caplan in *The Guardian* also referred to the Consort/Figment as an 'androgynous ballet dancer' (Caplan 1991). Neither does this necessarily relate to the actual sex, gender or sexuality of these performers. Nor is it necessarily a matter of author's intentions. Just as the undecidability of the hymen in 'Mimique' is a matter of syntax, the 'undecidability' of identity within *The Double Wedding* is a matter of *staging*, arising from the structuring of the show as a false quotation of itself and its subsequent dependence on an intertextual relation to theatre or 'the stage' as a discursive institution for its intelligibility. The resultant potentially infinite deferral of reference to 'reality' means that the show may be read as a literal repetition of phallic authority, which stages the performative fashion in which this authority operates. This staging can be read as an improper repetition that defamiliarises the basis of that authority by foregrounding the mimetic surfaces and processes that it needs in order to appear as 'real' and as such puts into question the decidability of the difference between these surfaces, those processes and that authority. However, phallic authority cannot be said to be abolished; it is simply shown to be undecidable, haunted by its own internal contradictions. The drag effect apparently produced by the show cannot then be definitely said to subvert dominant, heterosexual norms in relation to the sexed positions, only to open their basis in any 'reality' up to contestation as a matter of interpretation.

At first glance, the roles played by English and the Consort seemed to conform to the sexed positions as defined by the Lacanian masquerade, except that the term 'Consort' can refer to either a male or female partner. Also, in Act one, English appeared to 'have' the phallus, in so far as she wielded a magic wand, deployed as an instrument for discovering the mystery of their identity. However, English's role could be recuperated in terms of describing her as a castrating, phallic woman, and the position of the Consort as 'masculine' seems to be guaranteed in so far as, whereas in Act one English asked the rest of the cast 'What is The Double Wedding?', she asked him '*Who* is the Double Wedding?', assigning him the patriarchal power of naming. Yet this question was asked by a character in the process of performing in *The Double Wedding*, a show that has no original referent, so that any reference outside this show can only be made in terms of this show. As such, although he answered this question in the present, through reference to his own role in the fictional original version of the show, this turned out to be a description of his role in this production, which he had yet to perform. His 'phallic' authority was therefore literally performatively produced through reference to itself as a fictional ideal established in an irrecoverable past and via a process of imitation in the present that would not become fully apparent until the future, by which time it would once again be in the past. The same principle holds for the basis of the authority by which English, playing the role of author and director, asked this question in the first place, since, as one of the cast later remarked, while she may have identified a dilemma she is as much part of it as anyone else. Within this fiction, no actual identity is ever performed or made present, only the process of performing an identity as the repetition of something from the past that is itself purely mimetic. This is a literal repetition of the Lacanian masquerade, purely as a performative 'comedy of appearances', in which, if there can be no access to anything outside the symbolic from within the symbolic, the authorising authority can only be guaranteed by reference to its fictional effects. As such, in the process of repetition, roles can easily be reversed. In fact, the Consort described his role *as* Consort in Act one as 'peripheral', saying he would only come into his own as the Figment in Act two, in which he would do a lot of dancing. In this act, English took up the active role of the 'pursuer', a position in the narrative usually occupied by the 'male hero', as identified by both Propp (1968) and Mulvey (1975). The Consort then took up the 'feminine' role as the object of desire, and hence of 'being the phallus', and indeed as the 'Figment' he is no-thing, a nomination Lacan ascribes to the feminine. This role reversal is underlined by the fact that, in Act one, this couple danced a duet where the Consort took the masculine role and English took the feminine, and in Act two they repeated this dance with the positions reversed, so that the subject became the object and vice versa.

Nevertheless, this does not adequately explain the sexual ambiguity of these characters, since there are plenty of theatrical precedents for such carnivalesque role reversals in genres of comedy, particularly those which, like *The Double Wedding* and the Lacanian masquerade, end in a wedding. However, despite the fact that at first sight they appeared to be 'properly' dressed, according to certain performance conventions for signifying masculinity and femininity, the potential gender confusion implicit in the fluctuating roles they performed was reinforced in a paradoxical fashion by their costumes. In line with the multimedia format of the show, English's and the Consort's costumes, like those of the rest of the cast, were actually quoting different generic conventions. While English wore a 'showgirl' costume associated with variety, the Consort wore a short sequinned top, black tights, ballet shoes and a long black wig, all of which constitute traditional attire for a male classical ballet dancer. So, while their respective clothing remarked a gender difference between them, as a couple they were not properly asymmetrical in terms of vestimentary conventions. This juxtaposition defamiliarises these clothes, remarking them as generic, theatrical 'costumes'. As the history of the theatre going back at least as far as Ancient Greece demonstrates, a theatrical costume does not necessarily signify as reflecting either the actual sex or gender of the performer or the supposed sex or gender of the role they are playing within the fictional world of the performance. On the Shakespearian stage, for example, the audience were apparently quite happy to suspend their disbelief and perceive the boy player playing Rosalind in *As You Like It* as a woman pretending to be a boy, pretending to be a woman. Moreover, the costumes worn by English and the Consort were drawn from performance genres where form takes precedence over meaning, and so in their original context these costumes signify neither the 'interior' identity of a psychologically rounded character nor of the individual performer, but rather an abstract, stylised, artistic 'ideal' of masculinity and femininity. This generic theatricality makes these versions of femininity and masculinity easy to copy and appropriate, which may explain why, as the very existence of the term 'showgirl drag' indicates, costumes such as the one worn by English have a long history within drag performance. It is this same generic quality which, in Judith Butler's terms, can allow this style of costume when deployed as drag to appear as a subversive parody of femininity, since what is being imitated is already marked as a theatrical 'ideal' of femininity. Similarly, quoted outside the context of ballet, the same generic theatricality that informs the Consort's costume can allow it to be read as signalling 'effeminacy', if not femininity. Indeed, a very similar style of costume has frequently been employed in female to male 'travesty' roles, dating back at least to the seventeenth century, the vestiges of which are still evident in the dress of the British pantomime principal boy. The meaning of these costumes, then, *as* theatrical costumes, is context and function specific, and they can signify either the absence or presence of the 'real' thing. Within *The Double Wedding*, the audience may choose to read the meaning of these costumes through reference to the apparent 'actual' sex of the performers. However, the potential doubleness of these costumes is underlined by the suspension of reference to reality within the show and the crossing and confusions in the roles played by English and the Consort. As such, English's costume could actually have been deliberately citing the idea of 'showgirl drag', rather than 'actual' showgirls, or even both at once. To return to the comparison I made between Ru Paul and English in the previous chapter, Ru Paul has been quoted as saying 'I don't think I could ever look like a woman. They don't dress this way. Only drag queens dress this way' (Baker 1994: 258). In relation to

Rose English's costume in *The Double Wedding* and Ru Paul's for his *Christmas Ball*, he could be both right and wrong at the same time.

The potential for confusion implicit in English's costume was reinforced by the fact that it was actually cited as 'drag' at the start of Act two. In this scene, the Consort/Figment asked Rose how it (the show) was going, and English was praising the fantastically individual performances of the cast when the vortex curtain drew back to reveal them all performing imitations of her. These impersonations were supplements or 'poor copies' to her 'original', since although they wore similar wigs and dresses, several retained their own footwear or glasses. Her reaction was one of melodramatic outrage and her anger was particularly directed at Nigel, whom she accused of holding a 'little bit' of himself back, a comment that produced laughter in the audience since this 'little bit' seemed to be his penis, visible through the thin fabric of his frock. When English asked Nigel what he thought he was doing, he replied that he was doing what she told him to as author and director. English then asserted that she didn't want this derisory effort; she wanted him to 'be' her, to 'be like her'. Nigel responded, 'I don't see the point of even attempting to represent the real, isn't it bound to fail?' and she answered, 'Of course but the attempt is often interesting'. In fact nothing 'real' was even being attempted; the 'original' that Nigel was failing to impersonate properly was already marked as purely conventional and mimetic. The cast were pretending to imitate themselves in a previous performance, imitating English's own past performance which never took place, and in the present and they were miming back at her her own obviously performed reaction to their impersonations. As in drag, the 'masquerade' was apparently revealed through reference to the 'actual' sex of the male performer, visible through his feminine attire. However, Nigel's 'little bit' was already written into the show as part of a masquerade which can only reveal as masquerade something already marked as a masquerade, of a masquerade, of a masquerade. No-thing is being performed, only the 'idea' and process of performing identity as a process of repetition, and each repetition inevitably differs from the last, so that the 'original', which is itself a representation, not the thing itself, is continually displaced and resignified. Once again, this scene could be interpreted as an absolutely literal citation of the Lacanian masquerade as a 'comedy of appearances', even to the extent that the scene acknowledges the masquerade is bound to fail because the sexed positions are only fictional constructs based on the illusion that having the penis is equivalent to having the phallus. Yet, in this instance, the failure is genuinely comic rather than tragic because the idea of Nigel's 'little bit' standing for the phallus is clearly ridiculous. At the end of this scene, English states that 'even to speak of the absolute of opposites is a travesty'. 'Travesty' means to make ridiculous and may also refer to female to male cross-dressing, or 'drag'. The joke in this scene is actually on the phallus, since it can only appear through what Lacan insists it is *not* – for instance, an imaginary object (the figment or the magic wand), or the penis (Nigel's little bit) – in short, as a travesty, a parody of itself (see Lacan 1977: 287–8). It also can only function in travesty or drag when 'veiled' and visible through its 'opposite', the feminine 'surface', which like the phallus itself is no-thing. Therefore there is effectively a difference and no difference between the phallus and all these things, a difference 'without any decidable poles, without any independent irreversible terms' (Derrida 1981: 210). Wholly dependent on and therefore indistinguishable from the 'surfaces' and masquerades it supposedly commands, the authority of the phallus, like English's, is already 'inside the fiction', dependent on a process of repetition that undermines any and all author(ity)'s 'intentions' and within which there is no 'absolute' in reality to prevent roles being reversed.

The same issue of the decidability of the 'absolute' of opposites is also remarked in the Lido scene, which occurs later in Act two. This sequence involved the repetition of a Paris Lido style dance routine, for which the male performers were dressed in white top hats and tails and the Dawn/Fake Adagio sported a 'showgirl' feathered head-dress and sequinned bikini. In the first version, an argument developed as to whether the scene was 'shrieking with heterosexuality', or 'shrieking with homosexuality', or 'shrieking with both' and continued:

> HARRY: Well I think its deliberately mystifying. That the homosexuality has to reveal itself through the heterosexuality.
>
> SECOND HYPNOTIST: Exactly, it has to remain hidden to reveal itself, concealed and revealed at the same time.
>
> FAKE ADAGIO/THE DEW: Oh for God's sake stop it, it's none of that, we're not even doing it properly.

FAKE ADAGIO/THE DAWN: What? We are not doing the homosexuality revealing itself through the heterosexuality properly? We are not good enough homosexuals? We are not good enough heterosexuals? There is a quintessential homosexuality or a quintessential heterosexuality, that's missing from this scene?

FAKE ADAGIO/THE DEW: We are not good enough dancers!

FIRST HYPNOTIST: Would you say that the scenery is essentially homosexual because it both reveals and conceals itself at the same time?

OTTO: Yes the scenery should be arrested immediately!

In an 'original' Paris Lido context, the conventions performed in this scene supposedly represent a paradigm of heterosexuality, yet even in this context this is already remarked as a generic wholly theatrical representation of heterosexuality. Recontextualised and improperly repeated, because the performers are not good enough dancers, the stylised and conventional nature of such representations becomes apparent to the extent that they appear to signal the absence of 'real' heterosexuality, and hence potentially the presence of its 'opposite', homosexuality. This is not necessarily subversive, since it could simply reaffirm homosexuality as a 'poor copy' of heterosexuality's original. However, the 'original' here is already marked as a mimetic, 'idealised' and performative notion of heterosexuality. The central issue in this scene is not, then, whether these characters are 'quintessentially' homosexual or heterosexual, since there is no 'quintessential' identity in terms of human subjectivity being performed, evinced by the fact that the same effect can be produced by the dark, sequinned surface of the scenery. There is only the 'idea' of the process of performing these identity positions, enacted in a manner that foregrounds their 'staging', or rather their dependence on the surfaces which they need to appear, the membrane that both separates and joins them. As such, the scene does potentially shriek of heterosexuality and homosexuality at the same time because each identity position is dependent for its intelligibility on its other. Each both repeats as well as differs from the other, haunting the other as its own internal contradiction, both revealed and concealed within and through the other at the same time.

As I indicated earlier, within most traditional theatrical comedies, any such doublings, ambiguities and confusions are usually resolved, and 'order' is restored through a wedding. This is a ceremony that is a performative act of naming, which repeats and reinstates phallic authority, for the securing of identities within the patriarchal, heterosexual symbolic. This ceremony is therefore once again a surface upon which phallic authority depends in order to be staged. Once again, this ceremony is improperly repeated within *The Double Wedding*, in a fashion that allows it to appear as a parody of itself, remarking both a difference and a confusion of identities, including a difference and a confusion between phallic authority and that which it requires to appear. In a text in which he refers back to the Bible as the basis of *his* authority, Lacan describes this regulation of the law of mating in marriage as the 'primordial law', in which the prohibition of incest 'is merely its subjective pivot, revealed by the modern tendency to reduce the objects forbidden to the subject's choice, to the mother and the sister, although full license outside of these is not yet entirely open' (Lacan 1977: 66). This ceremony, according to Lacan, refers back to an irrecoverable ground, through a 'lineage of succeeding generations' and therefore describes a 'double movement' between the past and the present, the present and the future. It is also double in terms of being an act of identification and dis-identification, in which normative heterosexual identity is secured under the threat of the incest taboo, indicating that improper identifications (more various than modern tendencies allow) must have already been made in the past in order to be repudiated in the present. Lacan goes on to assert that this law is then 'revealed clearly enough as identical with an order of language' (1977: 66). Both literally and metaphorically, within *The Double Wedding*, the traditional marriage ceremony was simultaneously performed and not performed, or rather performed only as a *process* for securing identities by virtue of an authority which refers to no-thing, except to itself, in an act of 'perpetual allusion between the past and the future', 'under the false appearances of the present'. All the cast, except English and the Cantor, asked each other to marry them, one after another, regardless of sex or gender. Each one was refused and they promise*d not* to marry each other, took their place in a line, linked arms and joined in a dance accompanied by song that included the words 'I do and I do not'. Each proposal, refusal and song repeated the same formula but differed from the last through the addition of a supplementary character, so that the 'two' between which the ceremony was supposed to take place became three, then four, then five and so on. As such, this ceremony was repeated as identical to an order of language but it was an order of pure difference in which phallic authority, or rather the 'primordial law', was both reiterated and displaced, remarked and deferred to the past and the future. This authority was shown to be a matter of interpretation, its 'originality' and basis in any reality in the present put into question, through the very process of repetition on which it depended to appear at all. Within this process as performed in this show, every repetition differs from the last, producing a proliferation, an excess of identities, opening up in an unlicensed fashion, the full license implied by the prohibitive, 'primordial' law in the past, to generate an increasing number of improper couplings. They all do and do not marry each other, no one is pronounced either man or wife, and indeed they are all simultaneously in the position of being both man and wife and neither man nor wife. Therefore differences are remarked between them but these are differences that, from within this fiction, are without decidable poles.

At the beginning of this show, English asked, 'What is the difference between a void and a vacuum?' and answered, 'One is only empty and the other a deficit of emptiness, one is open and infinite, the other is hermetic and closed'. This could be taken to stand for the difference between the differing perceptions of the effects and possibilities of the same process of signification, represented by the proper names Derrida and Baudrillard, Derrida and Lacan, Lacan and Butler, along with the other authorities cited in this chapter, all of whom both repeat and differ from one another. If any of these authorities provides the key for the meaning of *The Double Wedding* – whether the show subverts or reinstates phallic authority, whether it is an argument for a political theatre or a critique of the evacuation of the political in contemporary culture, whether it is a deconstruction or parodies deconstruction, whether it deliberately resists interpretation or is just not about anything, whether it is 'writerly' or simply unreadable, a masculine or feminine form, feminist, queer parody, or playing it straight or both and all at once – all of this remains a matter of interpretation.

In a repetition of the same void, vacuum, formula at the end of the show, English said that this was a 'difficult package to tie up and a dangerous one to leave open', but she did just that and the show ended on the word 'openings'. *The Double Wedding* remains double;

if contestation is opened up, it is left open to be taken up by the audience as active agents in the construction of meaning. There is no synthesis, no revelation of authorial intentions, any final meaning is left entirely as a matter of reception and perception. Whether or not this show is 'political' or 'resistant' cannot be decided by anyone in advance and once and for all; its effect or lack of effect depends on the audience, in the past, and in the future. Yet, the meaning of the show is not simply relative, since defining it as undecidable is, in effect, a decision on meanings, and, as Derrida puts it, undecidability is always of a 'determinate oscillation between possibilities, possibilities which themselves are highly determined in strictly defined situations (for example discursive, syntactical or rhetorical but also political, ethical etc.)' (Derrida 1990: 148). In the final analysis, I think this show remarks the necessity to decide on meanings in the present, as a matter of responsibility that is both individual and collective, despite the knowledge that such meanings can only ever be provisional. As such, I believe that this show represents the working through of, as English will say in her sequel to *The Double Wedding*, *Tantamount Esperance*, 'a different sort of ethics', or rather the politics of undecidability – a concept that I will explore in the conclusion of this book.

Notes

1 All quotes from *The Double Wedding*, by Rose English, are from the unpublished version of the script, or from the live performance, or the video made of one particular live performance during the show's run at the Royal Court 1991, all copyright Rose English 1991. Titles of scenes were not announced within the production, and the show also included a certain amount of improvisation, so the script, the version of the show I actually saw and the video (of another performance) vary in minor ways. I have privileged the text as I saw it *performed* as much as possible, and for all these reasons I am not citing page numbers for quotes from *The Double Wedding*.

2 The cast was as follows: the Hostess/Hermit – Rose English; the Hypnotists – Thom Osborn and Roddy Maude-Roxby; the Cameramen – Otto, Steven Beard and Harry, Brian Lipson; the Fake Adagio: the Dew – Nigel Charnock; the Dawn – Wendy Houston; the Figment – Matthew Hawkins; the Nebula – Lucy Allen and Joanne Robley-Dixon; the Viscera – Giovanna Curati and Claire Roberts; the True Adagio – Paul Askham and Sharon Jones; the Cantor – Phil Minton. Music was composed and played by Ian Hill and Alex Kolkowski. Design was by Simon Vincenzi.

3 In *The Birth of Tragedy*, Nietzsche defines an opposition between the Apollonian (Socratic/Platonic) and the Dionysiac. The Apollonian in Greek culture is then said to cast 'a veil of illusion', or 'the veil of maya', over

humanity (see Megill 1987: 39–42). Artaud also talks a great deal of voids and vacuums and occasionally veils: see, for example, Artaud 1958: 71, or more or less any of *The Theatre and Its Double.*

4 In the interval (entitled 'trance partitions') between the two sessions of his essay 'The Double Session', Derrida includes a quote from Artaud that refers to the philosophers' stone, and 'a suspension of gestures on:– phallus' (Derrida 1981: 286). *The Theatre and Its Double* contains a section entitled 'The Alchemical Theatre', in which Artaud suggests 'there is a mysterious identity of essence between the principle of theatre and that of alchemy' (Artaud 1958: 48). I have not studied Nietzsche closely enough to identify explicit references to alchemy, but certain phrases and attitudes seem very closely related to this 'science', even though at other times he makes comments that would contradict such a reading; certainly such an influence would accord with his anti-Socratic stance. Alchemy was itself concerned with 'chemical weddings', or rather with the transformation and unification of opposites. It posited an original unity of all things with a divinity or the 'One', with differentiation only taking place upon becoming matter. All matter was then held to be composed of the same elements, which it was the alchemist's goal to identify. According to 'Anaxogaros', it was possible to see 'the infinitely great universe in the infinitely small atom', and this mirrors the Renaissance perception of the stage as a microcosm reflecting the macrocosm (A. 1925: 460). Equally, the classical conception of the function of art is mirrored by the alchemist's attempt to discover the secret of the mixing of these elements from nature, so as to be able to both imitate and improve on it. The search for the philosophers' stone was, then, for the substance that would produce reunification, a return to a prelapsarian perfection of all matter. This was represented by the concept of transmuting base metal into gold as a process of purification. In more recent times, alchemy itself came to be considered an 'impure' mixture of philosophy, science and mysticism, so that the author of the entry for Alchemy in the *Encyclopaedia Britannica* describes it as belonging to a period in the history of science where 'its various branches were confused and conflated' (A. 1925: 459). He also indicates that the alchemist frequently combined the roles of philosopher, savant and priest, and this corresponds to both Prospero's role in *The Tempest* and to English's triple role, of Hermit, Hostess and director within *The Double Wedding*. *The Double Wedding*, with its addiction to multimedia, may similarly be said to have been an impure mixture, a space of confusion and conflation and a work concerned with the unification of opposites.

5 'Everything becomes undecidable – this is the characteristic of the domination of a code, which is based everywhere on the principle of neutralisation and indifference. This is what the generalised brothel of capital is, not a brothel of prostitution but of substitution and commutation' (Baudrillard in Kellner 1989: 79).

6 Throughout 'The Double Session', Derrida constantly plays on the similarity between '*entre*' and '*antre*', which is Latin for 'cave', so that, like *The Double Wedding*, Mallarmé's 'Mimique' and indeed 'The Double Session' can both be said to start in Plato's cave.

4

The active consumer: Bobby Baker's *How to Shop*

How to Shop was performed in June 1993 as part of the London International Festival, at Tuke Hall, Regents College, Regents Park. As Bobby Baker informed us at the start of the show, this lecture theatre originally formed part of Bedford Women's College, established in 1849 and one of the first of such institutions in England. The piece was presented as a public lecture and included numerous slides and several sections filmed on location at the Co-op Superstore in Croydon. The stage contained a lectern, a piano, a screen, an oversize pointer for 'visual aids' and a table with an overhead on-line video camera, allowing the audience to view Baker's 'transformations' of the goods she found in the supermarket. For most of the show Baker wore her usual shortish, white, cross-over lab coat, white high heels, and a detail picked out by reviewers but not visible from my seat – a gold ankle bracelet. Also appearing in the piece were two 'stooges', one male, one female, placed for the most part in the auditorium.

The show fell roughly into two parts: an introductory section on the 'theory' and basic techniques of shopping drawn from years of experience and 'research', with reference to academic publications on the subject, followed by an exemplary trip to the supermarket shown on film and through slides, which, drawing on the structure of John Bunyan's *The Pilgrim's Progress*, was formulated as a quest, 'shopping for life' or 'shopping for enlightenment'.[1] This quest was for seven items, corresponding to seven virtues: parsley (Humility), anchovies (Obedience), shaving foam (Patience), an apple (Joy), oil (Courage), wine (Compassion) and bread (Love). Each item was introduced and framed by the telling of a personal narrative that usually touched on biblical imagery. Each one was then worked in some fashion on stage and used as a basis for a physical action

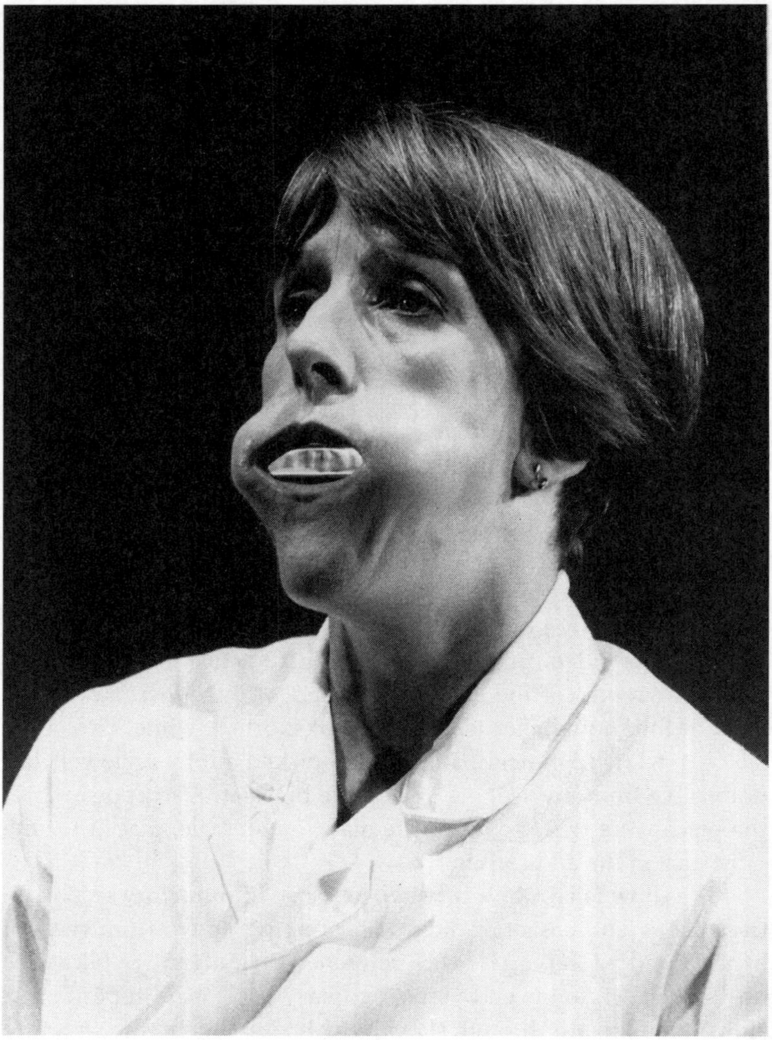

2 Bobby Baker: Obedience: *How to Shop*

played out on Baker's body, or in one instance the body of a male assistant brought out from the audience. The piece ended with Baker receiving a halo at the supermarket checkout on film and then on stage, by means of a flying harness 'ascending to heaven' in a huge plastic shopping bag together with her seven items. Although most of the show was funny and the early section demonstrating basket and trolley techniques was hilarious, as far as I am able to judge from reviews and from witnessing two different performances, certain moments of the show appeared to produce a sense of discomfort in the audience.

I am going to argue that, like *The Double Wedding*, *How to Shop* operates in terms of a 'double movement', that its meaning is very much a matter of reception and perception and also depends largely on how seriously the individual spectator decides to take the show. However, this does not imply that the two shows are in any way similar, nor, if both can be described in terms of a double movement, that this is exactly the same sort of double movement in each case. The most immediate and striking difference between them can be established through reference to the different sorts of drag that reviewers allude to in discussing English's and Baker's performances, represented on the one hand by Danny La Rue and on the other by Dame Edna Everage. The former represents 'showgirl drag', which I argued in the last chapter is a quotation of a generic idea of femininity that is already marked as theatrical and therefore a copy of something already framed as belonging to the realm of representation. The latter, as I indicated in chapter two, is viewed, by some critics at least, as 'realistic' and is generally taken as a caricature of a character type, rooted in 'everyday life'. Similarly, while *The Double Wedding* was literally and metaphorically staged within and through theatre as a discursive institution, *How to Shop* took place in a 'real' lecture hall which is contextualised historically, and the show took the form of a public lecture, containing citations from a 'real' academic publication. In so far as *The Double Wedding* referred to anything outside the Royal Court Theatre, it potentially referred to the entire history of the 'idea' of theatre, and as a result there were references in the show that could take the spectator anywhere from Plato's cave to Artaud's Bali. Conversely, references outside the lecture hall in *How to Shop* were specifically located through reference to Baker's love of shopping on Sidcup High Street and through the slides and filmed material which showed her pursuing her 'quest' in the Co-op Superstore in Croydon. In *The Double Wedding* there was no reference to the 'real', off-stage Rose English, only to the 'idea' of Rose English as the author and director of this production, whereas Baker apparently performed her 'self', drawing directly on her autobiographical experience as a housewife and mother. *The Double Wedding* foregrounded the performativity of performance, opening up to question the groundless ground of the authorities that inform theatrical conventions, and thereby the difference between the real and the mimetic. *How to Shop* focused on the performativity of social and cultural conventions, which in themselves may be said to be mimetic but which produce the illusion and, more importantly, the effect of *being* 'real', in the performance of everyday life. In both shows, then, the distinction between performance as a bounded act and performativity as a process, between agency and compulsory repetition, may be said to be both reiterated and opened to contestation. However, the very different ways in which this is achieved in each piece to a large extent encapsulates the opposing positions in the debates between feminism and postmodernism that I explored in the introduction.

How to Shop emphasises the material and psychological consequences of being sexed and gendered within everyday social reality, as marked upon and experienced through Baker's female body. Despite the personal nature of the material and its locatedness, this stress on the body, on 'experience' and on texts like the Bible and *The Pilgrim's Progress*, could be construed as an invitation to lapse into foundationalism and essentialism privileging sexual difference and obscuring the fact that this version of female subjectivity is *also* British, white, middle class and heterosexual. Alternatively, my Derridean-influenced reading of *The Double Wedding*, and I must emphasis that I am talking about *my reading* of this show, *not* the show itself, favours the linguistic, the discursive and (inter)textual over the social and material. As bell hooks has pointed out, subversion of dominant cultural forms happens much more easily in the realm of texts 'than in the world of human interaction' (quoted in Bordo 1995: 299). In fact, as I indicated in the last chapter, Derrida has been frequently criticised for deploying 'feminine' terms and textual strategies as part of a process of literary and philosophic deconstruction, while ignoring the 'reality of women' (see Elam 1994: 39). Indeed, although I defended his use of the signifier 'hymen' on the basis of it being both a masculine *and* a feminine term, it would be impossible to offer the same argument for his use of 'invagination', for example. That some sort of defence is necessary is indicated by Derrida's own insistence that such signifiers, 'at least in the context into which those words have been swept, no longer simply designate figures for the feminine body' and that they 'cannot be abstracted from the "performativity" that concerns us here', terms evoked by the 'labor of reading and writing' (Derrida and McDonald 1982: 74–5). Ironically, this statement seems uncomfortably close to Lacan's assertion that the phallus must *not* refer to the penis and as such constitutes an attempt at the type of mastery of the signifying system that 'undecidable' terms such as 'hymen' supposedly subvert. Not only have such words never 'simply' designated terms for the feminine body but 'hymen', in both its meanings, cannot be divorced from the ways in which women's bodies are culturally and socially regulated and defined as objects of exchange. Therefore, even though in theory I recognise the basis on which a 'deconstruction' is taking place in Derrida's 'The Double Session', in practice I remain uneasy about the fashion in which the piercing or penetration of the hymen is discussed throughout this piece in terms of 'violence', because I inevitably connect this to the violence so often performed on women's bodies in our culture. Whether this violence is repeated or resignified in 'The Double Session' may remain 'undecidable', but there is a very fine line between a purely literary notion of 'undecidability' and the sort of postmodern, playful pluralism or outright relativism which may actually represent a refusal to take responsibility for the role we play in reproducing the culture of which we are part.

It is on this basis that, in her book *Unbearable Weight*, Susan Bordo mounts a critique of certain postmodern, 'deconstructionist' feminist theorists who, under the influence of Derrida, celebrate an ideal of the 'choreography of the double movement of the signifier' as opening out infinite possibilities for the proliferation of 'non-binary, non-oppositional identities' or 'a multiplicity of sexually marked voices' (Derrida and McDonald 1982: 76). Clearly, these sort of Utopian notions, based as they are on the hypothetical possibility of moving beyond binary structures of thought, are far easier to enact in reading and writing or in cyberspace than in the supermarket or even in the lecture room. On a general level, Bordo is concerned that these ideas place too great an emphasis on strategies of cultural criticism or textual interpretation and can produce a flattening out of power relations in which 'resistant reading' appears as equivalent to public protest and political activism. This can result in an effacement of 'the arduous and frequently frustrated historical struggle that is required for the subordinated to articulate and assert the value of their "difference" in the face of dominant meanings'

(Bordo 1995: 261–2). With particular reference to feminism, Bordo suggests that such celebrations too often fail to acknowledge that we still live in a culture which is '*in fact* constructed by gender duality' and that, in Diane Elam's words, 'there is no escape from anatomy for feminism, even as feminism refuses to accept that anatomy is destiny' (Bordo 1995: 241 and Elam 1994: 60). According to Bordo, the theorists in question attempt to deny or transcend materiality altogether, subscribing to 'fantasies of disembodiment' which can eventually add up to a 'refusal to assume a shape for which they must take responsibility' (1995: 228).

In pursuing this argument, Bordo initially focuses on Susan Suleiman and Donna Haraway but later moves on to a discussion of Butler's *Gender Trouble*. Bordo claims that, despite Butler's citation of Foucault as a major influence, much of *Gender Trouble* represents a reworking of Erving Goffman's concept of the presentation of self in everyday life in a fashion that owes more to Derrida (Goffman 1959). As a result, Bordo asserts that Butler treats the body as a text, or rather as an 'abstract, unsuited, linguistic structure [...] whose meanings can be analysed in abstraction from experience, history, material practice and context' (Bordo 1995: 292). Therefore, Butler fails to share Foucault's and Goffman's concern for 'the institutional and everyday *practices* by means of which our experience of the body is organised' (291). Ultimately, the same might be said for my reading of *The Double Wedding* which does focus on the abstract and philosophical history of Western theatre, at the expense of the organisation of this theatre as a social institution. Consequently, while my reading of this show opens up the possibility of the deconstruction of sex, gender and sexuality *within* this production as a text, none of this necessarily reflects on these issues in terms of the material, everyday practices of the theatrical institution as a whole. Moreover, I barely acknowledge issues of race and class, despite the fact that these are significant factors in both the historical development of theatre as an institution and these diurnal practices. On the other hand, Bordo herself has pointed out that while 'selectivity' or 'centrism' is never innocent, it *is* inevitable, and finally her most significant criticism of Butler's work is that, unlike Foucault, 'who was resistant to identifying with any single theoretical position', Butler lapses into 'linguistic foundationalism' and, as a result, 'For Butler, contrastingly, there *is* one correct, unimpeachable position' (Bordo 1995: 222 and 290).

The majority of Bordo's criticisms of *Gender Trouble* are answered in *Bodies that Matter*. Butler's notion of a 'double movement' constitutes an approach which in theory, to quote Elam again, takes account of identity categories as 'neither pure abstraction (ideological construction) or raw bodies (real historical objects)' but 'both at the same time' (Elam 1994: 59). In practice, however, as I indicated in chapter two, Butler does still tend to give preference to the text over the context, the performer over the staging and the linguistic over the social, in a way that can produce a flattening out of power relations. This is partly because, albeit deconstructively, her argument is still staged primarily within and through the discourse of psychoanalysis, which places the artefacts she analyses mainly in relation to the symbolic, which is everywhere at once and nowhere in particular. Yet, Butler delineates very clearly and precisely the terms and limitations within which she is writing, and, as I understand it, *Bodies that Matter* is predicated on the notion that since we do at present live in a world constructed by dualities, it is impossible to speak of an identity, a theory or a politics that is not dependent in some degree upon centrism, exclusion or selectivity. For me, then, and I suspect for Bordo also, there is less of a problem with Butler's writing than there is with its reception and perception. Both *Gender Trouble* and *Bodies that Matter* sometimes do seem to have been seized upon as representing a single and 'unimpeachable position' which can be transferred across into any and all areas of existence in a fashion that ignores the specificity of the terrain that Butler covers. Further, Butler's writing does sometimes seem to have produced disciples who, as Bordo puts it, are 'intoxicated with the interpretative and creative possibilities of cultural analysis' and 'neglect to ask themselves what is actually going on in the culture around them' (Bordo 1995: 295). Looking at the culture directly around her, Bordo is anxious that there is a desire within academic feminism to achieve 'unimpeachable theoretical purity' at the expense of a retreat from 'female otherness' (229). She argues that this has resulted in an abandoning of tools that have been central to the ongoing feminist deconstruction of the phallologocentric world view and which have inspired many effective, pragmatic strategies for bringing about social change. She goes on to suggest that this retreat may indicate a desire on the part of professional women, working within the still patriarchal institution of academia, to dissociate themselves from certain types of behaviour that continue to be coded as negative and feminine. Bordo's work, then, serves as a useful reminder of the power of dominant institutions to recuperate 'resistance' by incorporating otherness as a process of inoculation. In a similar vein to Bordo, in *The Subject's Tragedy*, Linda Kintz counsels caution when feminists draw on theories derived from poststructuralist philosophy and linguistics, on the basis that

> once we have located ourselves in this conceptual terrain [of the play of signifiers] there is a need to stay vigilant to the continuing influence of the repudiation of the feminine, as that applies to the maternal, even in strategies on resistance. [...] The repudiation of femininity, however, may still be at work in a too quick understanding of the 'free play' of signifiers, both in masculinist appropriations of that free play in a textualised femininity that proves to find no place for women as speakers or writers or for studies of legal discourse or of the arrangements of working conditions for women that find the argument that gender is constructed can potentially, though not necessarily, reinforce a model of organisation based on requirements whose ideal subject is male. (Kintz 1992: 138)

In short, rather than being transcended, sexual difference may actually be being reinscribed as the same old story.

I am not arguing for Bordo and against Butler, or for Foucault against Derrida, or rejecting my own reading of *The Double Wedding* and offering a better, more 'theoretically pure' one of *How to Shop* since there are important areas where all these authors and my readings repeat as well as differ from one another. Nor am I implying that one show or one author is any more or less 'politically correct' or better in any other way than the other. The differences between them do not detract from the integrity of each one on its own terms but are of immense value in remarking the necessity for distinct modes of contestation, specific to particular times, fields and locations. These productive differences also indicate the impossibility and undesirability of preferring any single theoretical position or strategy of subversion or of deciding in advance on any single model for politics or political performance practice.

Despite my insistence on the 'undecidability' of *The Double Wedding*, my analysis did implicitly favour a positive, Derridean reading for the reviewer's comparison between English and Danny La Rue. Bearing in mind the differences between Danny La Rue and Dame Edna Everage, as well as those between *The Double Wedding* and *How to Shop*, I would like to commence by being more cautious about the comparison made between Baker and Everage. All four are perceived as 'funny', but with both English and La Rue, much of the humour is derived from the performer's evident and skilful manipulation of theatrical illusion, whereas the comedy with Baker and Everage appears to arise from the 'delusions', exhibited by their stage personas. With this pair, the 'joke' seems to be based on a reversal of social and cultural norms, in so far as the idea of an 'average', middle aged housewife and mother claiming the identity of 'superstar', 'artist' or even that of an 'expert' in her field is considered hilarious. The difference is, of course, that Barry Humphries *makes* the joke, while Baker apparently *is* the joke, a performer and artist who claims authority based on her experience as a middle aged housewife and mother. Indeed, as I indicated in chapter one, Baker was initially puzzled and upset to discover that she made people laugh, since she had set out to make 'serious' points. Whether or not this comment can be taken at face value, this comparison could indicate a 'repudiation of the feminine' on the part of the reviewers – particularly as 'that applies to the maternal' – that proves to find no place for certain types of women as speakers or authors. Humphries, whose imposture invites the audience to laugh *at* Dame Edna's claims to knowledge and authority, may be being invoked in order to reveal the laughable, groundless nature of similar claims on the part of Baker.

Alternatively, in her review of *How to Shop*, Susan Melrose uses this comparison to suggest that Baker may *herself* be performing a 'repudiation of the feminine'. She points out that Baker enacts the sort of 'self-mutilating savageries' on her own body which 'Dame Edna prefers to practice on others', and which 'speak of masculine controls performed by the female on the feminine: and nothing in the show, besides, suggests that she likes her female body. Is this why women shake with joy in the audience?' Melrose then goes on to ask whether this is 'subversive or precisely programmed and obedient?' (Melrose 1993). There is no doubt that Baker's performance demonstrated the sort of ambivalence towards her own body which, as Bordo indicates in *Unbearable Weight*, is a characteristic of the experience of being female for the majority of women within Western culture. Yet, as Bordo attests in this book, I think this is more of an 'ambivalence' than Melrose appears to allow, if only because, as her syntax indicates, the female and the feminine cannot be separated neatly. There were points in the show where Baker's performance suggested an obedience to the traditional, gendered, hierarchical, philosophic divisions between mind/body, active/passive, sadistic/masochistic, male/female. As such, this body was portrayed as the 'abject', that which must be repudiated and transcended for 'proper' subjectivity or 'true' knowledge to be achieved. Yet, there were other moments where a reversal took place and the 'inferior' terms in these binaries were privileged, so that her female body was celebrated as a locus of pleasure, and 'feminine' skills and knowledges were represented as offering the basis for subversion and resistance. And then again, there were points where Baker appeared to be performing both at once, or rather where contradictory images and identifications accumulated and were layered one on top of the other, so that her body became a 'battleground', a site or surface for the struggle over meanings (see Bordo 1995: 263). This struggle was staged within and through carefully delineated social institutions, personal experiences and everyday material practices, as much as within and through dominant cultural discourses. Therefore, while this body may be shown to be an ideological construct, it also always remains specifically located as a real historical object. This, then, is a body and a subjectivity formed in the spaces between the universal and the particular, the dominant and the subordinate, the textual and the everyday, theories and practices.

Actually, for much of *How to Shop*, Baker could be said to be identifying with masculine control in terms of 'demonstrating a wish for masculinity' in almost exactly the same terms set out in Joan Riviere's essay of 1929, 'Womanliness as Masquerade', not least because this concept was developed by Riviere through a case study of a woman who was an academic and lecturer (Riviere 1929: 303). This concept of masquerade describes how a woman who usurps 'masculine' prerogatives by taking up the position of 'speaking subject' may assume a mask of 'excessive womanliness' as a defensive reaction to avoid punishment. This strategic masquerade aims at 'disarming the avenger' by, among other things, offering herself to him sexually and also 'treat[ing] the situation of displaying her masculinity to men as a game – something not real, a joke', so that she can 'make sure of safety by masquerading as guiltless and innocent' (305–6). Paradoxically, while this subject's attitude towards 'the father' is described by Riviere as 'sadistic', above all this she seeks to placate this symbolic figure whose position she usurps, desiring from him, as Riviere puts it, 'absolution', a point that is particularly resonant in the light of the framing of *How to Shop* in relation to *The Pilgrim's Progress* (Riviere 1929: 312).

The radical aspect of Riviere's theory lay in the assertion that for her there is no difference between 'genuine womanliness' and this masquerade, thereby making a distinction between sex and gender and effectively representing a repudiation of the 'feminine' by the female (Riviere 1929: 306). However, 'sex' remains installed as the dominant factor in the organisation of identity, and the Freudian metanarrative that informs Riviere's analysis means that she assumes in advance that all desire, if not all activity, is male, phallic and heterosexual. Nevertheless, according to Linda Kintz, a Rivierian mimicking of 'excessive womanliness' potentially opens up 'a gap between women and the image of Woman', a space in which women can manipulate this image 'without being wholly caught in it' (1992: 133). Kintz asserts that this strategy 'defamiliarises female iconography in a masquerade that is more transparent to other women than it is to men' (134), which might explain the 'joy' that Susan Melrose suggests *How to Shop* produced in women in the audience. Yet, as Kintz implies, this 'gap' opens up because this masquerader plays both subject and object, active and passive, at the same time. Therefore, the defamiliarisation that is said to occur in Riviere's original masquerade does not become legible so much because this woman simply performs 'excessive womanliness' but because she does so while 'usurping' a position socially and culturally coded as masculine. It is this staging which, above all, allows her 'femininity' to appear as excessive and in turn her 'excessive' femininity that makes her masculinity appear as only a 'role'. This may implicitly confirm the proper speaking subject as male for both sexes of spectators. Alternatively, and to be more positive, it is the fact that this female subject apparently *successfully* occupies the 'masculine' place of speaking subject which creates the threat and the subsequent necessity for a defence. To some extent, then, this masquerade could be seen as a double bluff in which the female subject manipulates both masculine and feminine roles, using one to disguise the other so that there is, as it were, always one mask too many, creating an 'excess' which potentially defamiliarises both.

In *How to Shop*, Baker's occupation of the 'masculine' position of lecturer, like her identification with Christian from *The Pilgrim's Progress*, was certainly received as a joke. The audience laughed when she said she was offering a deconstruction of the shopping experience, read out a particularly dense passage from an academic publication and announced that, since this was a public lecture, she was going to address the 'lowest common denominator'. This may have been because, like the ridiculously oversized 'phallic' pointer she wielded, her performance of this persona was parodic, pompous and aggressive. However, she also constantly undercut her own authority, moderating into another persona who was breathy, if not 'lacking control', or, in the words of various reviewers, 'dotty', 'batty', 'self-effacing', 'cosy' and 'uncertain'. For example, she vigorously castigated the audience for their apparent ignorance of classics such as *The Pilgrim's Progress*, Thomas More's *Utopia* and *Everyman*. Yet, she then revealed that actually she herself had never read *The Pilgrim's Progress* and remembered the story only from her reading of the summary that accompanied the illustrations in a copy of the book she had as a child. Just as the pointer dwarfed her, her position of knowledge and mastery appeared to be highlighted as a game, a phallic imposture, masking an authentic 'feminine' self. Although she started the show by identifying with Christian from *The Pilgrim's Progress*, as she made clear in an ironic aside, Christian leaves his wife and children behind as the first stage of unburdening himself of impure worldly desires and temptations of the flesh.[2] Baker's quest, on the other hand, actually involved acquiring *more* worldly goods, and she was constantly distracted by concern for her family and by domestic detail. For instance, with 'Courage', a 'masculine' identification with King David being anointed with oil by Samuel before going to fight Goliath, an image taken from a biblical epic she saw on television, was undercut by a 'feminine' concern for laundry. She revealed that she was 'ridiculously obsessed with washing', an obsession that extended to both the hessian robe worn by the actor playing David and her own bra, which became stained when she imitated this action, pouring cooking oil over her own head. The portrayal of this excessively 'feminine self', which was essentially masochistic (the oil was allowed to dribble into her eye, causing visible discomfort) seemed to unmask the 'real' Bobby Baker, behind her assumed 'masculine' identification.

On the other hand, this 'feminine' self sometimes operated as a mask for an aggressive and castrating phallicism, which was also received with delight on the part of the audience. For 'Humility', Baker transformed the parsley into a 'sweet little bouquet', declaring that she found this easy as an 'artist' but 'some of you may struggle with it'. Despite this claim to 'mastery', when it came to demonstrating this virtue she insisted that she was naturally very humble and so 'humbled' a male performer drawn from the audience instead, throwing him the bouquet, at which point his previously aggressive, masculine stance was transformed into one of 'feminine' meekness. For 'Joy', Baker made toffee apples and then stripped down to a skin-tight, red dress to mime to a Dusty Springfield record, using the toffee apple as a microphone, licking and finally biting into it. Here she simultaneously 'offered herself sexually' and enacted castration on the phallic/apple/microphone. However, while all of these could be read as 'sadistic 'and 'disobedient' acts, they were still expressed in terms of an iconography which is easily recuperated to an 'obedient' model of heterosexual femininity where self-assertion and the expression of active desire in a woman demonstrates penis envy, a castrating wish for not only the masculine role, but for 'maleness'.

It is not so easy to unravel and recuperate the confusion of masks and identifications that characterised the sequence for 'Patience'. This was introduced through a dictionary definition of the term as, among other things, 'the capacity to calmly endure pain' and 'constancy in labour, exertion or effort' and from there on in became a Freudian nightmare. Using a tub of solid shaving soap and a brush, Baker started slowly applying foam to an oval, silver foil platter and commented on how much this reminded her of her father because 'I could smell it on his neck'. Saying that she could sense the audience's lack of patience with this slow and time-consuming method, she then switched to a 'modern' method, using an aerosol to create a smooth white mound. This was, in effect, the classic pantomime custard pie, which she carefully transferred to the front of her white overall, remaking the mound but now including a 'navel' to complete the illusion of pregnancy which, arm in arm with the male performer, she paraded proudly. This pregnancy was then 'exploded' by the man, spreading foam all over the stage, a mess which she aggressively ordered him to clean up. The practical connection between 'shaving' and 'labour' is not quite so obscure as it may at first seem since the practice of shaving women prior to their giving birth, whether this was necessary or not, was a fairly widespread procedure for much of this century and still continues in certain places. This shaving represented the perception of an adult woman's bodily hair as 'unhygienic' and was often experienced by women as a ritual of discipline and control which marked their disempowerment by the patriarchal medical institution. This image, then, of a pregnant, adult female visually and metaphorically reduced to a child-like status potentially forms part of a multi-layered series of identifications and dis-identifications in which Baker touches on a whole range of primordial taboos by acting out both masculine and feminine roles in reproduction. First she cites her/the father and connects him to the use of a shaving brush rubbed in the circular pot of soap producing 'foam'. She then 'usurps' him using the faster, more modern aerosol spray in order to 'impregnate' herself, literally by her own hand. This could be read as the expression of an Oedipal desire for the father and the wish to supplant the mother and bear his child. As such, it may be explained in terms of the simultaneous identification with, and repudiation of, the maternal through the internalisation of 'masculine control' which, according to psychoanalytical theory, is demanded of the female subject at the Oedipal stage. However, if the mother is supplanted in this particular case, the father is also 'castrated', so that Baker can wield the phallus/penis herself. While this may simply indicate 'penis envy', it could equally, and in line with Butler's reading of Riviere's case study, represent a desire for the mother by the female child which has been repudiated and so is in fact 'a refusal of a female homosexuality and at the same time the hyperbolic incorporation of that female Other' (Butler 1990: 53). Yet, actually, Baker enacts a refusal and incorporation of *both* the father and the mother at the same time. Therefore, this pregnancy is an immaculate self-conception, a sort of 'reproduction of self', or rather a self-portrait of the artist as a mother and/or mother as artist in which Baker occupies both masculine and feminine positions and during the course of which the maternal body is both celebrated and violently erased. Alternatively, it is none of the above, and Baker remains 'innocent and guiltless' because this act is clearly only a joke, a piece of good old-fashioned theatrical slapstick, and in fact I feel extremely silly offering such a convoluted interpretation of something that is so clearly simply a comedy of appearances. Yet to continue taking Baker seriously, this is potentially an incredibly complex sequence in which Baker fluctuates between the positions of Father/Mother/child/artist/clown/performer/castrator/castrated/subject/object/abject in a fashion that cannot be contained within the asymmetrical and mutually exclusive relationship between desire and identification, having and being, assumed by Freudian and Lacanian theory. In short, this sequence remarks the sort of 'incoherence' that, according to Julia Kristeva's *Powers of Horror*, is produced by the foregrounding of the 'abject', a concept and a work of particular relevance to *How to Shop* because of the show's religious content. According to Kristeva, 'Abjection accompanies all religious structurings and reappears, to be worked out in a new guise, at the time of their collapse' (Kristeva 1982: 17).

In this essay, Kristeva throws into relief the ways in which the modernist, 'scientific' discourse of psychoanalytical theory draws upon and remains imbricated within the historical discourses of institutionalised religion, particularly the Judeo-Christian tradition. Kristeva traces out the evolution of Old Testament purity laws as a process of creating rules and boundaries for an ideal 'clean and proper subject', fit to speak to his god. She argues that these laws, which were related both to hygiene and to the sacred, developed into a classification system of differences and oppositions separating out subject from object, masculine from feminine, heterosexual from homosexual, the spiritual from the corporeal, the clean from the unclean, inside from outside. According to Kristeva, this system then served to define the limits and borders of orderly, proper subjects, defined in obedience to cultural taboos, which must be maintained to achieve socialisation and provide a sense of the self as a discrete and unified whole. The abject marks these limits and borders which, when transgressed or even simply remarked, can provoke the recognition that this wholeness is only a construct, producing a sense of instability and incoherence or of being 'out of control'. Above all, the abject relates to a fear of the fragility, permeability and 'uncontrollability' of the body, and so the subject's 'wholeness' is threatened by the sight of blood, the appearance of other bodily fluids and the ingestion and expulsion of food, all of which serve as reminders of, and prefigure, the ultimate loss of self – death. Paradoxically, these same objects simultaneously serve as a reminder of birth and of the primary, physical and psychical process of separation from the maternal body, necessary to the achievement of this discrete subjectivity in the first place. As a result, within this process of classification, the feminine comes to be associated with the corporeal abject, and the abject with the feminine, so that for Kristeva food enduces abjection when it recalls the 'archaic relationship between the human body and the other, its mother' (Kristeva 1982: 75–6). However, as Kristeva puts it, abjection 'is caused by what disturbs identity, system, order. What does not respect borders, positions, rules. The in between, the ambiguous, the composite' (1982: 4). It would therefore be wrong to associate the abject *only* with the maternal feminine. In *Powers of Horror*, Kristeva then turns to the New Testament, where she explores the sublimation and recuperation of the threat of the corporeal/abject/maternal/feminine through its incorporation into the figure of Christ, a god made flesh, whose body is subsequently purified through physical suffering and death and then resurrected so that he is assumed 'whole' into heaven. By this means the abject/corporeal/feminine is inoculated and transcended through this figure, who thereafter represents an impossible, ideal model for achieving 'true', rather than 'symbolic', wholeness (Kristeva 1982: 120). Linda Kintz develops this idea in a discussion of what she identifies as a 'double pattern' in Western philosophy, where the embracing of femininity looks like progress but is in fact an appropriation of the feminine into an ideal, 'suffering' masculine figure, who engages with the 'abject' only to transcend and purify it. She exemplifies her argument with reference to Nietzsche, Artaud, Lacan and Barthes, and so her point might be pertinent to my discussion of Barthes in chapter one and of *The Double Wedding* in chapter three (Kintz 1992: 115).

Clearly, 'Patience', like much of the rest of the show, can be read as playing on social and sexual taboos in a fashion that borders on the abject in various ways – hence the contradictory, excessive, if not incoherent, nature of Baker's identifications. The tendency towards 'abjection' throughout the piece was often concentrated around the use of food products which were also quite specifically connected to religious iconography. Yet the attitude Baker demonstrated towards this iconography in the show was in itself ambivalent, ambiguous and contradictory. At times, this imagery seemed transgressive, foregrounding the historical, discursive abjection of the feminine within the Judeo-Christian tradition. At others, Baker appeared to accept her position as the feminine abject and at others again to identify with Christ as an ideal of unity and wholeness, unifying the split between masculine and feminine, the pure spirit and the sinful flesh. This may indicate a reworking of this religious structure at the time of its collapse, and, interestingly, it was the sections where Baker appeared to express genuine religious belief, rather than those that were more obviously transgressive, which seemed to evoke uncertainty, if not instability, within the audience. For example, just before launching into her exemplary shopping trip, Baker repeated the little prayer 'Lord send me', which she told us she always said before engaging in such activities. In contrast to the comic tone previously established, this prayer was delivered quietly and seriously, a switch of mood that caused a hiatus, after which Baker shrugged self-deprecatingly, muttered something inaudible and once again changed registers.

Yet 'Obedience', for which, following the prompting of her 'inner voice', the voice of the Lord, Baker placed an unopened tin of anchovies sideways in her mouth, was received with much hilarity despite its masochistic and Christian framing. This action was shown first taking place in a supermarket on film and then on stage where, still with the tin in her mouth, Baker performed a clumsy dance to the music of 'When the Boat Comes In', therefore obediently and/or ironically, dancing for her 'daddy'. The implicit, biblical reference to 'fish' was consolidated through linking this act to a story about friends swimming with a shoal of fish in Greece, but Baker also said she may actually have got this image from the film *Shirley Valentine*. This act was most definitely a mortification of the flesh, and yet Baker's personal anecdote dwelt on the pleasures of the senses. Moreover, *Shirley Valentine* is a story of a 'disobedient' woman who leaves her husband and rejects domesticity to 'find' herself through worldly physical experience, in a sort of reversal and repetition of *The Pilgrim's Progress*. Finally, enacting this gesture in the supermarket in itself was socially a transgressive and disorderly act that failed to respect not only the boundaries of inside and outside the body but also the 'rules' of the appropriate public behaviour. Similarly, for 'Joy', Baker mimicked Eve's original sin of eating the apple which brought death into the world, thereby quoting the Old Testament construction of the feminine as standing for, and enslaved by, the corrupt and corrupting temptations of the flesh. Yet her citation of this religious archetype was performed as a playful celebration of the body, if not a positive reclaiming of disorderly female desire. Yet again, this whole section was framed by reference to the experience of drowsing in an apple orchard on a late summer afternoon surrounded by the scent of windfalls, a highly sensuous image but one which in turn is not so far removed from notions of death and decay. These, then, like all the sequences in the show, were sort of double or triple exposures in which contradictory or opposite images, narratives and identifications were layered on top of each other, in a manner that was contiguous and overlapping, rather than dialectical. This produced clashes, convergences and dissonances that were somehow both obedient *and* disorderly, celebratory *and* troubling, simultaneously affirmations of life and *memento mori*.

This contradictory, dissonant layering was much in evidence with reference to the last two items on Baker's shopping list. Red wine, for Baker, stands for 'Compassion', and she said she needed a great deal of this to get through the day. She held up a corkscrew to the audience, flapping its arms and saying 'My friends say this is me'. Under the influence of the show's religious framing, this corkscrew seemed not only to signify 'out of control' femininity but also a crucifix. A film sequence used trick photography to show Baker being transformed into this corkscrew (the masculine position of penetration?) to open a bottle of wine in which she then swam apparently nude. This again, then, is a series of double images bringing together the masculine and feminine, the martyrdom of Christ with the 'hysterical' woman, the partaking of the cleansing blood in the ritual of the Eucharist with more mundane, literal consolations. This reference to the Eucharist was consolidated in the final action for 'Love'. Using 'Mother's Pride' bread and taking pains to let the audience enjoy the smell of frying garlic, Baker made garlic croutons which were placed in baskets, passed out and shared with the spectators. Of the ritual of the Eucharist, Kristeva says that, 'By surreptitiously mingling the theme of "devouring" with that of "satiating", that narrative is a way of taming cannibalism. It invites a removal of guilt from the archaic relation to the first pre-object (abject) of need: the mother' (Kristeva 1982: 118). This sequence was described by several reviewers as 'touching', but it is also potentially a reminder of the way in which Mothers are often 'devoured', both literally and metaphorically, and therefore, although presented as an act of love and willing self-sacrifice, it did not necessarily allow for the removal of guilt. In fact, *How to Shop* was shot through with moments when Baker foregrounded the self-effacement demanded by her role as mother and housewife as a sort of martyrdom. This is a mortification of both the flesh and the spirit, which is not entirely willing and happy – hence her need for courage and compassion and her ambiguous relationship to obedience. She was shown breathlessly rushing around the supermarket in order to fit in all her daily tasks, she said she never got to watch a film all the way through because she would always either fall asleep or be popping in and out of the room, and before picking up her halo at the end of the show she muttered darkly that, of course, 'You've got to pay'. In both the 'Love' sequence and in the final act of assumption, the image of the nurturing, everyday housewife and mother, weighed down and 'devoured' by mundane, domestic duty, overlaps simultaneously with Christian from *The Pilgrim's Progress*, transcending his body to reach the celestial city, the body of the abject, 'archaic (M)other', the image of Christ as an ideal of both loving self-sacrifice and 'wholeness', and also perhaps with that of the Virgin Mary who, like Christ, was bodily assumed into heaven. This final figure, venerated as a mother but only in so far as she achieved maternity without any recourse to sexual intercourse, again represents both an incorporation and erasure of the feminine at the same time. This layering and juxtaposition of contradictory imagery opens up a space of defamiliarisation to underline the ambivalent, if not incoherent, fashion in which the maternal feminine has been historically, discursively constructed and is concretely experienced by Baker in the practice of her everyday life.

However, since *How to Shop* is, above all, a performance, it would be a mistake to take some of Baker's 'masks' in this show as transparently reflecting the truth about her 'real life' subjectivity, while assuming others only to be part of the act, not least because the subjectivity performed is unstable and unreliable. To do so is to assume the meaning of the show in advance on the basis of Baker's apparent sex, gender and sexuality and paradoxically to close down the space of agency out of which, in Linda Kintz's terms, Baker is successfully manipulating these images. Since it is the proliferation of 'masks', identities and identifications Baker performs that produces this defamiliarisation, it is important to take all her 'roles' in this piece equally seriously or equally as jokes. This includes her identity as artist and her role as lecturer. As I indicated above, as with Riviere's original subject, the 'excessiveness' of Baker's femininity only becomes apparent through the staging of the piece intertextually in relation to the institution of 'art' and directly in relation to academia, both of which have traditionally been organised around a model in which the ideal subject is male. Paying more careful attention to the staging of the show within the lecture theatre as a social space and to Baker's role as lecturer allows for another reading of the piece to emerge which confirms much of my analysis so far but also places more emphasis on Baker's 'agency' as a socially and historically located subject.

As the lecturer, Baker stated that she was offering a 'deconstruction of the shopping experience' and that one particular source of 'inspiration' had been the book *Lifestyle Shopping: The Subject of Consumption* (Shields 1992), from which she read a quotation from Lauren Langman's essay 'Neon Cages: Shopping for Subjectivity'.[3] Examining this quote, its original context suggests that Baker has indeed studied this work which offers a deconstruction of the shopping experience, and that to a large extent *How to Shop* is a repetition, a reversal and a resignification of this work – in short, a deconstruction of this deconstruction. This reading is of course entirely based on information collected *after* seeing the show, but Baker did strongly urge the audience to take notes and gave enough information for us to follow up her citation of Langman's essay. She also stressed that she chose the lecture format because she felt that in previous pieces, like *Kitchen Show*, the audience became too relaxed and failed to pay attention to the '*very important points*' she was trying to make. In short, she invited us to accept the validity of her knowledge and her right to speak as an equal authority in a field where, as she remarked, the strength of academic interest indicates that 'an understanding of the shopping experience is central to any analysis of our modern society'. At the time the audience laughed, and it was left open for them to finally decide whether or not this authority was only a joke and whether or not to become active agents in the construction of meaning *after*, as well as during or before, the event.

There are three major 'themes' that feature significantly in all the essays in *Lifestyle Shopping* and, as far as I can tell, in most publications on the same area, as well as in *How to Shop*. Firstly, considering these works tend to be 'materialist', there is an absolutely astonishing proliferation of religious, specifically Judeo-Christian metaphors and imagery, a convention that can be traced back to the influence of works on consumption by Karl Marx and

Walter Benjamin. Secondly, the store or mall is continually discussed as a 'stage', a 'palace of illusions', a 'hall of mirrors' or a 'theatre' for the staging of the self, and these references owe much to, among others, Erving Goffman's theories on the presentation of self in everyday life. Both of these themes are often explored in relation to Foucault's notion of 'panopticism' and the internalised, regulatory gaze that ensures 'discipline' and social control. Finally, Foucaultian ideas are interwoven with theories of the 'practice of everyday life', from Edmund Husserl and Jürgen Habermas through to Pierre Bourdieu and, most of all, Michel de Certeau, to inform and develop a concept of the 'resistant consumer'. Interestingly, despite the 'materialist' tendencies of such works, there is seldom much discussion of class or indeed race.

All of these motifs occur in Langman's essay. The quote Baker read out in *How to Shop* makes up the second part of a paragraph which likens the development of the contemporary shopping mall to the building of the great cathedrals of Europe as places where society may 'celebrate and sanctify itself' (Langman 1992: 40). This comparison is a common one in academic works in this field, but what is unusual is the fashion in which throughout this essay Langman continues to draw heavily and punitively on Old Testament, religious imagery.

For Langman, the 'mall' is a post-lapsarian, postmodern Eden or, as she puts it, a false 'utopia of consumption' in which the consumer seeks a self that has been 'lost' (49, 65). This de-centred subject is, then, literally 'shopping for subjectivity' and, in her terms, searching for 'substantiation if not salvation' (68). Drawing on Goffman's work, she characterises the malls as 'theatres', stages where different subjectivities can be tried on and played out, subjectivities which are 'increasingly intertwined with popular images which at times become parodies of media images and celebrities' (63). However, she remains unconvinced that this sort of activity really represents a de Certeauian or Foucaultian style of resistance where such activities create 'microspheres of empowerment' through the appropriation and transformation of cultural practices (48). Langman is critical of de Certeau's notion of the consumer as 'artist', transforming commodities, claiming this is an 'art of the sacred', that literally, in Marx's terms, devolves on these objects 'strange, metaphysical powers' (42, 46). Conversely, for Langman these virtual selves are only commodified practices seeking recognition in the gaze of the other which is in reality the internalised, panoptican gaze of market forces. These consumers, then, have sold their birthright for a mess of empty signifiers, and indeed she claims that, 'If Nietzsche announced the death of God, Goffman's work announces the death of the soul or at least its conditions of sale' (65). These soulless 'self-presentations' now wander in a 'trance' caught up in a sort of purgatory, in 'an ever-changing Manichean range between the simulated good of the hyperreal and the Evil of the mundane' (46). As such, according to Langman, the location of George Romero's film *Dawn of the Dead* in a shopping mall makes perfect sense, since the resurrected Zombies are returning to 'the most important place in their earthly lives and what heaven is like in the next' (68).

Meanwhile, back in this life and suffering from the absence of self/God, the purchase of the 'right products' promises this subject 'the good life, good feelings and good selfhood and maybe a sign of God's blessing', while the purchase of the 'wrong products' can lead to a 'social fate worse than death' (47, 69). Langman defines the 'gratifications' produced through such consumption, feelings she argues that were once achieved through labour and production, as deeply selfish (69). The consumer is 'Cain', a figure characterised by postmodern envy, 'prone to anxiety and panic' and the 'abandonment of all concern for the collective good' (44, 69, 40). Langman's mall, then, exists firmly in a Baudrillardian postmodern universe where the 'Cathedral' is really 'the generalised brothel of capital', which is a 'brothel of substitution and commutation' and in which there is no possibility of resistance from 'the masses', because they are too busy mistaking the signifier for the thing itself (quoted in Kellner 1989: 64). In this soulless half-life, without a transcendental signifier to arrest the process of the exchange of signs, the confusion of categories, most particularly between the economic and the cultural, work and leisure, production and consumption, the social and the political, but also between categories of sex and sexuality, is a sign of decadence, if not transparently of 'evil' (see Baudrillard 1993).

Although in *How to Shop* Baker took up the Langman quotation after the reference to cathedrals, her first slide introduced moments later showed the high vaulted ceilings and subdued lighting of the entrance to the Croydon Co-op Superstore, and she said, 'Look at this magnificent entrance, Cathedral-like.' From this point on, *How to Shop* mimicked Langman's essay, but Baker introduced New Testament iconography in contrast to Langman's Old Testament severity. Baker admitted that the supermarket sometimes reduced her to a trance, a 'dream like' state, but, unlike Langman's Zombies, she retained knowledge of her fallen condition. In Christian philosophy such knowledge is the primary condition of the concept of free will, which posits that while all of us are born with the stain of Eve's 'original sin', our spiritual destiny is *not* fated or decided in advance but depends on whether or not we choose to accept God and follow the teachings of Christ. Baker therefore sets out to exercise her free will to transmute Langman's deadly, post-industrial capitalist sins into virtues. In identifying herself with Christian from *The Pilgrim's Progress*, Baker absolutely literally represents herself as a 'lost soul' but one in search of salvation through the *tran*substantiation of 'evil' mundane commodities, as substitutions for 'real' desires, into 'good' symbols for 'what we really need in life', in an 'art' very much of the sacred. As such, she may be 'David', fighting the Goliath of commodification that appropriates all social interaction to the market, taking on the role of the 'resistant consumer' as posited by de Certeau, who is involved in 'an entirely different kind of production (...) characterised by its ruses, its fragmentation, its clandestine nature, its tireless quiet activity, in short by its quasi invisibility, since it shows itself not in its own products but in the art of using those imposed upon it' (quoted in Shields 1992: 2).

However, de Certeau's analysis of the 'practices of everyday life' is not a simple, positive reclamation and celebration of consumption. As Langman stresses, the 'gratifications' that de Certeau identifies as accumulating through the appropriation and reinterpretation of cultural practices partly function as the bribes that society offers 'in order to get most of its work done and particularly the routine tasks that *mus*t be done' (Langman 1992: 54). In a similar fashion, the reference points in Baker's quest, such as *The Pilgrim's Progress* or *Everyman,* emphasise the notion of 'struggle', and she underlines her daily need for courage and compassion in undertaking the laborious, undervalued and quasi-invisible routine tasks of motherhood and housewifery. Yet *How to Shop* also celebrates this selflessness, exercised for the collective good, and foregrounds the 'artistry' and expertise that can be displayed in the accomplishment of these very routine tasks, which, as de Certeau puts it, constitute an 'art' that is anything but passive (de Certeau

1994: 483). This, then, is, as Susan Bordo puts it, a subject in the 'grip' of cultural meanings, inscribed through the dominant discourses, the practices and bodily habits of everyday life, but also one for whom those very discourses, practices and habits produce the means of subverting and rearticulating the meanings imposed upon it (Bordo 1995: 16).

Since academic writing is itself a commodity, subject to market forces, it is reasonable to suggest that, in *How to Shop*, Baker uses her 'art' to transform Langman's writings which impose on her a definition of her subjectivity, within which she is denied 'free will' or agency. Baker enters into both the physical and the symbolic space of academia, insisting that she, the housewife and mother, is not a blind, zombie consumer but that 'like my fellow academics, I know there is more to shopping than meets the eye'. In re-presenting the act of shopping within the frame of a performance, Baker accentuates the theatricality that academic theorists have affirmed as inherent to this activity. However, in appropriating the lecture hall as a stage for this re-presentation, Baker potentially also reflects the authoritative gaze of this discourse back on itself, pointing up the performative nature of academic discourse itself and putting into question the 'ground' on which that authority is based. If the shopping mall is a theatre, or a hall of mirrors, where lost, postmodern consumers try out subjectivities intertwined with popular images, then the same principle holds in the lecture room. In this fashion, the academic authority which places itself 'outside' that which it speaks may be put into question. Like Langman's subject, in *How to Shop* Baker tries out various subjectivities, some of which are 'intertwined with popular images' and becoming parodies of media images and celebrities, and these include the very images and metaphors that Langman herself cites and parodies in her discussion of 'the' consumer. These are mixed up with personal associations, activities from Baker's everyday domestic existence and childhood memories, to create a 'bricolage', a unique work made of 'found' objects (see de Certeau 1994: 480). Baker might be said to perform a subversive repetition of Langman's discourse from 'within'. The subjectivity she acts out repeats Langman's definition of 'the' consumer but reinscribes it as 'this' particular, individual consumer, who has experience and knowledge that is equally as valid, or equally as groundless, as that of academics. Nevertheless, if such academic authority is put into question, 'Baker' as a practitioner is not necessarily installed in the panopitican position of an outside 'authority' in its stead.

Since the show is presented as autobiographical, in Brechtian terms this 'bricolage' effectively represents the 'social gest' of Baker's own identity, revealing the 'apparatus' and process of its production and pointing up the contradictions within that identity. Yet, unlike the Brechtian model, since there is no discernible or decidable 'distance' between the performer and the 'character' performed, there is no stable place of authority from which Baker can be said to comment on this identity. Further, since the contradictions and processes pointed up *constitute* that identity, these contradictions cannot be synthesised into a 'whole', nor can the processes of production be arrested through reference to a single stabilising axis of identity, or a single metanarrative, or indeed to 'author's intentions'. This body and this identity are then shown to be formed on the borders *between* a whole range of texts, images, religious, historical and social discourses, and institutions and everyday practices, never fully escaping these discourses, institutions or practices, nor their psychic and material effects, but not delimited or defined by any single one of them either. As such, Baker's subjectivity as played out in *How to Shop* cannot be wholly appropriated to the panoptican gaze of market forces, or God, or the father, or psychoanalysis, or academia, or to feminist, feminist postmodernist or poststructuralist theory. In this show, Baker always performs one identity too many. Some of these identities are masculine, some feminine, some active and sadistic, some passive and masochistic, some are 'modernist', and some are postmodernist or social constructionist, some are feminist, some Christian, some camp or queer, some heterosexual, some cite archaic archetypes and some are local and specific. Indeed even her 'class' identity is not as straightforward as it might first appear, something hinted at in the gold ankle bracelet, not normally middle class, middle-aged British style. In sum, Baker performs a subjectivity which is at the same time not Bobby Baker and not not Bobby Baker, both a hyperbolic, theatrical character and the 'real thing', an ideological construct and a situated historical object, both entirely socially constructed and unique. As such, she effects a double movement inhabiting an identity category and opening it up to contestation, thereby producing a 'hiatus in iterability', a space of defamiliarisation. This 'hiatus' may represent the 'space of agency', the point at which Baker's subjectivity both repeats and reinterprets the norm of white, British, middle class motherhood. Yet, in practical terms it is also the space where the specificity, if not uniqueness, of this reinterpretation renders this subjectivity incoherent, abject, unintelligible, 'unreadable'. In the world of everyday experience, rather than that of texts or performances, this is usually a position marked by pain and rejection. Therefore, while *How to Shop* may at some level remark the desire for, and the possibility of, transcending the dualities of mind/body, active/passive, sacred/domestic, masculine/feminine, abject/object, Baker still performs a subject carrying out an existence caught up within these binaries, caught between theories and practices, between Utopian 'ideals' and exigent everyday realities. Hence, perhaps, the apparent fluctuation in the show between obedience and resistance, celebration and violent erasure, self-assertion and self-loathing and the anger and frustration which often seem to be behind Baker's 'dotty' mask of 'excessive femininity'. Hence also, perhaps, the ambivalent nature of the show's reception. It seems to me that the reviewer's comparison with Edna Everage indicates both a recognition of the incoherence and unintelligibility of Baker's subjectivity as performed and a recuperation of this unintelligibility to dominant norms. As such, it represents an identification which is in fact a dis-identification and a repudiation, a denial of the existence of Baker's text and of her authority, except as the sort of 'joke' which contains transgression and leaves the phallus installed in its 'proper' place.

If this show is taken seriously, it does offer some sort of pragmatic model for becoming 'artists of our own existence', in terms of participating as agents in the 'active production of self and society' (de Certeau quoted in Shields 1992: 4). This is a model which acknowledges that we are very much 'inside' that which we wish to critique. As such, it is also one in which 'agency' implies an acceptance of responsibility for the part we as individuals take in the construction of meanings and reproduction of our collective culture, inside and outside the lecture room, the home, the supermarket or the theatre. This responsibility requires the constant questioning of our own implicit assumptions and a taking up and onwards of contestation *after* the event, as a continuing struggle in which there are no 'unimpeachably pure positions' that can be decided on in advance.

Afterword

Revising this chapter in preparation for submitting the manuscript to the publishers, I came across an article in the *Sunday Times* for 29 March 1998, describing Dame Edna's latest show. Apparently, in this production Dame Edna founds a new religion and the piece ends with her assumption into 'heaven' by means of a flying harness. As Edna herself might say, 'spooky!'

Notes

1 All references from *How to Shop* are taken directly from the show, or from the video recording courtesy of artsadmin, copyright Bobby Baker 1993.

2 Interestingly, Christina, Christian's wife, makes her own, similar journey in the lesser known book two of *The Pilgrim's Progress.*

3 The quote reads:

> In the contemporary world the signifying and celebrated edifice of consumer culture has become the shopping mall which exists in a pseudo democratic twilight zone between reality and a commercially produced fantasy world of commodified goods, images and leisure activities that gratify transformed desire and provide packaged self images to a distinctive form of subjectivity. (Langman 1992: 40)

3 'Tits on the head', photo taken with Annie Sprinkle in the interval of *Post Post Porn Modernist*

5

Becoming part of the show, the I of the beholder: Annie Sprinkle's *Post Post Porn Modernist*

In March 1994 for two nights only, Annie Sprinkle performed her show *Post Post Porn Modernist* at the Centre for Contemporary Art (CCA) in Glasgow. The show was not widely publicised but even so we were lucky to secure the last thirteen tickets available. It is a six- to eight-hour round trip to Glasgow in a minibus, so this is a journey we only make for shows that are 'special events', such as Peter Brook's *Mahabharata,* or The Wooster Group's LSD: *Just the High Points*. These factors, plus the crossing of the border from England to Scotland, produce an aura of liminality for these trips, a sense of an escape from the routines of everyday life.

As I indicated in chapter one, Sprinkle has been reworking, revising and updating the same body of autobiographical material for over twenty years, and so most of my group had already encountered parts of this show in other forms, such as video extracts, articles and photography produced by both Sprinkle and others.[1] This meant we all had a good idea of what to expect in terms of the content of the piece and were eager to experience it and judge its effect for ourselves. The studio theatre at the CCA is small and intimate and was set up in a basic, end-on staging. Pushed forward by my companions, I found myself sitting in the centre of the front row only a foot or so away from the edge of the stage. The set was dressed as a bedroom cum dressing room in a flashy, trashy, glitter, ruffles and fake leopard skin style, which really deserves the term 'boudoir'. On one side of the stage there was a dressing table, on the other a working flush toilet, and just off centre stage left there was a bed. Otherwise, the space was filled with costumes on dressing rails or pinned up on the 'walls' alongside a profusion of 'sex toys'. The show was divided into two halves with an interval, during which the audience could buy a range of souvenirs priced between 70p and £3,400 or have a 'tits on the head' Polaroid photo taken with Annie for £3.50. In the course of the piece Sprinkle changed clothes and shoes several times and was often topless or completely nude. At some point, she made a joke about the legality of some of the content of the show in Scotland, a comment that may have been accurate, and we were warned that if we left the building during the interval, we would be refused re-entry. The performance started with Sprinkle introducing herself and going on to explain the purpose and function of some of the stranger looking and more obscure sex aids on the set. Explaining that she loves to be photographed and filmed, she invited us up on stage to take photos, arranging herself on the bed in a series of classic soft porn poses. This invitation was taken up by only two spectators, both male, one of them a gay man from my group. Significantly, the resulting photos were much less revealing and less provocative than my memory of this moment suggested. The rest of the first half was mainly dedicated to Sprinkle's transformation from dull, inhibited Ellen Steinberg to outrageous, exhibitionistic porn star Annie Sprinkle. This process was demonstrated through a series of before and after slides, which paralleled the before and after pictures from her 'transformation salon', shown later in the piece. Sprinkle explained the pros and cons of her life as a professional sex worker, introducing charts and diagrams containing 'pornstistics', such as 'Why I Did It', 'Hours Worked per Week', 'Amount of Cock Sucked'. She made it clear that while the financial rewards were important and not inconsiderable, she also found the work fun and enjoyed it for its own sake. After a brief interlude of 'dancing tits', enacted, if I remember correctly, to the music of the sugarplum fairy from *The Nutcracker Suite*, this section climaxed with Sprinkle peeing and then douching herself over the toilet, before inviting us to view her cervix in what she termed the 'Public Cervix Announcement'. Just before douching, she asked a member of the audience to help her off with her knickers, explaining this is a difficult task to accomplish by yourself without losing your balance if, like her, you happen to be wearing nine-inch stilettos. My position in the audience made me an obvious choice for her 'helper', and she allowed me to keep her black nylon knickers as a souvenir. Since we were expecting it, my mixed sex group was first up to view her cervix, and eventually about half the audience, male and female, lined up to see this part of Sprinkle's anatomy. The mood of the second part of the show was generally more sombre, partly because early on Sprinkle performed '100 Blow Jobs', an act that touches on the negative side of her experience in the sex industry. For this Sprinkle used a rack of different sized dildos, forcing her own head down on to them, to the accompaniment of a tape of male voices shouting abuse. Although she said she no longer found this enactment distressing, at the end of this sequence her eyes and nose were running and she took several moments to recover. Sprinkle then turned to her evolution from Annie to Anya, sex goddess and sacred prostitute. She showed slides and told anecdotes to demonstrate the enormous variety of types of lover that she has had over the years, many of whom were clients. These included one large black dog (not a client), people of all sexes, sexualities and races, and the whole range of physical types, including amputees and one man with extensive scarring all over his body from severe burns. One of these lovers, 'Les', was a female to male transsexual who had had a penis constructed but also retained his/her female genitalia, and Sprinkle spoke of having run into trouble for exhibiting Les at Coney Island Funfair. She then turned to the impact of HIV on her personal and professional life, her own escape from infection and the discovery of tantric 'safe sex' with one of her lovers who had full-blown Aids. In order to demonstrate this technique she masturbated and appeared to achieve multiple orgasm live on stage.

It would be an understatement to say that *Post Post Porn Modernist* is clearly a very different sort of show from *The Double Wedding* and *How to Shop*, and the framing of my brief description of the piece, in terms of a more personal account than I offered for the other two shows, has already started to reflect this difference. However, there are similarities between the way I have interpreted these two other shows and the fashion in which Sprinkle's performances have been analysed and discussed by other critics. For example, Linda Williams and Chris Straayer, in *Dirty Looks* (1993), read a number of Sprinkle's performances through Judith Butler's conceptualisation of gender as performative and her articulation of a political strategy of 'subversive repetition' in *Gender Trouble* (1990). Sprinkle's story of transformation from one identity to another, her 'repetition' in performance of certain types of roles and subject positions such as the 'hooker with a heart of gold', is perceived as a deconstructive strategy that operates to confuse, if not dissolve, the boundaries between good girl/whore, subject/object, masculine/

feminine, commodity/agent and heterosexual/homosexual. For these authors she is identified as using parody and pastiche to 'denaturalise', or rather to unveil, the theatrical, constructed nature of these identities. As I indicated in chapter one, it was under the influence of *Gender Trouble* that Linda Williams described Sprinkle's performance of 'Anya' as 'an imitation not unlike that of a drag queen' (Williams 1993: 187).

Paradoxically, while Sprinkle is defined as revealing the instability of the identities she performs, the subjectivity of both the actual and the implied spectator figured as engaging in her work by Williams, Straayer and others seems to be remarkably consistent and coherent. This may be because Sprinkle's shows tend to be discussed in the context of the sex industry and the discourse of pornography. In another chapter in *Dirty Looks*, subtitled 'Pornography's Academic Market', Jennifer Wicke points out that most academic analyses of pornographic works focus on the artefact as a site of stable meanings which are passively consumed, rather than on the reception of texts by individual readers and spectators (Wicke 1993: 68–71). While this is not *entirely* true of either Williams or Straayer, ultimately they both do tend to focus on Sprinkle as the producer of meanings and (re)discover exactly the same strategies and significations through time and across a range of different productions, in a manner that seems to suggest that these texts, their effects and the spectator on whom they operate are timeless, fixed and stable. In short, any 'subversion' is deemed to be intentional and accredited to Sprinkle as 'author', in a fashion that belies my description in chapter one of this piece as 'writerly'. This may actually be a consequence of the specific subject positions from which Straayer and Williams are writing and the conditions of viewing the material. Both operate chiefly within the field of film studies, an area dominated by psychoanalytic theory, so that while they draw on Butler to define gender as a socio-cultural phenomenon, both Williams and Straayer continue to discuss spectatorship in terms of universal 'male' and 'female' positions, privileging sex as foundational and conditioning all other identities. Wicke also indicates that the single generic term 'pornography' elides the differences between the enormous range of artefacts that are being produced and consumed, and a similar elision takes place in Straayer's and Williams's writings. Although both refer to a range of different types of Sprinkle texts, including her live performances, the formal distinctions between these texts and the varying relationships they construct between artefact and spectator are barely acknowledged. This seems a significant oversight, since it underestimates the distinction between consuming such work in the 'social' space of live performance as opposed to the 'private' space of the home viewing of videos or the anonymous darkness of the cinema auditorium. As a result, they fail to take account of the difference between the way in which, in the electronic media, the look of the camera directs and controls the gaze of the viewer and the 'tripartite' relationship operating in theatrical performance, where the look of the spectator is both freer and more likely to be distracted by their surroundings. Equally, they overlook the effect on the spectator of the episodes of audience participation that are a significant feature of Sprinkle's live work.

As I hope will become clear by the end of this chapter, it is not my intention to criticise these authors, only to establish the differences between my spectatorial position and theirs. In fact, even though I am going to place as much stress on the consumption of the artefact as the artefact itself, my reading will repeat important aspects of their analyses. I wish, then, to focus on how Sprinkle's live performance might be described as producing shifting and contradictory identifications in the *spectator*, in a manner that might produce a defamiliarisation through which they become aware of their own identity as discursively constructed. I have, of course, already engaged with this issue in relation to *The Double Wedding* and *How to Shop*, but in some ways this has been explored rather more in theory than in practice. Although I have acknowledged that the meaning of these shows may be very much a matter of individual interpretation, I have not pursued and explored in any detail the fact that the majority of the time 'I' am 'the' interpreter in question and therefore the subjectivity from which my own interpretations are produced. To put it another way, I have avoided offering much in the way of personal or autobiographical details that might illuminate and contextualise my own response to the shows. There are some good reasons for this and some not so good excuses.

Autobiography has always had an important place within all types of feminist practice and criticism. In the 1960s and 1970s, 'consciousness raising' stressed the importance of women sharing their experiences in order to understand that these experiences were not only personal and individual but were political, produced and affected by the prevailing social and cultural structures and systems. By the 1980s, under the influence of postmodernism and poststructuralism, there was a growing wariness in academic circles concerning autobiography as a literary and theatrical form. This wariness was based on a reaction against the traditional, modernist view of this form as the transparent product of a rational, stable subject, presumed to have the ability to stand 'outside' the social and cultural structures and signifying systems in order to uncover and communicate the 'truth' about themselves and the world in which they lived. Paradoxically, this same period saw a significant number of feminist and postmodernist academics starting to draw on overtly personal and autobiographical material in the writing of criticism. Such strategies were intended to deconstruct the notion of 'academic objectivity' and show that, in Bordo's terms, all viewing is 'perspectival and centric', informed and shaped by the particular subject position of the viewer (Bordo 1995: 222). As Nicole Ward Jouve put it, there was a realisation that all criticism is a 'scrambled form of autobiography, which seeks to conceal the self in writing' (Ward Jouve 1991: 37). Criticism that abandoned the traditional, supposedly inclusive, yet actually exclusive, academic 'we' in favour of 'I', and acknowledged that the positioning of the writer in terms of race, class, age, sex and sexuality inevitably coloured and inflected their work, was considered more honest and less authoritarian. Ironically, within some stratas of academia, this sort of attempt at self-revelation rapidly became a received convention standing for a new sort of 'transparency', a new, better and more 'truthful' way of writing. In its more sophisticated form, the writer using this approach foregrounds the instability of their own subjectivity. As such, they try to point up the fact that if criticism is 'like' autobiography, it is because both are already mimetic, always already inside the various 'fictions' that performatively construct our experience and can never finally reveal the truth about the 'self', or anything else. In both cases, consciously or unconsciously, this device, at times, took on the nature of a double bluff, masking the fact that while the authority of the writer was apparently being undermined, this authority was actually, performatively, being reinstated in a manner very difficult to challenge. Even though they were always drawing on and so reinforcing the authority of a particular body of theory on the nature of subjectivity and the world, often implicitly represented, as Bordo might say, as an unimpeachably pure, theoretical position, the writer was, after all, supposedly not generalising. They were only talking about *their* interpretation, which was not even 'theirs' in the first place. It is difficult to contest such interpretations because there is no 'one' to argue with and the theories deployed leave no grounds from which to argue. At their very worst, such strategies can represent an evasion of responsibility for the part the writer as an individual plays in the reproduction of both self and society. At their very best, they represent an attempt to accept the ways in which we are all at some level reproducing 'authority' and the acknowledgement of 'agency', despite the problem of having to constantly renegotiate what this might imply. This is to concede that the personal is still political and to embrace the obligation this places on the individual in the ongoing, collective struggle over meanings. It is in terms of this latter principle that I have interpreted Baker's use of autobiographical material in *How to Shop*. It is on the same basis (I hope) that, despite my reticence over personal details, I have for much of this book been drawing on critical approaches that deploy such strategies. However, if I have failed to engage with them fully it is because, like Susan Bordo as cited in the last chapter, I remain suspicious of too ready a perception of a dissolution or transcendence of borders, whether between performance and performativity, academic criticism and autobiography, or theory and practice. While in theory such distinctions may be artificial, and playing on the border between criticism, autobiography and fiction can most definitely be a useful 'deconstructive strategy', there are dangers as well as advantages in breaching borders, not least that all differences may be appropriated to the same, single authority or metanarrative. When 'like' is taken too easily to mean 'equivalent to', the complexity of the power relations that govern our daily lives can be underestimated, and we can end up back where we started, reinstating by other means that which we wished to subvert.

Having said this, I am also aware that at times my failure to locate myself more concretely in relation to my readings of *The Double Wedding* and *How to Shop* may have still given a false impression of 'professional' objectivity. To concentrate on just one of many possible examples, my Roman Catholic upbringing makes me feel certain that Baker's use of religious imagery in *How to Shop* is influenced largely by British Protestantism. If I am correct in this assumption, since it is my (rejected) Catholicism which informs and conditions my own response to this iconography, my understanding of its significance in the show may in fact differ in crucial ways from Baker's and many other audience members. This is fair enough, but my failure to reveal this may have dissembled the perspectival and therefore unreliable nature of my account. In discussing *How to Shop* and *The Double Wedding*, it is only too easy for me to underestimate the significance of this type of difference. Even while I have been talking about dis-identification, unreadability and incoherence, I actually identify fairly strongly with Baker and English and certain aspects of their work by dint of race, nationality, class and fields of interest, before even considering sex and gender. In my youth, I, too, sometimes shopped on Sidcup High Street and was an avid fan of Paris Lido style variety shows, live or on television, and indeed of Danny La Rue. As a prepubescent both the 'real' showgirls and 'showgirl drag' seemed to me to represent exactly the same wholly desirable model for femininity: I yearned to wear those frocks, those feathers, those wigs and gorgeous paste jewels – who was interested in what was underneath? This may, one way or another, say a great deal about my arguments in this book. More recently, when I go to see shows by English and Baker in London or Manchester, I am often familiar with by sight, if not to talk to, some of the audience as well as the performers on stage because to a large extent we are part of the same 'world'. As a result, even though I might define these shows as 'writerly', if not undecidable, I have felt confident in offering relatively 'authoritative' interpretations of both *The Double Wedding* and *How to Shop*, even if I know this authority may be founded on illusory transitivity. For all sorts of reasons, it was much harder for me to identify with Annie Sprinkle. This may have created a much more fundamental distancing or defamiliarising effect than those I have described as operating in these other shows. Certainly, in the course of *Post Post Porn Modernist* I found myself forcibly becoming aware of and questioning some of the pre-existing assumptions I held not only about her practice but also about my own subjectivity, in a far more challenging and confusing fashion than I had experienced with the British pieces. The outcome of this is that my reading of *Post Post Porn Modernist* is more obviously personal and maybe even less 'coherent' than my readings of *The Double Wedding* and *How to Shop*. Without doubt this uncertainty, although not necessarily entirely a matter of Sprinkle's author's intentions, is partly due to the nature of the piece. As Michel Foucault has argued, sexuality might, like gender and/or sex, be a discursive construct, but in this part of the twentieth century both sex and sexuality are still perceived by most subjects to be at the very 'core' of their identity. It is on a similar basis that Liz Kotz warns in another chapter of *Dirty Looks*,

> pornography represents a place where distance breaks down, where subjectivity is insistently engaged, even uncomfortably so. Even its incorporation into a project of critique is notoriously unstable, since even the most determined efforts to reframe pornographic representations as objects of a politically motivated examination, can go deeply awry, subverting authorial intentions in fascinating if problematic ways. (Kotz 1993: 107)

To a large extent this quote sums up my argument as both stated and 'performed' in this chapter, but if this statement is accurate, the same principle must hold for any 'politically motivated intentions' Sprinkle might have as an 'author'.

It is important to note that my own entry and access to Sprinkle's work has always been framed in relation to 'live art and performance', rather than specifically to pornography. A key text in the formation of this context is the section on Sprinkle in Elinor Fuchs's article for *The Drama Review*, 'Staging the Obscene Body', in which she analyses Sprinkle's contribution to Schechner's show *The Prometheus Project* (Fuchs 1989). Re-reading this article after seeing *Post Post Porn Modernist*, it struck me that what Fuchs is describing and acknowledging throughout is a sense of instability, if not crisis, produced by her own fluctuating identifications and dis-identifications in relation to Sprinkle. At one point, Fuchs describes an episode in which Sprinkle invited the audience to examine her labia and describe their colour and texture, an offer taken up by male spectators only. Fuchs's response to this is strong and personal:

> I shrink back from the spectacle in my seat, filled with rage at Schechner who is submitting me and other women to this assault on our bodies via this alien medium this ... who is she? Is she a woman like me? [...] the act becomes more threatening as Sprinkle offers to give a little demonstration of cock sucking. By now blind to critical judgement, whatever might be the case, I feel violated and furious at my entrapment. (Fuchs 1989: 43–4)

Psychoanalysts could have a field day with this quote. For Fuchs, Sprinkle's literal demonstration of her 'castration' to the male spectators seems to reveal the phallic imposture that has occurred, in the process of her taking up of the position of speaking subject within this performance. This unveiling discloses the fact that Sprinkle only 'has the phallus' on loan from Schechner, the absent, true 'author' of this act, so that Sprinkle is remarked as appearing to 'be' the phallus in relation to Schechner's 'having' of the phallus. In this 'part', as an 'alien medium', metonymically Sprinkle is used to effect an 'assault', a 'violation' on the women in the audience. Fuchs asks the question, 'Is she a woman like me?', apparently putting Sprinkle's sex into question and constructing her as different at the very moment when Sprinkle is offering biological proof of their similarity. Does Fuchs deny identification because it reminds her of her own positioning of 'being the phallus', her own erasure within the symbolic and so she 'shrinks' back? Certainly there is a loss of self, since when the 'real' penis threatens to enter the act, Fuchs finds herself 'blind to critical judgement', feels trapped and in the next sentence speaks of the impossibility of 'recaptur[ing] our autonomy'. Both in the specificity of the language and in the play between repudiation and identification it suggests, this mirrors Freud's account of the female experience at the Oedipal stage to an extraordinary degree. Within Freudian theory, the necessary transference of desire from the mother as primary love object to the 'father' takes place for the female subject through a simultaneous act of identification and dis-identification. She identifies with the mother, in so far as she recognises that they are both 'castrated' – there is literally 'nothing to see' in terms of their genitalia. This provokes a turning away from the mother in disgust, which is implicitly an act of self-disgust, to focus her libidinal energy on the father who can give her what she needs in order to compensate for her awareness of her own castration and subsequent penis envy. However, this in turn involves a further identification with the mother because for Freud this compensation, which is deferred until later, is not represented in terms of sexual relations with the father but by the promise that the daughter will become a mother herself (see Freud 1925, 1931, 1933). Is Fuchs's reaction of rage entirely directed at Schechner as the 'Father' and true author of this act or also at Sprinkle as the 'Mother', who is revealed as castrated and only exercising phallic authority through her relation to the Father?

It is interesting that while Sprinkle's later performances, including *Post Post Porn Modernist*, detail her own identity shifts in terms of traditional female archetypes, the Virgin (Ellen), the Whore (Annie) and the Goddess/Witch (Anya), there is no explicit reference to 'the Mother'. As with Freudian and Lacanian theory, then, there seems to be a repudiation or dis-identification from the 'maternal feminine', a disassociation said to be necessary for both sexes for the institution of 'proper', adult subjectivity. Yet, the apparent absence of this archetype seems to engender it, intertextually, as a powerful presence for the spectator. So Chris Straayer describes Sprinkle's subversive repetition of the 'whore' persona in terms of a 'collapsing' of Freud's mother vs. prostitute dichotomy through the figure of 'the mothering prostitute'. This seems to occur only for the 'male' spectator, since to support this argument she cites Chuck Kleinhans's assertion that,

> In (decidedly non Lacanian) Oedipal terms: she enacts the nurturing mother who encourages sexual exploration: a figure who allays performance anxiety while encouraging voyeurism as part of an acquisition of knowledge that can create a new straight male sexual subject. (Kleinhans, quoted in Straayer 1993: 161)

According to both Kleinhans and Straayer, the benefit here for the *female* spectator, who seems to have no need of either nurturing or knowledge, is apparently that the 'new', straight, male subject produced is one that they can 'comfortably live with' (Straayer 1993: 161).

A similar sort of collapse of the 'mother vs. prostitute dichotomy' could be described as occurring during the 'Public Cervix Announcement', when Sprinkle offered her cervix to the gaze of the audience by means of a speculum, an act which is the closest equivalent in *Post Post Porn Modernist* to the *Prometheus Project*'s labia episode. This body part is normally scrutinised in a medical rather than pornographic context, and it also has stronger Oedipal connotations than the labia since viewing the cervix is literally the closest we can come to seeing 'where we come from'. As a result, I am tempted to make much of the fact that looking at Sprinkle's cervix, I noted that it could described as looking like a blind(ed) eye, in so far as it was round and pink, with a red spot in the middle and veins radiating outwards. Sprinkle also remarked that this act is intended to prove that 'there are no teeth up there', a comment which did place it in relation to the discourse of psychoanalysis and framed it as aimed at a *male* subject in need of education and reassurance. As such, it offered the 'female' spectator the choice of either identifying with, and therefore accepting for herself, the role of mothering/prostitute for the male heterosexual subject or possibly, as with the earlier labia episode of repudiating this 'mother', inducing a sort of re-enactment of the female Oedipal crises.

Actually, as a feminist academic, I was tempted to read this moment, and indeed Kleinhans's assertion, through Luce Irigaray's discussion of the female subject as the 'sex which is not one' developed in *Speculum of the Other Woman* (1985a). This is, of course, a work that subversively repeats certain discourses mainly drawn from or related to psychoanalytical theory, in order to reveal the groundlessness of the authorities on which they are based. Irigarary employs the speculum as a central metaphor to indicate the means by which the male spectator/theorist/philosopher ostensibly considers 'woman' but actually perceives and describes only his own reflection. It is possible, then, to read this showing of the cervix as a 'subversive repetition' or even parody, revealing the absence of 'woman' within patriarchal discourse, except as a mirror for the male subject, the mimetic double to the male original, or, to put it another way, as a man in drag. Sprinkle appears to promise the male spectator 'enlightenment', a full disclosure of Freud's 'dark continent', and indeed the viewing of the cervix is facilitated by means of a torch. Yet at the moment of seeing the maternal place of origin, what this male spectator sees looking back at him is the blinded eye, a reflection of himself as Oedipus, the subject of the psychoanalytical tragedy.

Some time after seeing *Post Post Porn Modernist* and after completing several drafts of this chapter, I came across Rebecca Schneider's *The Explicit Body in Performance* (1997) and her discussion of this moment in Sprinkle's work seen at The Kitchen in New York. Although she implies that she approached this moment in search of some sort of reciprocal 'female gaze', her experience confirms an Irigarayan interpretation affirming the positioning of 'woman' as the 'blind spot', the unreadable or unintelligible within our cultural symbolic. She also likens Sprinkle's cervix to an 'eye' and found that queuing up to view it reminded her of waiting as a child to receive communion from the hands of her father, a Methodist minister. For her, this memory produced a chain of associations between the literal everyday family and the symbolic religious and psychoanalytical family models in a manner that appeared to restate and underline her excluded, 'abject' position as a 'daughter'. It is possible, in support of my own thesis concerning the intertextual presence of the 'absent' mother in *Post Post Porn Modernist*, to perform something of a slippery critical, double movement on Schneider's comments. Reading them through Kristeva's theory of 'the abject' in terms of its relationship to Christianity and the Eucharist explored in chapter four, it is possible to suggest that Schneider is also 'unconsciously' responding to the way in which the abject body of the absent (M)other is simultaneously remarked and erased through the 'body' of the communion wafer.

Yet, as I indicated in the last chapter, to define 'the abject' solely in terms of the maternal feminine is once again to privilege sexual difference at the expense of all other differences, an abiding problem even with theories that deploy psychoanalytical theory deconstructively. It is one of the central, and perhaps implicitly the most revealing, paradoxes of this book, that considering how much space I have dedicated to psychoanalytical theory, I am not by any means a 'believer' or even a fellow traveller of this discourse in any mode. As such, I do not feel comfortable with a 'collapse' of differences into sexual difference, families into 'the' family, mothers into 'the' (M)other, Oedipal or otherwise, nor women into 'the' feminine or into 'the female spectator', an identity position defined purely in relation to 'the' heterosexual male subject. Neither do I feel much reassured by Irigaray's and Lacan's suggestion that there may be an autonomous female subjectivity 'elsewhere', since 'here' is the place I have to live, or even by Schneider's concept of the 'blind spot', since for me this suggests a place where people get run down and killed. In short, like Fuchs at the labia episode, this section in *Post Post Porn Modernist* threatens to leave me feeling 'trapped' and robbed of autonomy and of agency. Sprinkle's address to the male subject implicitly positioned me as a 'female' spectator within a psychoanalytical discourse that demanded I either identify with or repudiate Sprinkle as the Oedipal mother. Within this discourse, the terms of both an identification and dis-identification are already decided in advance as either evidence of the acceptance of my own castration or a sign of my own self-disgust and penis envy.

Alternatively, since in principle 'the Mother' is only cited intertextually within Sprinkle's performance, its absence leaves space for the interpolation of the viewing subject – in short, for the production of a Mother other than Freud's Oedipal mother and the later variants on this theme. In my own case, during the 'Public Cervix Announcement', I found myself resisting the psychoanalytic frame, through reference to my own mother, Peggy, which, paradoxically, due to the particularity of her social identity, simultaneously reinforced and undermined a collapse of women into 'Woman' and mothers into 'the Mother'. It so happens that Peggy was a district midwife, engaged in home deliveries for over forty years. Reference to the cervix always evokes for me the phrase, overheard several times a week, 'the cervix is three fingers dilated', indicating the imminence of her departure for work and so synecdochically standing for her professional and social role in our local community. This professional role embedded in a specific time, locale and set of everyday practices produces a surplus identity that cannot be contained by the generalised figure of the Oedipal mother, just as the recounting of the specific details of her life as a sex worker in the United States in the 1980s produces a gap between Sprinkle and the concept of 'the Whore' as an archetype. On the other hand, midwifery, like prostitution, is regarded as an archetypically female realm, and the midwife as a figure has often been celebrated as an embodiment of specifically 'female' power and knowledge in a similar fashion to Sprinkle's reclaiming of the sacred prostitute. Since, as it dilates, the cervix becomes increasingly impossible to 'see' and so must be measured by touch, this itself invites the production of an essentialist, reverse discourse that opposes the 'male' privileging of sight in psychoanalytical theory as the source of knowledge with a 'female' language and knowledges based on 'touch' or contiguity. At the time (I think), I felt myself both resisting the collapse of my identity into the universal psychoanalytical 'female' spectator, by reference to my own identification with Peggy as a historical, social being, and simultaneously being drawn back into that position through the very specificity of that experience. The same double movement occurred with Sprinkle's performance as 'whore', in that the specificity of her own socio-historical subjectivity, her 'individuality', throws the constructed nature of this category into relief. Yet, in turn, the very force of this 'individuality', indicating a person of enormous wit and charm, encourages an identification with her for 'the female spectator', which threatens to obscure the specificity of her experience. My positioning was, then, neither entirely that of the universal 'female' spectator, nor entirely individuated and socially specific, neither fully escaping the psychoanalytic discourse, nor remaining within it, but rather moving between these positions in a contradictory and indeed confused manner. This produced not a 'collapse' of opposite categories but a hiatus, a moment of hesitation and indecision, of being aware of the inherent, internal contradiction in any position I might take up in relation to this act.

I think that in 'Staging the Obscene Body', Fuchs describes a similar sense of hesitation, indecision, contradiction and confusion, but this is both obscured and ultimately deepened by the fact that within this piece she defines herself in advance as 'the female spectator'. She then becomes caught up in a number of paradoxes produced through the clash of the specificity of her socio-cultural subjectivity in conflict with this blanket categorisation. As a feminist, she wishes to express a solidarity with Sprinkle in which they are both defined as female in opposition to Schechner and the male spectators. As such, she does not want to 'take away Sprinkle's voice' and 'deny her female authorship', and later she claims for Sprinkle the position of speaking subject as a 'successful working woman' (Fuchs 1989: 44). Yet at the same time Fuchs feels that this performance includes the 'visual rape and sexual objectification of my body by identification' (44). In this instance it seems that the giving of a voice and of authority to one woman is bought at the price of violence towards another.

This same double bind also operates later in the article, when she describes another performance in which Sprinkle shows before and after slides from her 'transformation salon' where 'ordinary' women are transformed into 'porn stars', a section also repeated within *Post Post Porn Modernist*. Fuchs analyses this as a 'dare' to the 'good girl' female spectator to examine 'her own self division':

> The female spectator, who energetically defends herself against being projected into the role as the other of male fantasy, is shown an image of her own replication of that pattern, her co-operation with it, in her own deepest terror of being contaminated by the other side of female life. Here she is caught before men with her 'other' showing (her other, 'other'). (Fuchs 1989: 52–3)

Watching *Post Post Porn Modernist* I found these images deeply depressing. 'Before', these *were* women 'like me' in so far as they were all very different, their bodies, hairstyles and methods of presenting themselves to the camera all telling different and complex stories. 'After', their individuality was wiped out, reduced to the banal, repetitive iconography of basques, crotchless panties, big hair and soft focus that supposedly represent 'sexual fantasy' within our culture. Yet, like Fuchs, I recognised that a dis-identification from these 'bad girl' images might easily support a cultural system that constructs certain identity positions and then defines those who inhabit them as 'abject'. Moreover, who am I (a middle class, white, lapsed Catholic, British feminist academic) to deny the validity of this experience as a liberating one for Sprinkle and these other women?

This part of the act *may* be read as a deconstructive comment on the construction of 'whore' and indeed a collapse of the categories 'good' girl/porn star, revealing how women are kept in a state of socially approved sexual 'goodness' through the terror of the possible consequences of being nominated as 'whore'. Yet, the much quoted phrase that accompanies this section of the show, 'There may not be a little bit of porn star in you but there is a little bit of you in every porn star', suggests a more essentialist view, in which intra-gender differences are always already subsumed within sexual difference. Like Fuchs in the labia episode, once again I felt a sense of 'entrapment' in that, as a 'feminist' spectator, I was being positioned so as to identify with these images but the framing of the episode demanded an identification with the 'after' pictures (woman as same), not the 'before' (women as different from each other). For me, the manner in which this socially and culturally constructed division between good girl/bad girl is produced, enforced, naturalised and internalised remained unquestioned and uncontested.

In a fashion very similar to Freud's description of the female experience of the Oedipal stage, it seems to me that Fuchs's comment on these pictures forecloses the terms of identity and identification in advance. The category 'women' is simultaneously represented by Fuchs as singular, embracing all women in a shared identity, and yet internally divided, embracing oppositional identities. However, since these divisions are defined solely in relation to, and only become apparent before and *for*, the single and 'whole' category 'men', any other differences *between* the women or indeed other divisions *within* these women cannot be explored and are in fact erased.

In other parts of her article, Fuchs does acknowledge intra-gender differences, clearly indicating that some of her ambivalence towards Sprinkle stems from 'class discomfort'. At one point she indicates a difference between seeing this type of work at the Performing Garage, one of New York's best known performance art spaces, as opposed to a burlesque hall. In the latter venue, she can become an 'invisible masquerading spectator of a separate male culture with its different kind of female' whereas 'in this space Sprinkle had entered my world'. In this, Fuchs's own world, Fuchs's own identity becomes constructed primarily through her sexual difference so that, 'If Sprinkle represented a female other, she was also not other enough' (Fuchs 1989: 47).

Ironically, it is partly Fuchs's class and cultural alliance with the male spectators and her *own* identity as 'working woman' which she must suppress in order to identify with Sprinkle, that 'return' to rob her of autonomy. When Fuchs asks, 'Is she a woman like me?', the answer is no, because this 'like me' means a feminist academic who studies 'performance'. As such, she probably has as much, if not more, in common with Schechner and many of the other male spectators in this venue than she does with Sprinkle. In this context, if the male spectators were 'other', they too were not 'other enough'. While it is her sex identification which creates her sensation of violation, it is this unexplored class identification, the internalised conformity to its codes of behaviour, that partly causes her 'entrapment' and prevents her protesting against this 'assault'. At the moment when Sprinkle exhibits her labia, Fuchs feels *physically* trapped because 'the seating configuration of the Performing Garage adds an element of coercion, it is impossible to recapture our autonomy and walk out of the theatre without crossing the playing area' (Fuchs 1989: 44). The impossibility of this act arises from the fact that she would have to transgress the social norms of this, her world, by which the audience do not disrupt the show and do not enter the playing space during the performance, except by invitation of the performers. Moreover, to do so would be to realise a threat to her *own* identity as a 'worker', that is already immanent in any identification she makes with Sprinkle. To physically enter the stage space would be to become 'a performer', the object of the critical gaze rather than an invisible spectator, and, ironically, to figure just as she does here in my own reading of *Post Post Porn Modernist* as part of the show. While it is her sex identification with Sprinkle which creates her sense of violation, it is these other unacknowledged differences from Sprinkle that render her powerless in her seat.

I hope that if, by some chance, Elinor Fuchs ever reads this analysis of her essay written well over a decade ago, she will forgive me if I seem to be scoring what, in retrospect, are easy points at her expense. Actually, I have undertaken this exposition primarily in order to explore why and how it was that, in watching *Post Post Porn Modernist*, I found myself frequently perceiving Sprinkle as not 'a woman like me', in a manner that both repeats and differs from Fuchs's experience. Before the show started, I asked the female friend next to me if she intended to join in the audience participation sections of the show, and she answered, 'You don't go to the fairground if you are not going to go on the rides.' Clearly, as Sprinkle's reference to having exhibited her lover 'Les' at Coney Island implies, there are aspects of the show that could be described as deliberately playing on and foregrounding the sort of voyeurism that operates in the traditional fairground or carnival 'sideshow'. Indeed, with reference to Mikhail Bakhtin, the central problem posed by Sprinkle's work seems to be whether it represents 'genuine' or 'licensed' carnival, inoculation or liberation. So, for example, Rose Ilett has written about Sprinkle's use of photographic imagery of some of her lovers/clients who have disabilities in terms of a deliberate shock effect which objectifies these subjects in an insidious way, reinforcing rather than subverting negative attitudes towards people with disabilities (Ilett 1994).

If my friend's remark struck me and remained in my mind, it is also because, as my description of the show at the head of this chapter was intended to imply, my companions and I did approach this show from the very first in some sort of spirit of the carnival. This spirit had a sense of fun and liberation about it but also more than a whiff of voyeurism, and this voyeurism related to 'class' in a fashion that includes but also exceeds the mode in which this term tends to signify in Bakhtinian influenced theory. I did 'go on the rides', helping Sprinkle to remove her knickers, queuing to see her cervix and paying for a 'tits on the head' photo. Yet, despite this participation, like Fuchs in the burlesque hall, I was at times aware of engaging in some sort of masquerade as a spectator of a separate culture, and this was not entirely related to Sprinkle's identity as a former sex professional. Although Sprinkle is now clearly defined as a performance artist, the world in which this show took place was still more 'mine' than hers because she is a North American and this was Glasgow and I am British. Before the event and throughout the piece Sprinkle was always, on some level, the object of my curious gaze as exotic North American other, part of a wild and whacky New York scene which I had read about but never experienced directly. In short, any identification I had with her as a female spectator was always potentially being alienated through the distancing lens of national identity.

In New York, Fuchs read Sprinkle's selling of souvenir items in the foyer in positive terms as evidence of her 'undismissable' subjectivity as an independent business woman. In Britain, this entrepreneurial activity signified in the same manner but also seemed the natural extension of a performance that constituted a classic narrative of the American dream. This is a story of commercial and artistic success based on the virtues of individual enterprise, self-determination and self-discovery, a reading reinforced by a statement in the programme notes which appropriates the format of the American constitution, to claim the right to sexual freedoms. Since this show is 'post post modern', it may well deliberately inhabit this territory as an ironic, subversive repetition. However, the term 'post post modern' is ambiguous and may in fact indicate a return to the very 'modernist' values that produced this American cultural myth, and so it is impossible to say whether this myth was being celebrated or critiqued, restated, parodied or pastiched. What is clear is that this particular reading of the performance is thrown into relief by viewing it in a British/European context. From this position, America is inevitably the 'other', usually the 'new' world (copy) to Europe's 'old' world (original), the 'hyperreal' to Europe's 'real', and it is no coincidence that two of the chief theorists of 'hyperreality', Jean Baudrillard and Umberto Eco, are both Europeans who developed their theories primarily through reference to examples drawn from North American culture. Equally, it is not surprising that for me much of *Post Post Porn Modernist*, particularly the 'serious', cathartic ending, did seem like sideshow shamanism and licensed carnival rather than genuine subversion or transgression. Nor is it surprising that I perceived much of the show as being staged within and through the discourse of psychoanalysis, since while this theory was 'invented' in Europe, it was in the US that it first took hold of the popular imagination and became part of many people's everyday life.

Within the show, any negative aspects of Sprinkle's experience are recuperated through the framing of the account teleologically as a narrative of progress towards self-realisation and self-improvement. The exploring of different archetypal identities corresponds rather neatly to the Jungian process of achieving psychological 'health' and wholeness through the process designated 'differentiation'. So the self-revelatory nature of the performance in itself becomes therapeutic, with Sprinkle describing the continual re-enactment of '100 Blow Jobs' as a means by which she has been able to transcend the pain it represented. Sprinkle's recounting of her own experience of the positive, physical, spiritual and economic benefits of sex combined proselytising and salesmanship in a manner that recalled the uses of personal testimony in American charismatic evangelical services, wild west medicine shows and talk shows on the lines of *Oprah.* As evinced in the programme notes, which includes '101 Uses For Sex, Or Why Sex Is So Important' placed alongside a price list for a number of souvenirs and products, sex is being sold as a magic elixir, a cure all for the problems of existence in the late twentieth century.

In short, rather than identifying with Sprinkle as a 'female' spectator, mostly I found myself denying Sprinkle's authorship and dismissing her subjectivity, perceiving her as an effect, rather than a critic of certain cultural myths. At the same time I became aware that these perceptions arose out of the part of my own subjectivity that is constructed through another set of imperialist, nationalist cultural myths. Watching the show, then, defamiliarised an aspect of my own subjectivity, in such a way as to leave me feeling robbed of my sense of autonomy as a 'unique' individual, since it was clear that this identity was so naturalised and internalised that I was unable to leave that seat. This sense of cultural and national difference became most acute at the literal and theatrical climax of the show. This section was introduced by the recounting of the deaths of friends and lovers from Aids. Candles were lit in their names and the masturbation was offered up as a dual act of commemoration and reaffirmation of life. Clearly, it was impossible to consider these deaths in any sort of ironic or parodic light, and there was nothing throughout this entire section in Sprinkle's outward demeanour or in the reaction of the rest of the audience to suggest that any was intended. Sprinkle then recounted her discovery of tantric sex with one of these lovers and offered this as a model of 'safe sex'. Taking on the role of 'sacred prostitute', she donned a costume copied from her research into historical documents, rubbed fake blood on her body and described how she would achieve orgasm. All this occurred to an accompaniment of New Age music, which gradually became louder and more intense as the lights were dimmed. While I was moved by the motivation behind this action, I rapidly started to feel manipulated by a ritual which seemed as fake, inauthentic and 'hyperreal' as the blood. The style of the dress was Cleopatra via Frederick's of Hollywood, the music banal and obvious, and while Sprinkle had implied that orgasm would be achieved through the 'natural' means of meditation and breathing, she actually employed a number of oversized artificial aids.

However, the critical moment for me arose through becoming aware of an element of dissembling, if not outright 'fakery', in my own response. For this part of the show the audience had been given plastic cups filled with lentils and encouraged to shake them as an accompaniment to Sprinkle's masturbation, an action again presented as a detail of 'original rituals'. On several occasions she made direct eye contact with those of us on the front row and I found myself energetically shaking my plastic cup and nodding back in an encouraging fashion, indicating that I was 'with her' all the way. I also noticed my friends behaving in the same fashion. The incongruity between the (US-style) self-revelatory, 'therapeutic' transgressiveness of Sprinkle's performance and the wholly hypocritical (British) 'politeness' of my response made me want to laugh, but I suppressed this desire because of the seriousness with which Sprinkle seemed to be acting and the apparent concentration of the rest of the audience. The 'gaze' had been returned: this should in theory have been either a liberating or a challenging moment, one in which all sorts of taboos could be broken. Yet above all, like Fuchs, I was conforming to the social conventions of this space in which one participates only as and if required and does not laugh except by some sort of cue or prompting by the performer or the rest of the audience because to do so is to risk drawing attention to oneself, giving up one's anonymity and invisibility as an observer to become part of the show.

One of my party did experience this part of the show primarily as a 'female' spectator, because of *where she was sitting*. The unknown man next to her started to masturbate along with Sprinkle during the final phase of the performance. Clearly, the show liberated *him* from the social and sexual taboos of this space, but for *her* the intrusion of this 'real' penis left her (like Fuchs) positioned in opposition to this man as 'the female spectator', objectified by identification with Sprinkle. I was surrounded by and identifying with my mixed sex and sexuality peer group and so my subject position at this point was, for the most part, defined socially and culturally in opposition to Sprinkle. From this seat, in defining Sprinkle's ritual as 'fake', I am inevitably, implicitly, positioning myself as the arbiter of the original and the authentic, and this is not without all sorts of 'class' overtones relating to my professional identity as an academic and so one who is presumed to know about historical 'authenticity'. Yet, unlike Sprinkle, I have never studied 'sacred prostitutes' and therefore actually I am in no position to challenge her authority concerning their rituals or costumes, unless on the basis that I do not believe she has really undertaken this research. Why should I disbelieve her on this point, while apparently taking many of other things she says in the show at face value? Actually the joke is on me in a double sense since, by dint of my professional identity, I am only too aware, as Sprinkle must be by dint of hers, that 'pornography' and 'performance' and even 'history' are fields where it is foolish to start bandying about terms like 'authentic', 'truth' and 'real'. So, why is it that I found myself outside the theatre, on the one hand laughing at the 'fakery' of the ritual she had enacted and, on the other, seriously debating whether Sprinkle 'really' experienced multiple orgasm or only faked it? Why should this question even arise when, after all, throughout the piece I knew Sprinkle was *always* performing and made no bones about the fact that both 'Sprinkle' and 'Anya' are fictional personas? Perhaps, despite all my talk about the 'distancing' effect of nationality and class and all my feminist, postmodern, poststructuralist smarty pants theory, there must have been some part of me occupying the position of the customer who goes to the 'confessions' of the porn star or to the sideshow or to the theatre, seeking some sort of revelation of 'truth'. Indeed, I *did* go to this show thinking, arrogantly, that I could be an invisible spectator at this event, in a position to decide 'objectively' on the politics of this contested piece. Despite my protests above, I discovered that my subjectivity was engaged by this piece, even uncomfortably so, sending my intentions awry and creating a hiatus in which I was aware that any position I might take was haunted by its own internal contradiction. It may be, then, that watching *Post*

Post Porn Modernist, I 'unconsciously' deployed certain aspects of my identity as a means of maintaining a distinctly undeconstructive distance from this performance, refusing to take it seriously. In doing so, perhaps I was simply trying to protect myself from the 'menace' that an identification with Sprinkle might present to my own social and professional identity. Indeed, the marshalling of defences I have described throughout this chapter against just such an identification might suggest a double movement, a dis-identification in which an identification has already taken place and been disavowed. It may even be that, despite my comments above, the 'gaze' *was* returned and I was confronted with my own reflection as the 'other', who is also part of the same, seeing myself as a masquerader, a 'performer' always already inside the fiction from within which there is no stable place or concrete ground from which I can finally speak with authority – even about my own response to this show.

In any case, it remains impossible for me to say one way or another whether my response to this show accords with Sprinkle's 'authorial intentions'. There is evidence to support an argument that the piece demonstrates a highly sophisticated, postmodern understanding of processes of objectification and that the show deliberately and subversively reflects back the objectifying gaze, forcing the spectator to confront the performative nature of her own subjectivity. Yet, there is also evidence to support a modernist and 'essentialist' reading, in which the show is an attempt to communicate certain 'truths' about human nature, women, sex and sexuality, which are far more normative than subversive. Which reading might reflect Sprinkle's 'intentions' or whether she intends 'both at once' remains undecidable, a matter of interpretation that will always be haunted by its opposite possibility, not least because this 'Sprinkle' herself is already inside the fiction. This nomination refers to a performance in a show of the self-acknowledged double of someone called Ellen Steinberg, who in the course of this show doubles with 'Anya', another wholly theatrical persona.

I could of course claim that, as author, 'Sprinkle', whoever this refers to, is deliberately and consciously performing a Butlerian double movement. However, there is always a slight problem with such an assertion, whoever makes it. Butler is referring to the process that foregrounds '*différance*', the differential trace in any interpretation which undermines all and every authority, all and every authorial intention. To accredit the deliberate genesis of such a movement to the name 'Sprinkle' or any other is to effectively recuperate it to pre-existing authority. Ultimately, I think that this indicates the problematics of claiming such performances definitely 'for' or 'against' *any* single 'pure' political or theoretical position once and for all. Yet, I do think that some sort of double movement *potentially* takes place with this show, but it occurs through the interaction of the performance, its staging and the various, located 'I's of the beholder(s), and as such, to paraphrase Artaud, it is a gesture that never occurs, and so never signifies, in exactly the same way twice – hence the differences between my readings and those offered by Williams, Straayer, Fuchs, Schneider et al. Yet, if there are also similarities in our interpretations, as opposed to, say, Rose Ilett's, it is because we are all primarily reading as feminists: that is, we are all concerned with the way Sprinkle performs the identity category 'woman'. Conversely, Ilett's chief concern and point of (dis-)identification with the show is the way it represents people with disabilities as an identity category. As feminists, whatever our material or theoretical locations, at some level we are *all* reading as 'female spectators', or rather we are simultaneously inhabiting this identity category, while engaging in an ongoing debate with this show, each other and the culture of which we are part, over its meaning, limits and parameters. As a result, I believe my hesitations, indecisions and sense of defamiliarisation in watching *Post Post Porn Modernist* arose through a combination of the show itself, its staging within and through certain discourses, traditions, everyday practices and personal experiences, the specific conditions of viewing and my pre-existing assumptions, which together created a clash which highlighted certain aspects of my subjectivity which usually remain veiled. This clash eventually produced the recognition that if Sprinkle was not a woman like *me*, she was also *not a woman* – like me. For each of us the space of 'agency' exists at the point where, although we cannot escape this identity category, in very different and yet similarly contradictory ways, we cannot be wholly defined by it either. Contrary to the ways in which it is often represented, even in this book, this is not a comfortable place. Finding yourself there can produce an awareness of the fineness of the lines between intelligibility and incoherence, repetition and subversion, resistance and recuperation. This is a border where it is a matter of interpretation as to whether a woman being perceived as a man masquerading as a woman might imply a defamiliarisation of the sex/gender binaries, or that they are effectively being denied existence as a speaking subject. As such, this is a point where audience laughter might indicate a recognition of subversion or a dismissal of, as Baker puts it, 'the very important points you are trying to make' as non-sense. There are no guarantees, yet at the same time this position of 'agency' stills implies an ethical responsibility for the meanings you might make, even if, in the final analysis, they are outside your control and any authority you might have or call upon is groundless. I shall elucidate this difficult position in the conclusion.

Note

1 There is some variation in her shows, however, and this means that all references in this chapter to *Post Post Porn Modernist*, rather than early work, come entirely from my memory of seeing this production once and once only, and therefore details may be inaccurate.

Conclusion
Closing words, opening questions: ethical activism, the politics of undecidability and Rose English's *Tantamount Esperance*

The problem with conclusions is that they offer the temptation to make grand sweeping gestures, a temptation that appears to have increased with the approach of the millennium. For instance, over the last three decades, possibly in an attempt to emulate the grandeur of Nietzsche's famous declaration of the death of God at the end of the last century, numerous academics have announced the deaths or 'ends' of things. These have included history, the author, the subject, the social, the political, the 'real', feminism, deconstruction, even theory and indeed postmodernism. Actually, these obituaries are usually more like notices indicating a change of address, but the rhetoric of such pronouncements implies that such moves have definitely occurred and are permanent, and that these things can now be found in a 'new' location, directly opposite where they used to reside. History was once facts and is now fiction, the social has been subsumed by the cultural, the political has become a matter of fragmentation and individualism rather than communities, the author has been replaced by the reader or spectator, production has become consumption, the speaking subject has become a product of language, the real has become the hyperreal which is wholly mimetic, feminism has become post-feminism in which women apparently 'control' and celebrate their own objectification, and under the influence of performative metaphors, theory often appears to have become practice. Yet, according to the post-structuralist linguistic theory that usually informs such ideas, this sort of resignification does not happen all at once and for all time. Rather, it occurs as part of a constant and continuing process which is not linear or teleological, in which signifiers and discourses do not 'end' or 'die' but rather are in a constant state of displacement and flux, the outcome of which cannot be predicted from within the present. Not only may conclusions on the death of these things, then, be a little previous, but these theoretical moves are reversals rather than resignifications, which is quite a different matter to continually working on the borders between oppositions so as to open them up to question. A reversal is only the first stage of deconstruction and can easily serve to reinforce and reaffirm the existing system through the creation of a new hierarchy, which gives the appearance and effect of being unimpeachable by means of reducing a double relation of interdependency to a single authoritative term. In short, an alternative metanarrative is created in which difference is once again reduced to identity, in a logic of equivalence that actually forecloses rather than opens up debate. As a result, while some of these pronouncements may have been intended as subversive and aimed at a transformation of our perception of the world, they do sometimes seem to have undermined the possibility of either a radical critique or active resistance to the prevailing late patriarchal, post-industrial, capitalist norms.

In my own field in Britain, it used to be necessary to argue that all representation was political and that oppositional political theatre did not just indicate the single model provided by Bertolt Brecht and his followers. This was particularly important in terms of teaching feminist theatre, since many female practitioners were beginning to experiment with 'female' or 'feminine' forms and focus on issues previously defined as personal and therefore outside the realm of the political. Nowadays, I sometimes find myself having to argue that not all theatre and not all of the personal is political in *exactly the same way* and to the same effect, in order to contest the idea that everything is equally political in an indistinguishable fashion and so, effectively, nothing is political, or rather that politics is purely a matter of individual interpretation and so entirely relative. Unfortunately, as a postmodern subject, I am aware that this problem of the slipping political cannot be addressed, as it was by Brecht, through reference to form, since to assume that a form always and inherently carries a particular ideology is to ascribe to a metanarrative based on an exclusive subject or reading position. In fact, as I demonstrated in chapter one, in practice it soon becomes clear that the same forms have often been understood to signify in quite different, if not opposing, fashions. Moreover, the prevalence of irony, parody and pastiche among many 'postmodern' works has further complicated matters, since irony and parody are always double and therefore always a matter of context and of individual interpretation. Yet, without recourse to form or history, reality, the social, authorial intentions or production, or to some notion of stable identity or subjectivity, it is very difficult to establish any ground from which to argue for one piece of performance or representation being more 'resistant', or more normative, than another. This may, in a sense, be theoretically and politically correct, except for the fact that we still live in a world governed by inequality, injustice and violence, justified through reference to these very concepts and bolstered up by the continual repetition of representations that normalise and naturalise racism, ageism, homophobia, misogyny and class hatred.

Focusing on these problems in relation to both postmodernism and feminism in *Subversive Intent*, Susan Rubin Suleiman attempts to grapple with the issue of assessing the subversive or normative value of art by '[d]isplacing the political effect of a work to its reading' (Suleiman 1990: 193). For Suleiman, this does *not* imply that this political effect is purely a matter of individual interpretation since she cites Stanley Fish's notion of 'reader orientated criticism' in which reading is perceived as a 'shared' activity, produced and undertaken by 'interpretative communities'. According to Suleiman,

> To be part of an interpretative community, one does not need a membership card; it is a matter of having learned, in the classroom or through scholarly exchange, or through more informal modes of communication, certain shared ways of approaching a text: asking certain questions of it, and elaborating a language and an interpretative 'strategy' for answering them. (Suleiman 1990: 192–3)

For Suleiman, this displacement 'has the advantage of moving the debate from the question of what postmodernism "is" to the question of what it does – in a particular place, for a particular public … at a particular time', which, she notes, 'can be a public of one, but as I have suggested every individual is part of a larger interpretative community' (193). She admits that this displacement 'does not, however, alter the basic questions about the politics of intertextuality or of irony, or more generally about the relation between symbolic and "real" action in the world. It merely displaces them from the work to its readings and readers' (193). In many ways these quotes delineate an approach not dissimilar from the one I have tried to practise in this book. Even so, I have some serious concerns about the mode in which it is expressed by Suleiman, not least because she admits that it fails to address the very questions that seem to me to be the crux of any discussion of postmodernism, feminism and political effect, most notably the relation between the symbolic and 'real' action in the world. The apparently democratic terminology of reading as a shared activity and of interpretative communities can easily gloss over the fact that 'in the real world' not all readers and not all such communities are equal. As Susan Bordo comments in her critique of John Fiske's writing on television, this sort of gloss can disguise the fact that the power wielded, for instance, by a viewer creating a 'resistant' reading in her own home cannot be compared to the sort of power wielded by television companies (Bordo 1995: 261). Some 'interpretative communities' have better access to the means of (re)production and dissemination and therefore have more influence on the sorts of questions that might be asked, the types of interpretative strategies and languages that may be employed and, as a result, the sorts of answers most likely to be produced – all of which can have profound effects on 'real' action in the world. I am not sure, then, that this displacement might not potentially represent a flattening out of power relations in a reversal, through which consumption is privileged and then represented as equivalent to production. Indeed, the specific terms of Suleiman's argument could be taken to imply that works have absolutely no meaning except those the reader/interpretative community brings to them. For instance, in approaching a work to find out what postmodernism 'does', the interpretative community interested in these matters must have defined the work as exemplifying postmodernism in the first place and therefore implicitly be working from some sort of definition of what postmodernism 'is'. On what grounds? Whatever they may be, the possibility that the work may turn out to be 'doing' something that contradicts this definition, or indeed doing something else altogether which may be unintelligible in terms of this reading strategy, has been already discounted. This renders the whole notion of the political effect of a work completely redundant since the 'answers' have effectively been decided in advance of the 'reading', and as such the work only serves to demonstrate the 'truth' of the interpretative community's pre-existing assumptions, so this community confirms itself on the basis of what it already thought it knew in the first place. To be fair, within this model I presume that it is through the clash of competing readings by different interpretative communities of the same works that the hierarchies and exclusions on which these communities themselves are based and the foundations of their knowledge are challenged. Even so, the work itself is virtually denied existence, the critical text is privileged over the artistic text as the source of political meanings and the fact that a work is itself a form of 'interpretation' is overlooked. Suleiman is scathing about the fact that the acknowledgement of the necessity of working within that which we would critique is often offered as an 'apology for postmodernism' as part of a strategy of 'anything goes', with the added proviso, 'as long as I recognise that I am not innocent' (Suleiman 1990: 196). Yet the notion of displacing the political effect from the work to its reading can easily imply that the object of criticism is solely a blank surface for the inscription of meaning. This accords art works a sort of 'innocence', as being outside the process of making meanings, and gives interpretative communities the freedom of 'anything goes' in terms of using works purely as examples of their pre-existing arguments, at the expense of paying attention to the specificity and complexity of the work itself.

Even the most multiple, contiguous, open-ended or ironic work of art or of criticism has been produced through a process of choosing one artefact, image or word over another, one form or set of conventions over another, one material, institutional, social and discursive location or context over another, all of which will influence the way in which a work is likely to be understood. None of the practitioners discussed in this book *have* to engage in live performance, and indeed their various non-theatrical backgrounds do not make that choice inevitable. The decision to do so places what they produce in relation to theatre as an institution, and the forms they have chosen to deploy, the types of venue they appear at and the artists they have collaborated with all place them within a tradition that questions some of the foundational assumptions of that institution and to a certain extent also prescribes the nature of their likely audiences. These choices may not be entirely free but they are not entirely predetermined either, and they operate alongside other issues, such as sex or gender, to condition the reception of their work. While the structure of *The Double Wedding* may *potentially* open up infinite possibilities for interpretation, the sorts of choices made in the making and staging of this piece mean that certain types of readings will inevitably predominate. For example, it would be an act of perversity that borders on violence in all sorts of ways to offer an interpretation of this show relating it directly to the issue of terrorism, in the same fashion as one might the work of Northern Irish artist Alistair MacLennan, whose practice is as 'open' and 'writerly' in its own fashion as English's. Equally, the decision to present *How to Shop* as a lecture inflected the meanings most likely to be made from this work, and the geographical location of the lecture theatre influenced what sort of interpretative communities might be represented within the audience. From the perspective of the audience, as individual readers we actually all belong to numerous different interpretative communities, and in approaching a work we have to make choices as to what particular 'interpretative strategies' we might prefer in this instance. Hence the dilemma of my reading of *Post Post Porn Modernist*, where the choosing of one reading position over another, for me, had all sorts of ethical and political implications. This dilemma was highlighted mainly by the combination of the geographical location of the show and Sprinkle's decision to 'interpret her life' through, and in relation to, a specific range of discourses.

I am most definitely not trying to reinstate the author as the source of meaning, but while I do *not* think making meanings and political effect is a matter of 'innocence' and 'guilt', I *do* think it is one of agency and of responsibility. To displace *all* political responsibility onto 'reading' by interpretative communities is much like saying that if subjectivity is a product of discourse, I cannot be held accountable for my actions since they are determined by forces and power relations beyond my control. The relationship between production and consumption is a complex one, particularly in the field of theatrical performance with its tripartite relationship and where 'works' do not have a permanent material form. However, creating a performance and creating a 'reading' are both kinds of production, operating within different yet interconnected discursive fields. The problem of 'difference', which is supposedly the driving force behind both postmodernism and feminism, cannot simply be solved by the displacement of responsibility for 'political effect' from one group to another in a single move. Aside from anything else, these groups are never absolute 'opposites' but exist in a relationship of interconnectedness, interdependence and therefore of mutual, 'shared' responsibility for the reproduction of the culture of which they are a part and hence for 'real' action in the world.

The political effect of any given work is not a matter of authorship or form, or of individual readers, or of interpretative communities, or institutional, social or material location, theories or practices, but of the specific dynamic existing between these diverse elements at a particular moment in time. It is impossible to pay attention to all these elements at once, but to reject or privilege any single one of them over the others in advance and as a general rule is implicitly to assert the authority and purity of one sort of 'interpretative strategy' over another. This fails to make space for differences or contradiction and thereby for questioning what is already thought or known and by what authority. This is a space which can only be opened up through a particular conjunction or clash of all these various elements of 'staging', and whether discussing alienation or a hiatus in iterability, if a formula for producing such effects can be established and its efficacy predicted or guaranteed, it has already been rendered familiar or iterable, already reappropriated to a pre-existing authority. It is for this reason that I worry about the recent popularity of drag, cross-dressing and butch/femme performance used as examples of the 'performativity' of sex and gender. It seems to me that often the 'subversive effect' of such performances is assumed in advance through reference to a particular interpretative strategy, at the expense of paying attention to the specific and often contradictory ways in which meanings are produced and negotiated in the performances themselves and through their reception and perception. Paradoxically, considering that this approach seeks to deconstruct the fixity of identity, as Carole-Anne Tyler suggests, this can effectively give the appearance of replacing the practitioner's 'authorial intentions' at the centre of the process of production (Tyler 1991: 54). In fact, what is dissembled in this process is that the authority actually being reinstated is that of an interpretative strategy. This tendency has also tended to produce a 'double movement', which can lead to a reductive confusion between 'performance' and 'performativity', where 'like' is represented as 'equivalent'. This is not a matter of objecting to 'my' field being raided and discarded, and in fact this tendency to confusion has been aided and abetted within performance studies by the spread of 'performance' as a keyword. As such, it has come to embrace an ever wider range of activities, many of which are more different than they are alike and some of which may better be described as being 'performative acts or utterances', rather than performances. The questioning of such boundaries is a useful and often effective political strategy, but simply assuming, in theory, that these borders have been finally deconstructed, dissolved or transcended and ignoring their continuing existence in practice, can lead to generalisations and over-simplifications, which fail to do justice either to the complexity of the activities under observation or to their potential political effect. As Judith Butler points out, simply extending a category can lead to a proliferation of differences with no means of negotiating between them (Butler 1993: 114). Alternatively, the ignoring of boundaries can conceal an attempt to define and describe a new single comprehensive category once and for all, a move that is always exclusive. Moreover, to fail to distinguish between different sorts of activities is to imply that the same monolithic law established through the same authority governs different material and discursive fields, thereby foreclosing in advance the possibility of agency, political contestation and a democratic struggle over meanings. It may be that the 'real' world can only be apprehended through the discursive, but 'discourse' is not singular. It is in the clash between competing discourses, the contradictions within and between discursive fields and the diverse and multiple ways in which power is reproduced and reinstated, that the possibility of political resistance, of active agency and of 'choice' occurs.

The problem is that, in *theory*, it is very difficult, if not impossible, to distinguish absolutely between performance and Butler's concept of sex and gender as performative, since performativity exists within performance. As I indicated in chapter two, Judith Butler makes a distinction between them in terms of performance being a 'bounded act', distinguished from her rethinking of performativity in so far as

> the latter consists of the reiteration of norms which precede, constrain, and exceed the performer and in that sense cannot be taken as a fabrication of the performer's 'will' or 'choice'; further, what is performed works to conceal, if not to disavow what remains opaque, unconscious, unperformable. (Butler 1993: 234)

Yet, as I have indicated, Butler constantly illustrates her argument through reference to examples drawn from literature, performance or other works that are already mediated, narrativised and theatricalised interpretations of 'everyday reality' and so have the appearance of being a 'bounded act'. It is only by virtue of this appearance, and because these texts can now seem to be fabrications of a performer's/author's will, that it is possible for Butler to reveal what in 'unmediated', everyday reality, remains unconscious, concealed and unperformable. Yet this is only an 'appearance', since literature, performance and film, whether a 'documentary' or a piece of pure fiction, depend for their intelligibility on the reiteration of pre-existing conventions, which precede, constrain and exceed the work, are historical and serve to reinstate an authority to which they refer in a fashion potentially infinite in its regression. In fact, as I understand it, and I may well be wrong, it is the operation of performativity as defined by Butler or Derrida *within* performance, literature or film that gives these artefacts the appearance of being 'bounded acts' and of arising primarily from the author's will because this is the 'dissembling' effect of performativity in general. It may be also in terms of identity that, because as subjects we are always 'within' performativity as a process, we can only perceive its operation in terms of its effects in the past and therefore through reference to already 'framed' or 'bounded acts', where the process of framing in and of itself inevitably represents the reinscription of some sort of authority. It is only under such conditions that this process can be shown to be conventional, historical and therefore contestable.

As such, performance can usefully serve to reveal and contest the normative operation of performativity in the realm of the social, but in practice, and in the terms of Judith Butler's argument, this can only be achieved when the difference *and* the interdependence of performativity and performance are both remarked and preserved, not where they appear as identical. There is no doubt that some performances can actually do what Butler posits may be possible to achieve in the realm of the social by rethinking the occupation of sexed positions through a concept of performativity as a process of citation – which is to open up to contestation the difference between the real and the mimetic, original and copy, while of necessity marking that difference. However, Butler's concept of performativity and that of performance, do not remark this difference in exactly the same way and, more importantly, to the same effect. In order for a performance to be intelligible as such, it must in the first instance and in some way give the appearance and effect of being mimetic. Butler's notion of sex/gender as performative, on the other hand, refers to something the intelligibility of which depends on it having the appearance and the effect of being 'real', or there would be no point in 'deconstructing' it in the first place. The intelligibility of both performance and performative acts or utterances, then, depends on a process of remarking of the opposition between the real and the mimetic. Yet what remains, as Butler puts it, 'dissembled, opaque and unperformable' in one is a dependence upon a notion of the 'real' as its own internal constitutory exclusion and in the other a dependence on a notion of the 'mimetic'. This is a very fine distinction and ultimately one that is without independent terms or irreversible poles. However, the conventions cited do not signify in the same way in each case, and what matters is the different ways these appearances are interpreted on the level of reception and perception and the resultant *effect*, whereby one is read as a second order symbolic action and the other as action in the 'real' world. It is by virtue of this difference that a man in a frock or a 'bearded lady' on stage may provoke laughter, while the same phenomena on the street constitute enough of a 'menace' to provoke abuse and violence. To simply equate Butler's idea of performativity with performance is not only to ignore this issue of effect but to miss the point that what is really at stake is the process through which, and the grounds on which, this difference is decided.

To equate performance and performativity is simply to produce a reversal of the traditional hierarchy, privileging the mimetic over the 'real', in a potentially undemocratic fashion. This precludes any possibility of a 'hiatus in iterability' and of contestation, since everything, everywhere is rendered intelligible in advance in exactly the same fashion – that is, as always already mimetic. Therefore, while the 'real' may be that which can never be defined or described, it may be a concept or category that we cannot do without, as the possibility and condition of the groundless ground of contestation. Indeed, Linda Kintz argues that the impossibility of enforceable identity as expounded by theorists like Butler might be read as *proof of the real*, 'a real that reveals itself as interruption' (Kintz 1992: 111). In fact, it is the way performance refers to the real from within the mimetic, *not* the way it remarks the mimetic, which potentially causes an 'interruption' or a hiatus and makes performance useful in theorising the politics of performativity. No performance can ever finally decide on, or transcend, this opposition because the intelligibility of any given performance, as a performance, depends upon the idea of its differing from 'reality', the existence of which can never be proved within its own terms since any reference to reality within a performance is always already marked as mimetic. Therefore, while the absolute nature of the difference between the real and the mimetic may be put into question within performance, this question cannot ever be definitely answered one way or another. Yet every time a performance is staged and perceived and received as such, some sort of decision has actually been made concerning the difference between the real and the mimetic. Since the existence of the 'real' can never be either confirmed or disproved *within the terms of a performance*, this is a decision performatively produced, without definite grounds or decidable poles. Self-reflexively, foregrounding the conventions of a given performance may produce a moment of indecision or alienation, but it does not necessarily create a 'hiatus in iterability' since this can simply reinforce the fact that it is by its very nature mimetic, differing from, but dependent upon, the 'real'. In order to produce such a hiatus, this difference must be remarked as undecidable, in so far as it is performatively produced through a process of citation 'potentially infinite in its regression', in which the ground of the authority which informs this decision 'is constituted as perpetual deferral' (Butler 1993: 108). In short, the production of such a hiatus depends on the foregrounding of the making of a decision between the real and the mimetic as a continuing *process*, which is historical and through which the 'real' can never be transcended or negated but rather remains 'open' as a possibility and therefore as a permanent site of contest. Because there are no absolute, a priori grounds for making this decision once and for all, the process of making it is one in which both the performer and the spectator are deeply implicated as having ethical and political responsibility for the struggle over making meanings in the reproduction of the culture of which they are part. There can be no fixed rules for producing this effect – but not because it is simply 'relative'. As Derrida points out, undecidability is always of a 'determinate oscillation between possibilities, possibilities which themselves are highly determined in strictly defined situations (for example discursive, syntactical or rhetorical but also political, ethical etc.)' (Derrida 1990: 148).

Deciding on the difference between the real and the mimetic, like that between performance(s) and performativity, resistance and subversion, the readerly and the unreadable, involves just such an oscillation between possibilities. As such, these are differences which cannot be decided upon outside, and without reference to, highly determined, strictly defined situations, including all the various locations and contexts within and through which acts and actions are staged. These, then, are decisions which are not entirely 'free' but which are not wholly predetermined either. It is the fact that they cannot be made once and for all, even, for example, with reference to one particular performance or set of performance conventions, but must repeatedly be made again and again, that allows space for change, for agency and for 'acting otherwise'.

This brings me to the final paradoxes of the many and, no doubt, extremely irritating paradoxes that have structured and informed this book. For the sake of intelligibility, and by virtue of the strictly defined situation in which I am writing, I have chosen to use certain terms and concepts, such as feminism, postmodernism, performance and performativity, as starting points for discussing and analysing a number of shows. However, rather than simply using the shows as 'examples' of these terms and concepts, I have tried to let the shows interrogate the unity, coherence and integrity of these terms. As such, I have been working on the conflicts and contradictions both within and between the theoretical perspectives and within and between the shows because it is the differences, alongside and in combination with the similarities, that open up the possibility for contestation and render their combination politically productive. I have, then, been trying to, in Butler's terms,

> map out the interrelationships that connect, without simplistically uniting, a variety of dynastic and relational positionalities within the political field. … to find a way to both occupy such sites *and* subject them to democratising contestation in which the exclusionary conditions of their production are perpetually reworked (even though they can never be fully overcome), in the direction of a more complex coalitional frame. (Butler 1993: 115)

In sum, I have been trying to find connections between feminisms and postmodernisms or even post post modernisms and post-feminisms, performance and performativity, theories and practices, without suggesting a single all-inclusive and therefore reductive meaning for any of these terms individually, or that because the terms in each pair may be interrelated and even interdependent, they can be treated as equivalent. Yet, in order to achieve this, it was necessary first to attempt to decide on some sort of unifying, limited and exclusive definition of terms, and second to identify connections between these terms and concepts and between the shows. One of the things that I have suggested connects the three shows studied in this book is the fashion in which they offer the audience the opportunity to participate actively in the process of making meanings, through the operation of a certain paradoxical 'undecidability'. This means I have been suggesting that the political effect of these shows is not entirely a matter of form, or of author's intentions, or of individual interpretation, but again of a variety of relational positionalities in strictly defined situations. I have therefore tried in my readings to accept such opportunities without denying the work an existence outside and beyond the grasp of my interpretations, treading a fine line between taking responsibility for the meanings I have made and allowing space for my own authority and the authority of the theorists on which I have drawn to be subject to democratising contestation. As such, I have been defining these live performances as ones which present the interpreter/audience with choices that might be called 'ethical', while simultaneously trying to explore and interrogate the 'ethics' of interpreting such performances. It is tempting simply to end here and suggest, in line with recent fashion, that this book is 'performative', in so far as it performs and fails to transcend its own contradictions (which it does). But of course, despite my insistence on difference and contradiction, I have produced something approaching a coherent thesis concerning the politics of these performances that does privilege a particular theoretical strategy. This was inevitable due to the demands of the form in which I am writing and of course reflects my not very unconscious and not very subversive desire to offer something that is intelligible as a 'proper' and authoritative academic publication – to ensure that I will be taken seriously.

In the final analysis, my thesis repeats and reiterates ideas best summed up through reference to a combination of Judith Butler's theories and Diane Elam's notion of 'ethical activism' or the 'politics of undecidability', which, like Butler's writings, is heavily influenced by both feminism and poststructuralist theory and in particular by Derridean deconstruction. These are, then, the theoretical authorities which this book tends to privilege, but actually I believe that to a large extent my methodology could be equally, and even more easily, understood through a close reading of Rose English's sequel to *The Double Wedding*, *Tantamount Esperance* (1994).[1] This show is internally contextualised directly in relation to the millennium and is deeply concerned with history, theatre and identity, and, like *The Double Wedding*, it can be seen as both a reinscription and a critique of certain postmodern and poststructuralist philosophical concepts. However, since to explore this complex piece fully would entail a whole new chapter and this book is already long enough, in contradiction to everything I have said so far and for reasons that will become clear presently, I am going to draw on this piece as an 'example'.

For Elam, the notion of a politics of undecidability is dependent on the production and understanding of, as English said in *Tantamount Esperance*, 'a different kind of ethics' or what Elam calls 'ethical activism' (Elam 1994). This implies a reworking of modernist ethics that does not depend on a notion of a rational, stable, knowing subject, just as the politics of undecidability does not depend on a priori laws, rules, pre-existing assumptions, universal truths or appeals to absolute authorities. In *Tantamount Esperance* English appeared in full, Edwardian male drag with convincing facial hair, apparently playing a 'proper' consistent theatrical character and so finally fully accepting her position 'inside' the fiction, already literally 'inside' that which she would critique, although she did at one point refer to having ended up 'with spirit gum on my face'. In some ways the historical nature of this costume and her role in the piece suggested an impersonation citing the rise and fall of classic humanist male subject or philosopher, coming to terms with his own illusions, his own contradictions. We were told that it was Tantamount who in the past had given the characters their names and once upon a time had functioned as Imogen Grave's mentor, but he had now had to come to terms with his own lack of mastery. He realised that he could only tell Imogen what she already knew and was 'tormented' when she told him that her name had no meaning but was not meaningless, was the 'template for her soul' but did not ultimately express or contain her, was neither fully one thing nor the other. Like *The Double Wedding*, this show is concerned with the interdependence of opposites, and in this interdependence there is the possibility of transformation and therefore something equivalent to hope (tantamount esperance). In the final analysis, the piece constitutes an attempt to offer 'the representation of [unrepresentable] possibility', through a series of juxtapositions that foreground the permanence of the apparently ephemeral and the ephemerality of the apparently permanent. To put it in rather more Derridean or Butlerian terms, the show works on the border between the material and theoretical, to explore the materiality of ideas and the ideality of the material.

According to Elam, ethical activism and the politics of undecidability represent the search for the rule that may do justice to the particular case, even though this politics also includes the recognition that justice is always both unrepresentable and impossible, that there are no absolute grounds on which to base this search and so therefore this task is necessarily endless (1994: 107–20). ('Representation is both futile and heroic' – Imogen Grave.) For Elam, this approach is bound up with a notion of ethics because 'ethics reminds politics that no social form can be instituted that will put an end to the problem of justice' (106). As such, the political is conceded as a realm of continual negotiation and permanent contest, in which here can be no perfectibility, no ultimate synthesis and no final solutions ('If the secret is that there is no secret, then that is the secret we must keep' – Tantamount). This, then, is a form of politics which, like the characters in *Tantamount Esperance*, strives to discover the 'perfect point of balance between wild hope and total pessimism', in order to deal pragmatically with the fact that we are always within that which we would criticise without falling into passivity or relativism.

According to Elam and Derrida, the politics of undecidability does not mean that decisions cannot or should not be made but, as I indicated above, highlights the process of negotiation by which they are and *must* be made. It also implies an acceptance of the responsibility to continually make decisions because they cannot be avoided by applying a pre-existing law and cannot be made once and for all time (Elam 1994: 87). In *Tantamount Esperance* it is acknowledged that 'The moment has no monument' and 'there can be no monument to immortality' and so 'the onus is entirely on us'. While this show is scathing about 'nostalgia', it affirms the importance of history, on the principle that 'we need a space from behind and in front in order to be able to think', even while acknowledging that 'history' is not an absolute. There can be no 'graven image' or monument to the (present) moment because the present can only be apprehended once it is over, has become a bounded act and so is already in the past. There can be no monument to the (past) moment because the past can only be apprehended in relation to the present or to the future from which it must differ. There can be no monument to immortality because immortality refers to something that has yet to occur, is always in the future and so remains unthinkable and unrepresentable in the present, except in relation to the past. In short, the piece remarks the interdependence of the past, present and future as concepts defined in opposition to each other. The 'responsibility' or 'onus' is on us because the relationship or difference between these concepts and hence their 'meaning' is 'undecidable', yet in the present we must make decisions based on the past or the future, conditioned by, but not wholly defined by, the past and already conditioning, but not defining, the future. In the absence of absolutes, as Elam puts it, 'we have to try to do the right thing here, 'just where we are in our pragmatic context and no transcendental alibi will save us' (Elam 1994: 108). This is without any guarantee of making the right decision and yet in the knowledge that 'we cannot be excused from our own role in history because we could not know, so as to be reassured that we were right in advance' (Cornell, quoted in Elam 1994: 118–19).

In *Tantamount Esperance*, this responsibility or onus could be said to be signified in the first instance by the way in which the show forced the spectator to choose whether to focus on the dialogue, the activities of the 'close up' magicians performing constantly back stage left, or other dazzling and often astounding tricks, illusions, dances and musical activities simultaneously occurring elsewhere on the stage. It is impossible to watch all of the show at once, and where the spectator chooses to focus at any given time will inevitably affect the meanings they make from the piece. In the second instance, this could be said to be signified by the bank of lights that were shone on the audience at regular intervals, reflecting back at them their own role in the performance. Further, it could be said to be represented by the gradual stripping away of the numerous illusions that made up the show, until the spectator was confronted with an empty space and the bare walls of the theatre building. As such, we are left literally to contemplate our own role within the mimetic machine and our responsibility for making meanings, particularly in relation to a piece of work so dense and so distracting and so self-consciously concerned with illusion and the ephemeral that it is constantly slipping away from the spectator's grasp.

Like *The Double Wedding, Tantamount Esperance* was also to a large extent a meditation on identity. As 'Espiritu La Verdad' put it, the piece represented an exploration of the 'complex identities' of the characters through reference to the process of naming by which 'the template for the soul is in the sound of your name'. We were told that because these characters were 'mortal and not yet immaterial', they 'still need their names' which appeared to determine their identities and roles in the show. So generally Tantamount was concerned with history and the future, Espiritu La Verdad with 'truth' and the soul, Imogen Grave with words and images or 'representation' and so on. However, as Imogen remarked later, 'there is no graven image', there is no fixity of identity because it is made up of 'multiple memories', 'separate forms', of the 'material and the immaterial and we have no preparation to make them adhere'. Yet for her, her name is still a rock to throw herself against because 'the object needs an advocate, it cannot argue if it is not noticed'.

In a rather poetic fashion this can be related to the concept of identity as discussed by both Elam and Butler. Both accept that being named a woman is a material and an immaterial process, discursive and concerned with real located historical objects, tangible and intangible, that it is not a matter of choice, and in that process of naming 'women are defined and determined'. However, since this is a continuing process, not a single event, there is the possibility of transformation and resignification. Indeed it is the contradictory ways in which 'women' have been and continue to be defined and determined, 'which cannot be made to adhere', that renders the meaning of 'woman' undecidable and therefore as a site of possibility and agency. Elam acknowledges that identity politics are not just going to disappear and cannot simply be transcended, just as *Tantamount Esperance* remains articulated through both modernist and postmodernist discourses, both theatre and 'performance', of necessity reworking past traditions and therefore owing a debt to them because it can only make sense in relation to these traditions which it repeats and differs from at the same time ('the souls of the dead in the very drapes of the stage crying out "remember us, remember us"'). Neither can identities be abandoned as sites of resistance because such politics continue to inform and support the power structures that dominate our culture and so, like Butler, Elam suggests, working on the weakness within the norm. 'Woman', then, is treated as a necessary but provisional and questionable category (no graven image) that can never be fully described or defined because this term refers to something both material and immaterial which is always multiple. As Elam puts it, 'As feminists we are all concerned for women, yet we don't know what they are. And what binds us together is the fact that *we don't know*' (1994: 84). For Elam, then, feminism operates as a groundless solidarity, which recognises that there are differences between those placed under the category 'woman' and that 'they arise, always more of them' (84). 'All these differences must be respected but we will never come to an end of them' (85). The aim is not to find a more inclusive definition of 'woman' but rather, as Butler puts it, to provisionally institute an identity and at the same time open that category as a site of permanent political contest (Butler 1993: 222). This feminism works through locations based on a temporary stability that is constantly destabilised because of the difference contained both within and without it, a difference that works to destabilise any clear separation between individual and community, between self and other. As such, this feminism goes beyond simply being concerned for 'women', and Elam makes it clear that she is not positing a notion of solidarity which privileges sexual difference. Rather, this is a form of feminism in which 'sexual difference is one difference among many – not the only or always the most important difference, not the absolute mark of otherness' (1994: 118). Neither does she conform to the notion that a hierarchy of such differences can be established in advance, or that the differences that constitute a particular individual can all be named and separated out. To quote Espiritu La Verdad, 'we are necessary to each other [but] we seek no ascendancy'. Instead, this is an approach which attempts to articulate the interconnectedness, the interdependence of differences and identities, and here Elam quotes Trinh Minh-ha: 'Difference does not annul identity. It is beyond and alongside identity.' So the term 'woman' 'articulates upon the infinity of "woman" as entities of inseparable I's and Not I's' (75). To put it another way, 'identity' expresses an infinite number of situated, interdependent, yet provisional relationships, in which the self and the other, the community and the individual, the material and the immaterial, the physical and the discursive, masculine and feminine, the real and the mimetic, like all oppositions, can never be fully finally distinguished because they are not in 'absolute' opposition but defined and perceptible only within and through each other. Contained within I there is always Not I, not as an absolute other but as a dis-identification which at some level is always already an identification that has been made and denied. This, then, is a notion of a multiply split subject or infinite self-difference, which is not necessarily, as Lacan suggests, tragic evidence of our 'lack' and our impossible isolation from one another. As Linda Kintz suggests, it can be interpreted as 'the very proof not of tragic isolation but, instead, of sociality, intersubjectivity, in short, of community, as proof of the *impossibility* of solitude, rather than condemnation to it' (Kintz 1992: 111) – and also the proof of the responsibility and obligation which we owe to one another. Since these interrelationships are not abstract or stable but both situated and constantly shifting, there is no way of deciding once and for all time how justice may be done to this obligation or responsibility, since we can never know in advance who this 'self' or 'other' might be. In Elam's and Derrida's terms, there is an obligation to history and to otherness which cannot ever be paid once and for all but 'is rather to commit oneself to an endless work of reparation without the final solace of redemption' (Elam 1994: 110–11).

There are immediately several potential objections to attempting to realise this approach in practice. In the first instance, while Elam expounds her ideas in relation to a coalition between 'deconstruction and feminism', it could be said that actually her ideas imply the 'end' of feminism, or rather the transformation of feminism into ethical activism and politics of undecidability. Considering the influence of Jacques Derrida on these ideas, this might make some feminists suspicious, but personally I do not see a problem with this in terms of the *future*, since feminism, like other movements concerned with equal rights, has always been politics which aimed to do away with the necessity for itself. Moreover, Elam's approach embraces the recognition that this particular 'future' has yet to happen and that here and right now there are circumstances when it might be necessary to decide, provisionally, that sexual (or racial, or class, or sexuality) difference is the difference that counts and to continue to struggle on this basis. Like

Butler, then, Elam is not denying the significance of identity positions within a process of political activism but opens their absolute nature to contestation and, like Butler, indeed implies that 'it may be only by risking the *incoherence* of identity that connection is possible' (Butler 1993: 113). I have to say, with reference to Butler's own argument in *Bodies that Matter*, that this still is a risk that in the 'real' world is more often imposed on 'other' people to the detriment of their existence. Where it is a matter of *choice*, it is one which those in positions of power seldom take unless in a 'playful', 'theatrical' fashion which avoids responsibility and is easily recuperated.

Unlike Butler, Elam focuses more on 'staging' and context than on the 'performer' and offers specific examples that concentrate more on the social than the textual. She suggests, for instance, how the politics of undecidability or ethical activism could operate in relation to issues such as abortion or surrogacy. However, Elam's ideas, like Butler's, remain difficult to understand in terms of a 'coherent' political movement or set of practices, because as Elam admits, it is 'somewhat difficult to grasp what it might be to proceed without foundations since the words patriarchy have left us for this are anarchy and chaos' (Elam 1994: 109). As a result, this is a politics which, in Spivak's terms, looks forward to 'revolutions that have no model' (quoted in Elam 1994: 84). The crux of the matter is that the politics of undecidability refers to a politics which acknowledges that a transformation of the political is in the *process* of taking place but that the outcome of this process cannot be fully realised, defined or decided upon from within the present without limiting the possibilities of this transformation in advance. On the other hand, it is worth remembering that whatever may be said of its successes and failures, initially, feminism, like many other 'minority' rights movements, was once considered not to be properly political, partly because recognising it as such demanded a redefinition of the 'political' and partly because it did not conform to pre-existing models of political organisation. This does not mean that feminism is a model for 'revolutions that have no model', but simply that such transformations are possible. Moreover, the politics of undecidability, like Butler's notions of subversive repetition, accepts the necessity of working within what already exists and 'forging a future from resources inevitably impure' (Butler 1993: 241). As such, it may be necessary to refer to such models as a starting point for contestation and negotiation, even while interrogating these models. Indeed

Elam, like Butler and Derrida, frequently uses variations on the term 'democracy', which does not mean that the politics of undecidability refers to our current understanding of democracy, only that some of the questions posed by this politics are: what has democracy meant, what does it mean now, and how can its meaning be opened up so that it may possibly signify differently in the future? Yet, admitting the need to work within that which we would critique means that the politics of undecidability acknowledges the impossibility of theoretical purity or perfectly politically correct practices. At the same time, it does not offer absolution from the responsibility for making meanings in the culture of which we are a part, and, as Derrida has remarked, 'responsibility is excessive or it is not a responsibility' (quoted in Elam 1994: 119–20). On this basis, it bothers me that Elam constantly uses the authoritative, inclusive, academic 'we' while speaking about the need to 'negotiate outside of the horizon of authority' and indicating that the notion of 'we' is itself groundless and contingent (120). Yet my own use of 'I' is no less contradictory, no less 'impure', and neither of us is actually working without a priori assumptions, since clearly we both have an a priori commitment to certain political positions. The trouble is that, like Butler and Derrida, we are defining certain things (justice, the future, the abject, the real) as unrepresentable, and yet the very process of doing so constitutes an attempt to represent them. This is why, of course, performance, which, as I noted above, depends wholly for its intelligibility on its 'opposite' and on something that in its own terms can never be represented, proved to exist or made manifest, has proved so useful as a metaphor and as an 'example' in attempting to articulate such ideas. However, what applies to politics must equally apply to both the politics of performance and the politics of theorising and writing about performance. If differences are to be respected and made productive, the specificity of any given performance and all the various aspects of its staging and location must be acknowledged and observed, even though, since, as I indicated in the introduction, all viewing is perspectival, this in itself is effectively an impossibility. This also suggests that there can be no theoretically pure paradigm for a politics of performance in theory or practice, nor can there be a once and for all time distinction *or* confusion between practice and theory, since it is through conjunction, contradiction, contrast and conflict that any sort of contestation occurs. Equally, the terms 'performance', 'performance art', 'live art' and 'theatre', like the terms 'feminism', 'postmodernism' and 'performativity', can only ever be provisional categories, the departure point for discussion and debate, not absolute definitions – no rules for subversion or resistance, no guarantees of efficacy, only a process of communication, interpretation and making provisional decisions, which are always invested with power relations, always 'ethical' and always haunted by their own internal contradiction.

My final paradox is that, as indicated above, I have been, to use Jill Dolan's terms, 'raiding and discarding' Rose English's show *Tantamount Esperance* in a very generalised fashion to illustrate the notions of ethical activism and the politics of undecidability (Dolan 1993: 419–20). Yet, even within the quotes from the show I have selected and cited, there is much talk about the 'soul', 'eternity' and 'immorality', concepts which at first glance seem decidedly essentialist and metaphysical, refer to absolutes and so are incommensurate with the whole notion of the politics of undecidability. It may actually be that such references are intended as purely allegorical, particularly since English's drag and the idea that 'the template for your soul is the sound of your name' suggests a more performative, discursive approach to identity. In fact, such references, like the rest of the show, are very much open to interpretation, and actually, like *The Double Wedding*, the piece could be read through a whole host of other, completely contradictory theoretical positions. However, if I have raided this show it is because actually I wanted to use it, not so much to exemplify the notion of the politics of undecidability, but to open aspects of this theory to question. In the course of writing this conclusion, thinking about *Tantamount Esperance* made me take another, closer look at some of the quotes from Derrida and the language that Diane Elam uses in expounding her ideas. Placing these quotes in relation to this show highlights the way that, in defining his position, Derrida stresses that he is *not* speaking of 'eternity or immutability', or an obligation or responsibility arising from a '*divine*' law but a law and a responsibility which can neither be defined definitely as human or inhuman, all of which leads Elam to talk about debts that must be paid with no possibility of 'redemption' (Elam 1994: 109–20 and 111). Speaking deconstructively, these denials and choice of terms may actually suggest that Derrida's and Elam's thinking, and hence Judith Butler's and my own, while being very much part of a tradition that owes much to

Nietzsche's pronouncement of the death of God, remain fundamentally caught up in metaphysics. As I implied in my discussion of *How to Shop*, the notions of 'agency' and responsibility being posited are not unlike the paradoxical Christian concept of 'free will', where the subject has a choice of possibilities within highly determined, strictly defined situations. This free will is exercised under the stain of original sin, which constitutes an obligation to 'history' which cannot ever be paid once and for all but rather demands 'an endless work of reparation', yet it also allows for the possibility, though not certainty, of redemption through belief in a god whose mercy is said to be 'infinite' and therefore, presumably, unconditional in the first place. Within Christian doctrine this paradox cannot be resolved or synthesised but, as with the politics of undecidability, requires a leap of faith in an undefinable future (immortality) and in something that, by its very nature, can never be represented. In short, despite the fact that the politics of undecidability appears to be anti-teleological, it does seem to posit a hope for the future which is implicitly teleological and, despite its denial, to offer the possibility of the solace of redemption in which, as Tantamount puts it, 'all will be well, all will be love again' between the self and the other, the double and the 'one'.

This religous structuring is of course inevitable because God, or some sort of concept of a god, did not actually suddenly die everywhere and for everybody at one moment in the nineteenth century. Moreover, to quote *The Double Wedding* again, 'even to speak of the absolute of opposites is a travesty', and, as is clear in *How to Shop*, religious discourse and, most particularly in the West, those discourses arising from the Judeo-Christian tradition are still very much part of the fabric of our everyday lives, whether we are aware of it or not. Derrida *is*, of course, very much aware of this, but even so I think a close reading of Elam's reading of Derrida's ideas through *Tantamount Esperance* may be useful in exploring and putting into question the implications of some of the assumptions on which these ideas depend and some of the paradoxes and contradictions by which they proceed. After all, English, like Baker and Sprinkle, is an auteur who, over a twenty-year period, has, much like Derrida, been exploring the limits of representation. As such it seems to me that it is worth taking Sprinkle, English and Baker equally as seriously as Jacques Derrida or Jacques Lacan or Judith Butler or any of the other theorists cited in this book and that to privilege the authority of one over the other in advance is to miss an opportunity for genuine debate. If I do have a slight personal prejudice in favour of English, Baker and Sprinkle, this may be to do with my own subject position as a theatre studies academic. Studying their shows has forced me directly to think about my own assumptions and investments and even my own phallic impostures in a similar fashion to studying Derrida's or Lacan's or Butler's writings. However, unlike Derrida's, Lacan's or Butler's writings, despite Derrida's use of parody, Lacan's emphasis on the comedy of appearances and Butler's on subversive laughter, these shows also made me laugh even when I had not fully understood them, whereas the theorists often leave me in a state of despair at my own ignorance and the impossibility of ever understanding them. Sometimes this laughter may have been at the expense of some 'other', but sometimes it has been at my own unintelligibility, at the very impossibility of ever fully understanding, as a shared condition in which ultimately there are no authorities. Maybe this difference is literally a matter of interpretation and something has been lost in the translation of these theoretical works from French to English, or from philosophy to theatre studies, in the same way that the comedy of the shows has been lost in my translation of them from live practices into the language of academic discourse. Be that as it may, and to end on an undeniably grand, if not sentimental, gesture, comedy, the sort that makes you laugh, is a 'social form', far less concerned with the individual than other forms and far more with interrelationships. It is also far more obviously dependent on staging, location and context and so, as any practitioner will attest, far more contingent, unpredictable and difficult to get right.

Note

1 All quotes and references from *Tantamount Esperance* come from seeing the show at the Royal Court Theatre Upstairs, London, and also the Contact Theatre, Manchester, in June and October 1994 respectively.

Bibliography

A., J. (1925), entry on Alchemy, in *The Encyclopaedia Britannica*, 9th ed, Edinburgh, A. and C. Black.

Adshead, K. (1988), *Thatcher's Women*, in M. Remnant (ed.), *Plays by Women*, London, Methuen.

Ansorge, P. (1975), *Disrupting the Spectacle: Five Years of Experimental and Fringe Theatre in Britain*, London, Pitman.

Arditti, M. (1992), 'Riding with the Valkyrie', *Evening Standard*, 6 August.

Armistead, C. (1992), 'Measuring up to the World's Longest Eyelashes', preview of *My Mathematics* by Rose English, *The Guardian*, 1 August.

Artaud, A. (1958), *The Theatre and Its Double*, trans. M.C. Richards, New York, Grove Press.

Auslander, P. (1987), 'Towards a Concept of the Political in Postmodern Theatre', *Theatre Journal*, 39:1, 20–34.

Auslander, P. (1997), *From Acting to Performance*, New York and London, Routledge.

Baker, R. (1994), *Drag: A History of Female Impersonation on Stage*, London, Cassells.

Banks, M. and Swift, A. (1987), *The Joke's on Us: Women in Comedy from Music Hall to the Present Day*, London, Pandora.

Baudrillard, J. (1988), *Jean Baudrillard: Selected Writings*, M. Poster (ed.), Cambridge, Polity Press.

Baudrillard, J. (1993), *The Transparency of Evil: Essays on Extreme Phenomena*, trans. J. Benedict, London, Verso.

Beatty, M. (1990), *Sphinxes Without Secrets: Women in Performance Art*, published in co-operation with the New York Council for the Arts, the National Endowment for the Arts and the New York City Department of Culture and the Arts.

Benjamin, W. (1992), *Illuminations*, trans. H. Zohn, London, Fontana.

Bordo, S. (1995), *Unbearable Weight: Feminism, Western Culture and the Body*, Berkeley, Los Angeles and London, University of California Press.

Brecht, B. (1987), in J. Willett (ed.), *Brecht on Theatre*, London, Methuen.

Brunette, P. and Wills, D. (1989), *Screen/Play: Derrida and Film Theory*, Princeton, Princeton University Press.

Butler, J. (1990), *Gender Trouble: Feminism and the Subversion of Identity*, New York and London, Routledge.

Butler, J. (1993), *Bodies that Matter: On the Discursive Limits of 'Sex'*, New York and London, Routledge.

Caplan, B. (1991), review of *The Double Wedding*, *The Guardian*, 9 July.

Carlson, M. (1996), *Performance: An Introduction*, New York and London, Routledge.

Case, S.E. (1988), *Feminism and Theatre*, London and New York, Routledge.

Case, S.E. (1989), 'Toward a Butch-Femme Aesthetic', in L. Hart (ed.), *Making a Spectacle*, Ann Arbor, University of Michigan Press.

Cixous, H. (1981), 'Sorties' and 'The Laugh of Medusa', in E. Marks and I. de Courtivron (eds), *New French Feminisms*, Brighton, The Harvester Press.

Cixous, H. and Benmussa, S. (1979), 'Portrait of Dora', in *Benmussa Directs*, London, John Calder Press.

Connor, S. (1989), *Postmodernist Culture: An Introduction to Theories of the Contemporary*, London, Basil Blackwell.

Craig, S. (1980), *Dreams and Deconstructions: Alternative Theatre in Britain*, Ambergate, Amber Lane.

Daniels, S. (1984), *Masterpieces*, London, Methuen.

de Certeau, M. (1994), *The Practice of Everyday Life*, Berkeley, Los Angeles and London, University of California Press.

Derrida, J. (1978), *Writing and Difference*, trans. A. Bass, London, Routledge.

Derrida, J. (1981), 'The Double Session', *Dissemination*, trans. B. Johnson, London, Athlone Press.

Derrida, J. (1990), *Limited Inc.*, Evanston, Northwestern University Press.

Derrida, J. and McDonald, C.V. (1982), 'Choreographies', *Diacritics*, 12:2, 66–76.

Diamond, E. (1988), 'Brechtian Theory/Feminist Theory: Toward a Gestic Feminist Criticism', *The Drama Review*, 32:1, 82–94.

Diamond, E. (1989), 'Mimesis, Mimicry and the True Real', *Modern Drama*, 32:1, 59-72.

Diamond, E. (1995), 'The Shudder of Catharsis in Twentieth Century Performance', in A. Parker and E. Sedgwick (eds), *Performativity and Performance*, New York and London, Routledge.

Dolan, J. (1987), 'The Dynamics of Desire: Sexuality and Gender in Performance', *Theatre Journal*, 39:2, 156–74.

Dolan J. (1988), *The Feminist Spectator as Critic*, Ann Arbor, University of Michigan Press.

Dolan, J. (1993), 'Geographies of Learning', *Theatre Journal*, 45:4, 417–41.

Dollimore, J. (1991), *Sexual Dissidence: Augustine to Wilde, Freud to Foucault*, London, Clarendon Press.

Elam, D. (1994), *Feminism and Deconstruction: Ms en Abyme*, London, Routledge.

Feral, J. (1987), 'Alienation Theory in Multi-Media Performance', *Theatre Journal*, 39:4, 461–73.

Ferris, L. (1993), *Crossing the Stage: Controversies on Cross Dressing*, New York and London, Routledge.

Fiske, J. (1989), *Television Culture*, London and New York, Routledge.

Forte, J. (1990), 'Women's Performance Art: Feminism and Postmodernism', in S.E. Case (ed.), *Performing Feminisms*, New York and London, Routledge.

Foster, H. (ed.) (1985), *Postmodern Culture*, London and Sydney, Pluto Press.

Fraser, N. and Nicholson, L.J. (1990), 'Social Criticism without Philosophy: An Encounter between Feminism and Postmodernism', in L.J. Nicholson (ed.), *Feminism/Postmodernism*, London, Routledge.

Freud, S. (1925), 'Some Psychical Consequences of the Anatomical Differences between the Sexes', in *The Standard Edition of the Complete Psychological Works (S.E.)*, 19, London, Hogarth Press and the Institute of Psychoanalysis.

Freud, S. (1931), 'Female Sexuality', *S.E.*, 21.

Freud, S. (1933), 'Femininity', *S.E.*, 22.

Fuchs, E. (1989), 'Staging the Obscene Body', *The Drama Review*, 33:1, 32–53.

Garber, M. (1992), *Vested Interest: Cross Dressing and Cultural Anxiety*, New York and London, Routledge.

Goffman, E. (1959), *The Presentation of Self in Everyday Life*, New York, Doubleday.

Goldberg, R. (1988), *Performance Art: From Futurism to the Present*, London, Thames and Hudson.

Gray, F. (1994), *Women and Laughter*, London, Macmillan.

Grosz, E. (1990), *Jacques Lacan: A Feminist Introduction*, New York and London, Routledge.

Hughes, H., Shaw, P. and Weaver, L. (1989), 'Dress Suits for Hire', *The Drama Review*, 33:1, 132–52.

Huyssen, A. (1990), 'Mapping the Postmodern', in L.J. Nicholson (ed.), *Feminism/Postmodernism*, London, Routledge.

Ilett, R. (1994), 'Deconstructing Disability: The Performance Works of Annie Sprinkle', *Performance Art into the 90s*, London, Arts and Design Magazine, Academy Group Ltd.

Irigaray, L. (1985a), *Speculum of the Other Woman*, trans. G.C. Gill, Ithaca, Cornell University Press.

Irigaray, L. (1985b), *This Sex Which Is Not One*, trans. C. Porter and C. Burke, Ithaca, Cornell University Press.

Jameson, F. (1991), *Postmodernism or the Cultural Logic of Late Capitalism*, London, Verso.

Jenks, C. (1986), *What is Postmodernism?*, London, St Martin's Press.

Juno, A. and Vale, V. (1991), *Angry Women*, San Francisco, Re-search Publications.

Kaye, N. (1994), *Postmodernism and Performance*, New York and London, St Martin's Press.

Kellner, D. (1989), *Jean Baudrillard: From Marxism to Postmodernism and Beyond*, Cambridge, Polity Press.

Kleinhans, C. (1994), 'Taking Out the Trash', in M. Mayer (ed.), *The Politics and Poetics of Camp*, New York and London, Routledge.

Kintz, L. (1992), *The Subject's Tragedy: Political Poetics, Feminist Theory and Drama*, Ann Arbor, University of Michigan Press.

Kotz, L. (1993), 'Complicity: Women Artists Investigating Masculinity', in P. Church Gibson and R. Gibson (eds), *Dirty Looks: Women, Pornography, Power*, London, BFI.

Kristeva, J. (1982), *Powers of Horror: An Essay on Abjection*, New York, Columbia University Press.

Lacan, J. (1977), *Ecrits: A Selection*, trans. A. Sheridan, New York and London, Tavistock.

Langman, L. (1992), 'Neon Cages: Shopping for Subjectivity', in R. Shields (ed.), *Lifestyle Shopping: The Subject of Consumption*, New York and London, Routledge.

Levy, D. (ed.) (1992), *Walks on Water*, London, Methuen.

Lyotard, J.F. (1979), *The Postmodern Condition: A Report on Knowledge*, trans. G. Bennington and B. Massumi, Manchester, Manchester University Press.

MacRitchie, L. (1996), 'Rose English: A Perilous Profession', *Performance Research*, 1:3, 58–70.

Mayer, M. (ed.) (1994), *The Politics and Poetics of Camp*, New York and London, Routledge.

Megill, A. (1987), *Prophets of Extremity: Nietzsche, Heidegger, Foucault, Derrida*, Berkeley and London, University of California Press.

Melrose, S. (1993), review of Bobby Baker's *How to Shop*, *Hybrid*, 4, 33.

Modelski, T. (1991), *Feminism Without Women, Culture and Criticism in a 'Post-Feminist Age'*, London and New York, Routledge.

Moi, T. (1985), *Sexual/Textual Politics: Feminist Literary Theory*, New York and London, Routledge.

Morris, M. (1994), 'Feminism, Reading, Postmodernism', in J. Storey (ed.), *Cultural Theory and Popular Culture*, New York and London, Harvester Wheatsheaf.

Mulvey, L. (1975), 'Visual Pleasure and Narrative Cinema', *Screen*, 16:3, 6–18.

Parker, A. and Sedgwick, E.K. (eds) (1995), *Performativity and Performance*, New York and London, Routledge.

Parker, R. and Pollock, G. (1987), *Framing Feminism: Art and the Women's Movement 1970–1985*, London, Pandora.

Patton, C. (1995), 'Performativity and Spatial Distinction: The End of AIDS Epidemiology', in A. Parker and E.K. Sedgwick (eds), *Performativity and Performance*, New York and London, Routledge.

Performance Magazine Survey (1985), 'What Performance Artists Are Thinking', *Performance Magazine*, 37, 7–14.

Phelan, P. (1993), *Unmarked: The Politics of Performance*, London and New York, Routledge.

Pollock, G. (1991), 'Kitchen Show: A Reading', in *Kitchen Show* by Bobby Baker, London, artsadmin.

Probyn, E. (1993), *Sexing the Self: Gendered Postions in Cultural Studies*, London and New York, Routledge.

Propp, V. (1968), *The Morphology of the Folktale*, Austin, University of Texas Press.

Read, A. (1993), *Theatre and Everyday Life: An Ethics of Performance*, London and New York, Routledge.

Riviere, J. (1929), 'Womanliness as Masquerade', *International Journal of Psycho-analysis*, 10, 303–17.

Rogers, S. (1986), interview with Rose English, *Performance Magazine*, 42, 29–32.

Schneider, R. (1997), *The Explicit Body in Performance*, New York and London, Routledge.

Schuldt (1981), 'Soho Women's Performances', *The Drama Review*, 25:2, 110–16.

Shields, R. (ed.) (1992), *Lifestyle Shopping: The Subject of Consumption*, New York and London, Routledge.

Singer, L. (1992), 'Feminism and Postmodernism', in J. Butler and J.W. Scott (eds), *Feminist Theorize the Political*, New York and London, Routledge.

Slater, N. (1995), 'Nurse, the Screens! It's Time for Choc Shock', review of Bobby Baker's *Take a Peek*, *The Observer*, 9 July.

Snitow, A. (1990), 'A Gender Diary', in M. Hirsh and E. Fox Keller (eds), *Conflicts in Feminism*, London, Routledge.

Spencer, C. (1993), review of *How to Shop*, *Daily Telegraph*, 3 August.

States, B.O. (1996), 'Performance as Metaphor', *Theatre Journal*, 48:2, 1–26.

Straayer, C. (1993), 'The Seduction of Boundaries: Feminist Fluidity in Annie Sprinkle's Art/Education/Sex', in P. Church Gibson and R. Gibson (eds), *Dirty Looks: Women, Pornography, Power*, London, BFI.

Suleiman, Rubin S. (1990), *Subversive Intent: Gender, Politics and the Avant-Garde:* Cambridge, Massachusetts, and London, Harvard University Press.

Tyler, C.-A. (1991), 'Boys Will Be Girls: The Politics of Gay Drag', in D. Fuss (ed.), *Inside/Out*, London, Routledge.

Ulmer, G.L. (1985), *Applied Grammatology, Post(e) Pedagogy from Jacques Derrida to Joseph Beuys*, Baltimore and London, Johns Hopkins University Press.

Wandor, M. (1986), *Carry on Understudies*, London, Methuen.

Ward Jouve, N. (1991), *White Woman Speaks with Forked Tongue: Criticism as Autobiography*, New York and London, Routledge.

Wicke, J. (1993), 'Through a Gaze Darkly: Pornography's Academic Market', in P. Church Gibson and R. Gibson (eds), *Dirty Looks: Women, Pornography, Power*, London, BFI.

Williams, L. (1993), 'A Provoking Agent: The Pornography and Performance Art of Annie Sprinkle', in P. Church Gibson and R. Gibson (eds), *Dirty Looks: Women, Pornography, Power*, London, BFI.

Wright, E. (1989), *Postmodern Brecht: A Re-presentation*, New York and London, Routledge.

Index